Project Management

Project Management

Harvey Maylor

Lecturer, Cardiff Business School

Foreword by Professor Dan Jones

PITMAN
PUBLISHING

To those who said it could be done, especially Kara, with love.

PITMAN PUBLISHING
128 Long Acre, London WC2E 9AN

A Division of Pearson Professional Limited

First published in Great Britain in 1996

© Harvey Maylor 1996

The right of Harvey Maylor to be identified as Author
of this Work has been asserted by him in accordance
with the Copyright, Designs and Patents Act 1988.

ISBN 0 273 61236 0

British Library Cataloguing in Publication Data
A CIP catalogue record for this book can be obtained from the British Library

10 9 8 7 6 5 4 3 2 1

Typeset by Pantek Arts, Maidstone, Kent
Printed and bound in Great Britain by Clays Ltd, St Ives plc

The Publishers' policy is to use paper manufactured from sustainable forests.

CONTENTS

PREFACE

I have just seen bricklayers spend a day erecting ornamental pillars on the top of which decorative concrete spheres are to be mounted. On delivery of the concrete objects, it is found that the pillars are too wide. The skip arrives and the builders begin to demolish their work, presumably so that they can start again. This is waste. In this case it is visible, obvious and noxious; it doesn't make business, humanitarian or ecological sense. Yet this kind of waste goes on about us every day in all industries, in all sectors. Most of the time it is not so obvious but the effects are just as damaging. One of the key tasks of project managers is the elimination of such waste.

Project Management is currently not overburdened with theory, but is practically based on the many conclusions which have been drawn from empirical study.

I believe that we are facing a new management agenda which has been set by:

- the end of Taylorism and the rise of participative management;
- the realisation that organisations cannot be treated as stable systems and the recognition of the effects of chaos theory;
- the popular adoption of quality management and other elements of the Toyota Production System;
- decline of the formal organisation;
- the empowerment of customers (whose demands have had far-reaching consequences, from the shortening of product and service life-cycles to the emergence of formalised quality systems).

The approach I have taken has attempted to include many schools of thought. There is the subject of management, which has grown from an offshoot of investigations into human behaviour, into a vast discipline. There is the technical specialism, not only of the area in which the project is taking place, but of the techniques associated with project management. The emergence of bureaucracy, initially as a means of control, but latterly associated with the application of quality systems, also is included. The project manager needs to be able to grapple with the conflicts caused by all of these.

The people who have helped in the compilation of this book include all the reviewers of the proposals and sample chapters. Their input provided much-needed direction when I was 'too close to the coal-face to see the wood for the trees' (J. Hooker, 1989). Without whom ... Peter Race and Peter Schmidt-Hansen at Brunel University; Dr Emmannuel Ogbonna, Dr Peter Hines, Dr Alun Isaacs, Prof. Mick Silver, Dr Ken Peattie at Cardiff Business School, and the many contributors especially Prof. Dan Jones, Bob Gibbon, Mark Goode and Helena Snee, Helen Lowe, Ian Haig, Chris Scantlebury and Tony Martin. At Pitman Publishing, the support and professionalism of all the staff has been refreshing and particular thanks to Penelope Woolf and Maria McLoughlin. The whole project would not have been achieved without the unerring enthusiasm and energy of Kara, who read, edited and generally pummelled into shape the many editions of each of the chapters, as well as taking on many tasks to release me to write. Any errors or omissions are, however, my responsibility.

As a student, one of my lecturers once admitted that his management book had been the worst managed project ever. You always feel you will do better and that your book will not suffer from the same problems, without any real knowledge of the particular challenges involved. Had I known . . .

This text will be the subject of continuous improvement, based on the study of the responses from students and fellow academics, as well as an ongoing study of emerging issues in the field. All feedback is gratefully received!

By the way – the project was delivered on-time and within budget. The quality I will leave to you to judge.

Harvey Maylor
Cardiff Business School,
University of Wales, Cardiff
July, 1995

FOREWORD

Project Management is no longer about managing the sequence of steps required to complete the project on time. It is about systematically incorporating the voice of the customer, creating a discipline way of prioritising effort and resolving trade-offs, working concurrently on all aspects of the project in multi-functional teams, and much more. It involves much closer links between project teams and downstream activities, e.g. in new product development integration with manufacturing, logistics and after-sales support – in this case 80 per cent of costs are determined before they take over!

There are huge opportunities for eliminating wasted time and effort in almost every project. In manufacturing, Toyota estimate that only 5 per cent of activities actually add value, 35 per cent are necessary but do not add value, whilst the remaining 60 per cent is pure waste – Muda in Japanese! By halving the effort in designing a new car, they show this Muda can be reduced by good project management. Every project manager in the future has not only to manage their own project but to seek new ways of eliminating the Muda in their systems so they can do more for less, and more quickly next time!

This book takes a fresh look at the new techniques used by best-practice companies to improve their project management performance. It shows how the disciplines used by Toyota and the Deming approach to management can be applied to any kind of project in any industry. Students will find the mixture of academic debate and practical case studies helpful and teachers will welcome the discussion questions after each chapter.

Professor Daniel T. Jones,
Director,
Lean Enterprise Research Centre,
Cardiff Business School,
University of Wales, Cardiff

Co-author *The Machine That Changed the World.*

CHAPTER 1

The nature and context of project management

Mention project management and to most people the image that is conjured up is of large-scale construction projects – the Thames Barrier or the Channel Tunnel. Whilst there is much to be learned from studying such cases, every day managers from every kind of activity tackle smaller, but no less important projects. On a personal level, we all have a number of projects ongoing – pursuing a course of study, buying a house or organising a holiday. The level of complexity differs, the underlying principle of delivering the result to a defined customer at a given point in time remains the same. At a commercial level, the effectiveness of the project management process will determine whether or not those projects play a role in providing a source of competitive advantage (or even continued existence) for an organisation. There is good practice to learn from all sectors. It is those organisations that are the most resourceful in seeking out best practice and making those aspects work for them that will be most successful. The individual too can succeed by looking at what the best are doing and adapting it to themselves.

CONTENTS

1.1 CURRENT ISSUES IN PROJECT MANAGEMENT

There is only one consistent feature of modern business and that is change. The view in many progressive organisations is that 'to stand still is to go backwards'. Organisations are constantly required to change what they do and how they do it. The most successful commercial organisations are those that have become best at changing. World-class performance is seen to be possible through the development of excellent management, one significant part of which is the management of projects.

This book discusses the concepts of change and the methods by which the 'process of change' or 'project' can be managed. No single industry or function has a monopoly on project management expertise; the average manager now spends upwards of 50 per cent of their time on projects or project-related issues. Their line responsibilities (finance, marketing, design) involve them in a variety of day-to-day activities plus longer-term projects. The skills and techniques used in the line-management function will differ from those required in projects. The more enlightened organisations will provide a basic skills grounding in the best ways to run projects.

At one time it was accepted that there was no substitute for experience and a fundamental part of management was the acquisition and demonstration of this. The need for innovation, together with the ability to establish and maintain high rates of change, is now what is required from managers.

Recently, the nature of project management has changed. It has ceased to be dominated by the construction industry, where much of the case material under this heading is based, and is now applicable in all organisations. Harrison (1992) states that project management is now an advanced and specialised branch of management in its own right.

1.2 SPECIFIC OBJECTIVES OF THIS BOOK

The specific objectives of this book include:

- to introduce the idea of a systematic or project management approach;
- to provide a set of tools and techniques that will set out possible mechanisms for the management of the project through the various stages of its life-cycle;
- to consider the specific role of the project manager in the organisation and management of people;
- to highlight specific examples of world-class performance and to take generic lessons from these;
- to provide a path for the individual to seek self-improvement in their project management expertise, through the study of both good and poor performance (through recognising where mistakes were made and avoiding these in future) from case studies.

1.3 DEFINITION OF PROJECT MANAGEMENT

A project can be defined as a 'non-repetitive activity'. This needs augmenting by other characteristics:

- it is goal oriented – it is being pursued with a particular end or goal in mind;
- it has a particular set of constraints – usually centred around time and resource;
- the output of the project is measurable;
- something has been changed through the project being carried out.

Project management includes planning, organising, directing and controlling activities in addition to motivating what are usually the most expensive resource on the project – the people. Planning involves deciding what has to be done, when and by whom. The resources then need to be organised through activities such as procurement and recruitment. Directing their activities towards a coherent objective is a major management role. The activities also need controlling to ensure that they fit within the limits (e.g. financial) set for them.

'PRINCE' (PRojects IN Controlled Environments) – the standard project management methodology for government information technology departments – defines a project in terms of its products. These are categorised as:

- management – the planning, documentation and control actions of management;
- technical – the planning, documentation and review of technical aspects of the project;
- quality – the planning, documentation and review of the quality control of the project system.

PRINCE is a project management shell or structure within which plans can be formulated and actions controlled throughout the project life-cycle. Its major benefit is providing a degree of methodology standardisation between projects. This allows managers to concentrate on details of their specific project, confident in a recognised and proven method.

1.4 THE PROJECT AS A CONVERSION PROCESS

The approach that will be considered in this book is a systems approach. The project is viewed as a conversion or transformation of some form of input into an output. As Fig. 1.1 shows, the inputs are some form of want or need which is satisfied through the process. The project will take place under a set of controls or constraints – those elements generally from outside the project which either provide the basis for any assumptions, or limit the project. The mechanisms are those resources that make the transformation process possible.

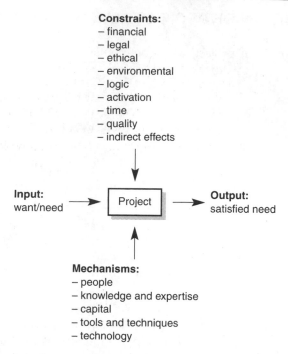

Figure 1.1 The project as a conversion process

Inputs

For projects of even moderate complexity there will be some form of project brief – a document which provides a statement of the want or need that is to be transformed by the project. There will be both explicitly stated requirements (original needs) and those which emerge during the course of the project due to the customer's changing needs or perceptions (emergent needs).

It is tempting to think of a project brief as an unequivocal statement from the customer. In practice this is rarely the case and there will always be a degree of interpretation required from the project team. Where there is a large creative element required of the project, the brief will need to provide guidance as to what the nature of the desire is, without putting unnecessary limits on the way it is achieved.

Constraints

The brief will also set out the constraints, which may take the form of:

- financial – the amount and timing of release of capital to the project, and the revenue or other benefit it should generate;
- legal – this may not be explicitly stated but there will be legal constraints, e.g. a building may not be constructed unless the planning permission for it has been obtained;

- ethical – a 1994 Mintel survey has shown that UK consumers are becoming as concerned about the ethical behaviour of the companies they buy from as they are about the environmental friendliness of the products they buy. Whilst this is at present limited to certain sectors of the community, the need to behave in an ethical manner as well as being seen to behave ethically is a factor in the way that projects are managed;
- environmental – the deluge of environmental legislation that has been generated by the European Union has changed the role of environmental control from a subsidiary issue to one which is at the forefront of management thinking;
- logic constraints – the need for certain activities to have been completed before a project can start;
- activation – actions to show when a project or activity can start;
- time – the biggest constraint for most projects (see current environment);
- quality – the standards by which both the product (the output of the process) and the process itself will be judged;
- indirect effects – it is practically impossible for any change to take place in isolation. There will be ripple effects which will need to be taken into account at the outset. The output of the project will be in the form of:
  - converted information, e.g. a set of specifications for a new product
  - a tangible product, e.g. a building
  - changed people, e.g. through a training project, the participants have received new knowledge and so are part of the transformation process as well as being a product of it.

Outputs

Figure 1.1 describes the output as a 'satisfied need'. This is a very wide interpretation of the possible outputs of a project and includes, for example, a new building as an output from a construction project; processed information, e.g. in the form of engineering drawings or a report; and people with the necessary skills for a task (the output of a project involving training). The outputs may be tangible or intangible.

Mechanisms

The means or mechanisms by which the output is achieved are as follows:

- people – those involved both directly and indirectly in the project;
- knowledge and expertise – brought to the project by the participants and outside recruited help (e.g. consultants);
- capital – the money that provides the resources;
- tools and techniques – the methods for organising the potential work with the available resources;
- technology – the available physical assets that will be performing part or all of the conversion process.

1.5 THE PROJECT ENVIRONMENT

There is the view that 'work can be done almost anywhere'. The new Mazda MX5 (Miata) car, for example, was designed in California, financed in Tokyo and New York, tested in England, assembled in Michigan and Mexico using components designed in America and made in Japan. Shipbuilding – a predominantly project-based environment – has faced competition coming from parts of the world that 20 years ago had little or no capability in this area. Traditional not-for-profit organisations (including the National Health Service) are now required to meet performance targets and individual activities are being subjected to previously unthinkable commercial constraints.

Within the expanding European Union, trade barriers have fallen and the number of international collaborative ventures has increased. Projects have become more complex as:

- generally the simplest ideas have been exploited first – it is becoming more difficult but more vital to be innovative;
- businesses are becoming more complex – it is less likely for a company to provide a commodity, product or service, but to provide a 'package' which meets an entire need rather than just part of that need;
- projects are moving towards turn-key contracts – where the end user does none of the interfacing between the different parts of the system, but deals with a single supplier in the provision of an entire system.

In addition:

- effective quality management has been shown to be the basis of many organisations obtaining a competitive advantage. Your quality system carrying a recognised certification (such as BS–EN–ISO 9000) is becoming a requirement for supplying goods or services into many markets – not just aerospace and defence where the standards originated.

The change in the competitive environment in which the majority of organisations operate has necessitated a major re-think of the way in which projects are managed. The effects of the changes on projects and their managers include:

- time has become a major source of competitive advantage, whether it be in the construction of a road or the development of a new product;
- human resource management has moved from considering that members of a project team should be treated as anonymous cogs in the machine to the idea that individual creativity can be harnessed. The concept is often heard expressed in the form 'with every pair of hands you get a free brain';
- rates of change in technology and methods have increased – not only is the change continuing, but the speed at which changes are occurring is increasing;
- organisations are having to become customer focused and exceed rather than just meet customer requirements. Customer expectations of the way products and services are delivered are increasing all the time;

- there is a trend towards integration and openness between customers and suppliers. Company information that would previously have been closely guarded secrets is often shared in a move towards partnership, rather than adversarial relationships;
- the most fundamental change in management has occurred through the investigation of the Toyota production system. Toyota was seen to have achieved significant competitive advantage in the automotive market through its management philosophy and the application of associated tools and techniques. The principles have been taken and applied in many unrelated business areas with considerable benefits;
- the service sector has been the biggest growth area in the past ten years. The economy of the majority of European Union countries has had to cease its dependence on manufacturing and rely on the growth of the service sector to provide employment and economic growth.

One view of the future of the economies of Western countries is that the depression of the early 90s will continue (Davidson and Rees-Mogg, 1992). This will necessitate the start of a much lengthier process of change. Environments are going to become even more competitive as the same number of companies fight for a smaller overall market.

The environment may be summarised by the four Cs, as shown in Fig. 1.2:

- complexity;
- completeness;
- competitiveness;
- customer focus.

1.6 THE COMPLEXITY OF PROJECTS

Not all tools, techniques and management ideas are univerally applicable – the project that takes one person a week to complete clearly has very different managerial requirements from the multi-site, high budget project. In order to provide meaningful consideration of the function of management in such a variety of settings, two classifications will be applied – complexity and the typology of projects. In general there will be a high correlation between the level of complexity of a project and the strategic level.

The level of complexity of an activity is a function of three features:

- the number of people, departments, organisations and nations involved, i.e. the organisational complexity;
- the volume of resources involved, time, capital, processes, i.e. the resource complexity or scale;
- the level of innovation involved in the product or the project process, i.e. the technical complexity.

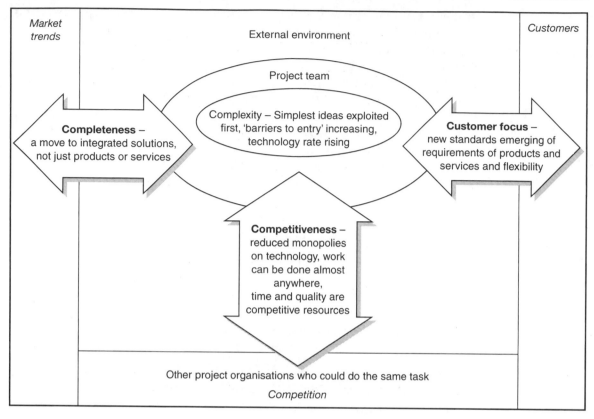

Figure 1.2 The external environment

This complexity model is shown in Fig. 1.3. As the overall complexity in-creases, so will the difficulty of the management task to ensure that the goals of the project are reached. Therefore the degree of formalisation of the project will increase. Project plans will need to be explicitly stated in writing and for-mal procedures for evaluation and justification of the project derived. This bureaucrary is neither appropriate nor necessary for the less complex projects, where the additional resources required to formalise matters would more than outweigh any benefits from the additional activities.

The scale of projects can be further described using the following typology – is the project strategic, systems-based or operational? Characteristics of each are given in Table 1.1 and examples of these types of project are given in Table 1.2.

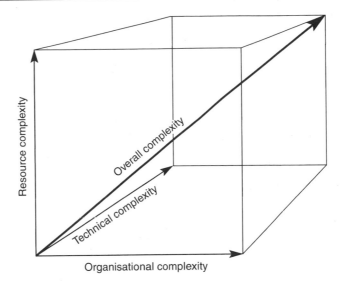

Figure 1.3 Defining project complexity

Table 1.1 A typology of projects

Type	Timescale	Degree of change to customers	Likely complexity	Effects of project	Change to customers/ users of output
Strategic	2-5 years	High	High	Impact felt throughout organisation and beyond	Change what is done
Systems	1-2 years	Medium	Medium	Impact limited to most parts of the organisation	Change to the way that things are done
Operational	Up to 1 year	Low	Low	Impact limited to the function within which the project was undertaken	Change who, where, when and the means by which something is done

Table 1.2 Examples of the use of the typology of projects

Type of project	Manufacturing e.g. lighting fittings manufacturer	Service e.g. general hospital	Retail e.g. supermarket	Construction e.g. housing developer
Strategic	Develop new products	Add or remove facility, e.g. accident and emergency department	Move store to new location	Develop designs for a series of standard accommodation units
Systems	Implement quality system	Contract out cleaning services	Implement electronic point of sale (EPOS) system	Use contractors rather than employees to manage projects
Operational	Change operating procedures on the shop-floor	Find new supplier for surgical supplies	Shelf-stackers to act as relief cashiers	Cross-train decorators and plumbers

1.7 THE RELATIONSHIP BETWEEN PROJECT MANAGEMENT AND LINE MANAGEMENT

Figure 1.4 shows a conventional management hierarchy with the lines on the diagram representing lines of reporting or responsibility. At the head of each of the major functions within an organisation there will be functional or line managers. These managers have the responsibility for the people who work under them in their departments.

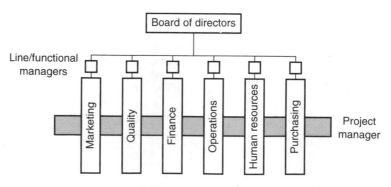

Figure 1.4 Project organisational structure (for project of medium complexity)

The project manager may have a line management role as well, but is responsible for projects that may run across several functions. The figure shows the project manager being responsible for people drawn from every function in their activities in relation to that project.

The project manager's role differs from that of the line manager in the nature of the task being carried out. Table 1.3 gives the major differences.

Table 1.3 Project versus Line Management

Line management	Project management
• responsible for managing the status quo	• responsible for overseeing change
• authority defined by management structure	• lines of authority 'fuzzy'
• consistent set of tasks	• ever-changing set of tasks
• responsibility limited to their own function	• responsibility for cross-functional activities
• works in 'permanent' organisational structures	• operates within structures which exist for the life of the project
• tasks described as "maintenance'	• predominantly concerned with innovation
• main task is optimisation	• main task is the resolution of conflict
• success determined by achievement of interim targets	• success determined by achievement of stated end-goals
• limited set of variables	• contains intrinsic uncertainties

As Fig. 1.5 shows, the split between tasks that can be considered as maintenance (maintaining the status quo) and innovation is changing. On the figure, the trend is for the line AB to move downwards – increasing the degree of innovation activities required from line managers. The result of this is a change in the role of line managers and a reduction in the difference in the roles of line and project managers.

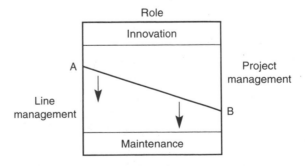

Figure 1.5 Innovation/maintenance activities in line and project management

The major change in the practice of project management has been its emergence as a management specialism in its own right – just as financial management, operations and marketing have done. For many strategic projects, the function of project management will involve many elements including:

- financial management – through the preparation of a financial case to meet the needs set out in the project brief;
- personnel management – the identification of skills required, the selection of staff, their motivation and welfare;
- operations management – there are often parts of a project that are repetitive in nature and so can be treated as individual operations;
- purchasing and logistics – the identification of material and service needs, suppliers, their selection and the management of the logistics (location and transport of materials);
- technical specialisms – e.g. new product development, engineering, programming, quality management;
- marketing – projects generated for both internal and external customers will need to have explicit statements of needs drawn up and then be 'sold' to the customer.

1.8 THE HISTORY OF PROJECT MANAGEMENT

Projects, as outlined above, have always been carried out in forms of varying complexity. The study of the subject, however, where the performance and methods are analysed, appears to have begun just prior to World War II in the chemical industry (Morris and Hough, 1987). It was in the 1950s that further development took place towards establishing a methodology that would be recognisable today as project management.

Whilst the focus of activities during the 1950s was in the process and construction industries, the heavy engineering and defence sectors (the US in particular) began the development of the numerical techniques which today are viewed by many as central to the subject. This part of the subject draws heavily on the work of operational research (OR) or management science, which is the mathematical treatment of complex situations such that understanding is achieved through numerical analysis and hence decision-making is enhanced.

This focus on mathematical reasoning has prevailed until very recently. The continued development of this area has lead to a fragmentation of the subject, to the point where rather than just having project managers, there are specialists in particular areas of the mathematics, e.g. risk management.

The more recent approaches of the emerging area of technology management have brought in other management specialisms such as human resource management. This element has expanded the scope of project management, making it the management specialism that we see today.

1.9 CONTINUOUSLY IMPROVING THE PROCESS

One of the leaders of the change in management thinking to concentrate on quality rather than quantity of output was Dr W. Edwards Deming. His original work was centred on the operational aspects of quality management – in particular the use of statistical data in controlling processes. This work was adopted with far greater vigour in Japan than in his native America, but latterly has been given more prominence in Western management study. He is famous for producing his 14 management points. The fifth of these points is:

> 'Improve constantly and forever every activity in the company, to improve quality and productivity and thus constantly decrease costs'.

> (Deming, 1986)

The means by which this constant improvement is achieved is by the approach to projects shown in Fig. 1.6.

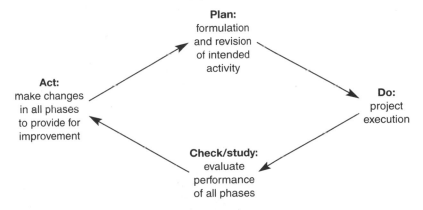

Figure 1.6 Deming cycle for project management (PDCA)

The *planning* stage involves the formulation and revision of statements of intended activity, whether formalised or otherwise. The *doing* is the time when the project is carried out (the direct value-adding phase). The *check/study* phase involves a critical appraisal of both the project output (was a good result achieved?) as well as the process (was it carried out as well as it could have been?). The *act* stage is that phase when the project process is considered to see how the lessons learned and gleaned from the review could be channelled back into the people involved in the process. As a result all parts of the process can be improved, e.g.

- planning – the experience of one activity shows that a particular element took considerably longer than planned and cannot be noticeably improved. This factor must be built into future estimates;

- project execution – the operational procedures of the project can be improved by finding what worked best and under what circumstances;
- project evaluation – were the right processes investigated?
- action for improvement – did previous reviews provide improvements in methods?

Using this cycle, the framework for this text has been developed as shown in Table 1.4.

Table 1.4 The application of PDCA to project management

Activity	Phase	Key issues	Fundamental questions
Plan	Project planning and analysis	Goal definition, planning, estimating, resource analysis and justification	How should a project be planned and the plans evaluated?
Do	Project execution	Organisation, control, leadership and decision-making	How should the day-to-day running of a project be undertaken?
Check/study	Project review	Assessment of results, feedback of performance, change in the light of results	How can the 'management process' be continually improved?
Act	Continuous improvement activities		

Models for success

It is appealing to try to find a single model of success for projects, i.e. that if you run your project in a certain way, it will be instantly successful. The reality is that:

- whatever can go wrong, will go wrong (Murphy's Law);
- whatever can be misunderstood, will be misunderstood;
- constants aren't;
- project activities will always expand to fill the time or resources available (Parkinson's Law);
- a project will spend 90 per cent of its time 90 per cent complete;
- a carelessly executed project will take three times as long as planned – a well executed one will only take twice as long.

These predictions can become self-fulfilling if the attitude and determination to succeed in achieving the goals for the project are completely ignored. The attitude is, that no matter what action is taken, there is going to be a degree of failure. This can be justified by its most ardent proponents with many cases. What is within the control of the project manager and what is not? Whilst there is no universal project superperson that can be called upon to revive projects that should have been killed off previously, management will be considered as having a very positive role to play.

There are three main criteria by which the success of a project may be judged. These are the timeliness, its cost and the performance of the output (*see* Fig. 1.7). It was at one time acceptable to express these in terms of trade-off relationships between the three, i.e. the project could be accomplished at minimum cost, but would need more time and may not achieve the goals set for it.

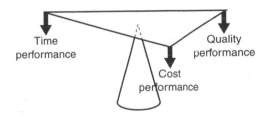

Figure 1.7 Trade-offs in project management

Investigations into the practices of Japanese management (*see* Womack *et al*, 1990 and Schonberger, 1986) showed that the trade-offs between these critical three areas had, to some extent, been removed. The evidence that there was a positive influence made by the managers in this environment seems undeniable. The philosophy centres on the removal of waste from all processes – not just manufacturing. This concept of analysing all activities to identify and eliminate any that are not value-adding will be a central theme here.

There have been many examples of projects achieving results against expectations. Whilst there are some that would be considered to have been successful due to luck, others are genuinely down to the effort of the project team members. These Super-Human-Effort (SHE) projects can be set aside from the rest, but the techniques and lessons learned will have to applied. Whilst it is not possible for every single project to demand 110 per cent of its participants, the situation that the majority of companies find themselves in demands that they have to do more with less resources. This is excellently described in Handy (1994) where he quotes the chairman of a large pharmaceutical company:

'1/2 × 2 × 3 = P – half as many people [working] in the core of his business in five years' time, paid twice as well and producing three times as much, that is what equals productivity and profit.'

For the purposes of describing the various levels of success for a project, the following categorisation will be applied:

- result achieved which meets the stated needs;
- result achieved within the given constraints;
- result achieved at minimum cost;
- result achieved with benefit to the project team;
- result achieved with benefit to all stakeholders (*see* Chapter 2).

Failure of a project may be likewise described:

- project ran over time
- project ran over budget
- project output does not meet the needs of it. This is due to the original need either not being defined or being incorrectly defined (by passing the information through too many sets of hands, for example, before it got to the people, who were going to carry out the transformation process, i.e. the project team), or another emergent need not being accommodated.

There is risk associated with projects that does not generally encroach on line-management areas. This is caused by the uniqueness of many project activities, and it is a general statement that this risk increases with increasing project complexity. The risks are that the project will fail in one way or another.

The reasons for success or failure (especially failure) have been the subject of much analysis. Morris and Hough (1987) quote the results of 33 studies, which took in thousands of projects from around the world. The majority showed that costs and time had overrun considerably – up to 780 per cent in one case. One study of 71 UK aerospace projects quoted, showed cost overruns to be considered normal. The principal reasons given for this included insufficient work in project definition, lack of concurrency and high risk elements (particularly in the development of new materials).

1.10 INTRODUCTION TO THE FOLLOWING CHAPTERS

This chapter has given an overview of the environment in which the project manager operates and some of the structures which can be applied to the subject to enable understanding and hence management. This approach is continued in Chapter 2, which starts to put in place some of the detail as to how a systematic approach to projects can minimise the risk of having too many unknowns causing problems. This shows the benefits of what will be termed the project management approach and includes some of the techniques for describing both the technical (the hard elements) and human (the soft elements) of projects.

Chapter 3 begins the discussion of what, for many, is the most important area of a project manager's responsibility – the planning process. The discussion starts to look at the trade-offs inherent in this management process-within-a-process, before moving on to discuss the basic tools of the project manager's trade – the logic of critical path analysis and other graphical techniques. Chapter 4 then builds on this quantitative analysis to show how the information can be used in the management process, and how the inevitable financial element of projects can be included. The process of justification in financial terms is shown to be less simple than on initial inspection, but is worth mastery if the project manager wishes to be taken seriously as a management specialist in their own right. Financial discussions should not just be the domain of the accountants – profit is too central a motive for projects taking place for any responsibility to be abdicated by the project manager.

Chapter 5 begins a more detailed discussion of how to organise one of the project's most expensive variable resources – the people. When the first books on management were written, it was attractive to treat the human input as some form of automatic activity which could be mechanistically determined. This is a major field for study by the practising and potential project manager. Chapter 7 continues the theme of the role of management and leadership in a modern project organisation.

Chapter 6 considers the information that will be needed in medium- to large-scale projects in order to maintain a degree of control over ongoing activities. It is, after all, of little practical use to find at the end of a time period that all the tasks have run late and that, as a consequence, all subsequent activities cannot start as planned.

Decisions should be made on the basis of good information, but what constitutes good information? Also, what should a manager do with that information once it has been received? The various approaches to problem solving and decision-making are discussed in Chapter 8.

The Deming PDCA cycle has already been shown to be useful in ensuring that processes are continuously improved. The review and feedback provided through short- and long-term reviews, and the role of world-class projects is covered in Chapter 9.

1.11 FUTURE ISSUES

In discussing the future issues in project management, Turner (1994) cites the study of 'risk management' as an emerging area for academic study, based on journal submissions. Whilst it can be said that the further development of technically specialist areas will certainly take place, the project manager's role will almost certainly move from that of a technical specialist, who has taken on the role of coordinator of a project, to that of 'change agent'. The function that they perform will be recognised as increasingly important for the survival of organisations in all sectors, by the management of all stakeholders in projects.

In addition there is the search for new management structures. Chapter 5 discusses the ways in which the project organisation can dovetail with the conventional line management hierarchy, but all of the forms currently recognised have appreciable shortcomings. Leading practitioners and academics in the subject of project management will be at the forefront of this debate.

PROJECT MANAGEMENT IN PRACTICE: **THE CHANNEL TUNNEL PROJECT**

Several years late and coming in at double the initial budget (around £10 billion as opposed to the estimated £5 billion) set for the project, the Channel Tunnel was opened to passenger and freight traffic during 1994. At several times during the work, the company which was funding the tunnelling work (Eurotunnel) itself ran out of money and had to return to the stock market and its banking financiers to seek new funds. The openings of the various services, attended by the world's press, were not without hitch either. Trains 'failed to proceed' at the times indicated, and had to be replaced, and there were well publicised laxes in security arrangements by the operations staff. Tales were recounted of how the tunnel, dug simultaneously from the French and English sides, was intended to meet in the middle, but did not. Add to this the loss of life during the project (ten people were killed during the tunnel construction), and the ongoing debate as to the desirability of the high-speed rail-link through Kent (trains are environmentally friendly until they are routed through your back garden), and the general public would be forgiven for thinking that the project was very badly managed. They have short memories, however, and the media focus has shifted to the way in which the business of transporting people, vehicles and freight is run.

The station at Waterloo, the terminal in Kent and the French stations have had to be constructed too, but have gained far less publicity. The Waterloo Eurostar station has won various awards for its architecture as well as praise from users who are more used to the drafty, dingy stations of the UK rail network.

By the start of 1995, the service being provided was getting good press reports, and the passenger transport side of the business was running ahead of predictions. Many of the earlier operating problems appear to have been rectified, though when one train was cancelled and the passengers offered alternative transport on the ferries, the tannoy announcement by the captain of the ship taking them did have more than a little of a sense of gloating about it! The airlines and ferry companies have not been slow to respond – the entrance of another player into a highly competitive market has been unwelcome to the industry, though not unbeneficial to the customers.

The trains

The Eurostar service is the passenger carrier, with each of the high-tech trains carrying more than the equivalent of two jumbo-jet loads of passengers at one time (over 800). It is owned by a consortium of British, Belgian and French railways. The trains themselves, over a quarter of a mile long, are fitted out so that they resemble the interior of an aircraft rather than a train. The chairs are reclining and individual reading lights are provided. The train can travel at 186 mph (298 kph) on specially adapted tracks in Northern France and around 100mph through Kent. The engines for the trains were specially developed by GEC-Alsthom, the Anglo-French company and can run on the four different power systems that the train will come across – French, Belgian, British and the tunnel itself. Much of the rest of the train design comes from the highly successful French trains – the TGV (train à grande vitesse).

Le Shuttle is the part of the service for cars, caravans and coaches – the box-like carriages transport the vehicles with their occupants remaining within the vicinity of their vehicles during the journey, currently from Folkestone to Calais. The competition for the ferries is that this service is virtually weather-proof and only takes 35 minutes from platform to platform. The safety systems against one of the greatest fears of all – fire – are where the greatest application of technology has occurred. The fire breaks, detection systems and procedures for dealing with an outbreak are way in excess of anything previously related to a train. The freight service for taking lorries and containers through the tunnel runs on different trains to the above services.

The tunnel

At the outset of the project, the technology involved and the sheer scale of the tunnel digging meant that it would not be possible for it to be undertaken by one company. A consortium of ten companies (five French and five British) was formed and had to coordinate the digging of three tunnels (one each way and one service tunnel) as well as the 1200 suppliers and 15 000 workers. Once this had been achieved, the tracks (over 130 miles in total) were laid, and the control system for the running of the trains installed. From an engineering point of view, the sheer scale of the project and the fact that it has been achieved at all shows the project to be an immense success.

The project appears to have achieved what it set out to achieve – there is now a fixed transport link between the UK and the rest of Europe, one that it is hoped will encourage the kind of union that many feel is needed if Europe is to continue its economic growth.

Case discussion

1 Identify the major components of the Channel Tunnel project.
2 Using the terminology of the model given in Fig. 1.1, identify the inputs, outputs, constraints and mechanisms. Are there any cultural constraints that may affect the progress of the project?
3 Distinguish between the project management and the line management functions which have been described here.
4 Describe the complexity of the project.
5 Discuss the issues that would make you believe that the project has been a success or failure.

PROJECT
MANAGEMENT
IN PRACTICE:
**IMPLEMENTING
BS-EN-ISO 9000
IN A HEALTH
SERVICE
ENVIRONMENT**

The international standard for quality systems BS-EN-ISO 9000 defines the way in which an organisation should set its own standards and provide procedures for reaching those standards. It concerns the way that an organisation operates, rather than the standards of the output itself (products, services, etc.). The environment in which the unit was operating was that of intense financial pressure, coupled with the indication that the functions of the unit would be put out to commercial tender in the near future (through market-testing). It was also hoped that the discussion of quality and the formalisation of parts of the organisation would give accountability and help focus on customer needs.

The move to bring their method of operating within the requirements of the standard came as part of the measures to give them an advantage in any future competitive tendering situation for health services. The project was set a target of achieving the necessary certification within two years in some areas, and longer in others. Staff would need to be trained and the necessary documentation (detailing all working procedures) would have to be prepared.

The project was started and a new project manager (called the quality manager) recruited to provide both knowledge and a degree of independence from the other functions within the organisation. Across the organisation, there were pockets of enthusiasm, but otherwise annoyance from departmental managers who saw the changes as being bureaucratic and as interference from outsiders in the way they ran their departments. Above all, there was resistance to change which was both obstructive and destructive. The common feeling was that people had enough to do already, and this was an additional workload.

The result of this was that the areas which took the new standard on board and made it work in their way, got through the process earliest and with greatest benefit. On reviewing the implementation, it was shown that one of the reasons that people had opposed the changes was a lack of comprehension as to what they would mean in practice. They could not see how the documentation of, adherence to, and continuous improvement of working processes, would improve their lives, or improve the organisation.

Case discussion

1 What was the need and how did the project go towards meeting this?
2 Describe the complexity of the project.
3 How might identifying all the people who could hold up progress earlier in the project have increased the speed of achieving the project goals?
4 Why might recruiting an external project manager be beneficial, and what risks would there be?

**SUMMARY OF
KEY POINTS**

● project management is about the management of a process of change and differs from the normal requirements of the line manager's role;
● a project is any non-repetitive activity which can be modelled through analysing the inputs, constraints, outputs and mechanisms (ICOMs);
● the environment in which all organisations are operating is characterised by the four Cs – competitiveness, complexity, completeness, customer-focused;

- complexity may be defined in terms of the organisational, resource and technical complexity;
- projects may be further categorised according to their nature – strategic, systems or procedural;
- utilising the PDCA cycle of Deming, the project manager can seek to continuously improve the performance of the organisation;
- success or failure of a project can be evaluated both through the achievement of desired end results and the way in which it was able to operate within the given constraints.

KEY TERMS	project	inputs, outputs, constraints and mechanisms
	management	complexity
	change	maintenance
	line management	innovation
	world-class performance	continuous improvement
	systems approach	

REVIEW AND DISCUSSION QUESTIONS

1 Identify a personal project that you have completed in the recent past – this may be a piece of course-work, a DIY project, etc. Consider the way in which the project was planned, carried out, the results analysed and then acted upon. What would you do differently if you were doing it all over again?

2 Explain the differences between project and line management.

3 Why should 'motivating' be included in the list of roles of the project manager?

4 Taking the example of a personal project that you have recently completed (as for Q1), identify the inputs, outputs, constraints and mechanisms for the project. What is the importance of defining the nature of constraints on a project prior to starting work on it?

5 How would you describe the competitive environment of the following organisations:
- automotive industry;
- construction industry;
- banking;
- further/higher education.

What constraints does this place on projects being carried out in such an environment?

6 Why is it necessary to define the complexity of a project?

7 Identify the likely complexity of the following projects:
- the development of a new office block;
- the development of a new office complex where a radical new design is proposed;
- a project to put a new telescope in space by the European Space Agency;
- implementing a robotised assembly line in a manufacturing company.

8 Why is it necessary to consider the continuous improvement of the processes by which projects are carried out?

9 Identify the criteria for success or failure of the projects that you discussed in Q1 and Q3.

10 'A project manager should not have other managerial responsibilities'. Discuss.

11 Show how developing a new product, for example a new range of vehicle engines, could benefit through the analysis of previous development projects.

12 Categorise the following projects in terms of whether they are strategic, systems or operational:
- the construction of a new warehouse complex for a manufacturing company to be nearer its customers;
- the installation of electronic point of sale (EPOS) equipment into a retail environment;
- changing the suppliers of medical equipment to a hospital.

REFERENCES

Davidson, J. D. and W. Rees Mogg (1992) *The Great Reckoning*, Sidgewick and Jackson.

Deming, W.E. (1986) *Out of the Crisis – Quality Productivity and Competitive Position*, MIT Centre for Advanced Engineering Study, Cambridge, MA.

Handy, C. (1994) *The Empty Raincoat – Making Sense of the Future*, Hutchinson, p.9.

Harrison, F. L. (1992) *Advanced Project Management*, 3rd edition, Gower.

Morris, P. W. G and G. H. Hough (1987) *The Anatomy of Major Projects*, Major Projects Association, John Wiley, p.3 and pp. 8–11.

Schonberger, R. J. (1986) *World Class Manufacturing*, Free Press.

Turner, J. R. (1994) 'Project Management: Future Developments for the Short and Medium Term', *International Journal of Project Management*, vol. 12 no. 1, pp. 3–4.

Womack, J., D. Jones, and J. Roos (1990) *The Machine That Changed The World*, Macmillan.

FURTHER READING

Badiru, A.B. (1993) *Managing Industrial Development Projects*, Van Nostrand Reinhold.

Bradley, K. (1993) 'PRINCE: A Practical Handbook', *Computer Weekly*/Butterworth Heinemann.

Kerzner, H. (1992) *Project Management*, 4th edition, Van Nostrand Reinhold.

Lock, D. (1992) *Project Management*, 5th edition, Gower.

Yeomans Software Consultants/Micromatch Limited, *IDEF0 Workshop Guide* (further exposition of the ICOM activity modelling methodology)

International Journal of Project Management, Butterworth-Heinemann.

Further information

Internet – the International Association of Project Managers
85 Oxford Road, High Wycombe HP11 2DX

The British Deming Association
The Old George Brewery, Rollerstone Street, Salisbury SP1 1DX

CHAPTER 2

Life-cycles, roles, interfaces and systems

The understanding of any subject comes from:

- *the logical deconstruction of a complex whole into its constituent elements – breaking down those elements until each is comprehensible in its own right;*
- *living with the subject so that the elements are intrinsically understood, but never analysed.*

Each of these is a valid approach and represents the two philosophical approaches to understanding. The first is the hard, analytical or scientific approach. The second is often referred to as the soft or romantic approach. For the purposes of the academic study of a subject, the hard approach is usually taken.

In this chapter, the subject of project management will be deconstructed using a series of frameworks in order that the process can be analysed, studied and improved, on an ongoing basis. Readers will need to become familiar with the language of the project manager.

2.1 PROJECTS WITHIN PROJECTS – WORK BREAKDOWN STRUCTURE (WBS)

The breaking down of large activities into comprehensible or manageable units is a fundamental part of project management. Figure 2.1 shows how a systems project – the installation of a new computer system – was broken down into elements that one person or one department could tackle as an activity in its own right.

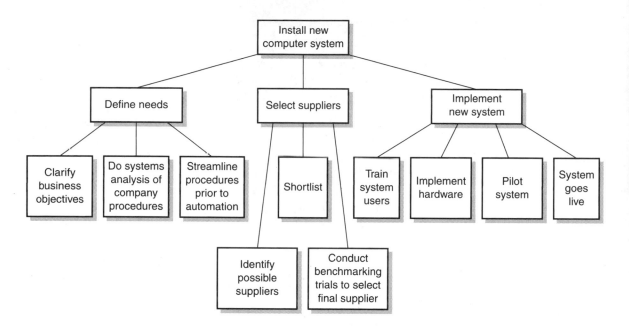

Figure 2.1 Example of a work breakdown structure (WBS)

WBS is also known as 'chunking' or 'unbundling'. This is attractive as it gives people responsibility for a manageable part of the project. WBS also facilitates financial control activities, as individual parts can have their consumption of resources tracked. The sensitivity of such control is preferable to keeping track of a single large activity.

The major drawback is that people naturally try to optimise their own part of the project and lose the holistic view of the project. Positions can become entrenched and destructive when improvements in one area upset the running of another, e.g. introducing new accounting procedures may greatly streamline the running of the accounting department's role in projects, but if it doubles the administrative workload for another function, the result is that neither the project nor the organisation as a whole has benefited.

The role of WBS is to create a linked, hierarchical series of activities which are independent units but at the same time still part of the whole. The hierarchical structure can be represented using the input, output, constraints and mechanisms model from Chapter 1. This form of activity model has been used effectively for a number of years, having been originally developed by the US Air Force. Models are created at a number of levels which are essentially static representations of the reality of project situations, i.e. they are a true representation of reality at one point in time (*see* Chapter 8).

The same technique can be applied very effectively in line-management situations where previously the description of procedures would have to be written longhand. Process mapping techniques, such as those discussed throughout this book, work far better and greatly cut down the amount of documentation required, whilst improving the usefulness of the end result.

2.2 THE PROJECT LIFE-CYCLE

In Chapter 1 Deming's PDCA was applied to the project environment with the objective of continuous improvement. The generic life-cycle for a project involves the consideration of how the level of activity varies with time. This is illustrated in Fig. 2.2 and shows how the level of activity is relatively low during the planning phase, increases through the doing phase, and decreases through check and act phases.

This pattern is reflected in the graph of cumulative expenditure against time (Fig. 2.3). Outgoings are generally low in the early stages, but grow rapidly during the execution phase. The graph also demonstrates why the check and act phases are so vital – by the time the majority of the doing phase is completed, the probability is that in excess of 98 per cent of the total project

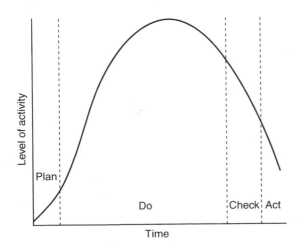

Figure 2.2 Graph showing how level of activity varies with time

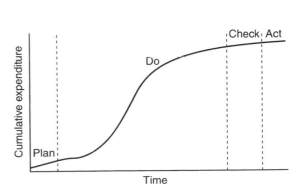

Figure 2.3 Graph of cumulative expenditure against time

expenditure will have been incurred. The last two phases are the time when the project team themselves can benefit from the process and ensure that lessons (good and bad) are applied in the future.

The life-cycle may be further broken down as shown in Table 2.1

Table 2.1 Development of the project life-cycle

Stage in project life-cycle	Activity	Description
Planning	Conceptualisation	Generate explicit statement of needs
	Analysis	Identify what has to be provided to meet those needs
	Proposal	Show how those needs will be met through the project activities
	Justification	Prepare and evaluate financial costs and benefits from the project
	Agreement	Point at which go-ahead is agreed by project sponsor
Doing	Start-up	Gathering of resources, assemble project teams
	Execution	Carry out defined activities
	Completion	Time/money constraint reached or activity series completed
	Handover	Output of project passed to client/ user
Checking	Review	Identify the outcomes for all share-holders
Acting	Feedback	Put in place improvements to procedures, fill gaps in knowledge, document lessons for the future

Table 2.2 shows how a new management information system was supplied to a hospital through a software company.

2.3 THE PROJECT BRIEF AND PROPOSAL

There is no single route for the development of the project brief and subsequent proposal. Formalised processes are most commonly required where the customer and the supplier are in different organisations (as in Table 2.2). Common practice is for the customer to provide a brief (a written document presented

Table 2.2 MIS project

Phase of project	Activities
Conceptualisation	Software house receives an outline from the MIS department of the hospital; various pieces of information and points of clarification are requested.
Analysis	The concept is converted into the terminology of the software house (every organisation has its own set of jargon). An initial feasibility check is carried out to see what could be achieved at what cost. Objectives are set for the system to be developed and the interfaces with other systems studied. The analysis phase was completed by an appraisal of the capability of the company to provide what was being asked for by the client.
Proposal	The proposal document is submitted for approval by the client's MIS department in terms of whether or not it would meet the requirements set out in the initial request. The client organisation is offered the opportunity to visit the software house's premises and existing clients to view their systems.
Justification	There are two parts to this process – firstly the software house doing their financial analysis to show whether or not it is feasible for them to undertake the project. The MIS people at the hospital need to provide evidence that the new system will provide a return. This has to be agreed by the financial managers.
Agreement	After the justification has been prepared by both sides, the formal act of preparation and signing of contracts can take place. This is the basis of the agreement between supplier and customer. The terms and conditions will have to go through each of the party's legal advisors (see Chapter 6).
Start-up	The software house starts to gather resources as soon as the contract looks likely to go ahead. Formal commitments are not made until the deal is formally signed. A project manager within the company is allocated to provide a single point of contact for the customer. The project team is gathered, external programmers hired and resources (development computers, pre-written software) procured. The project elements are allocated to individuals and specifications written for what each of the elements must achieve.
Execution	The project team starts work on the system – this is a mixture of importing existing code, modifying other parts and writing totally new elements. At the completion of each section of the work, the modules are tested to ensure integration. Gradually the system is pieced together, and de-bugged. The client is involved in the process, with modules being demonstrated as they are completed, so that amendments are made at the time, rather than at the end of the entire process.
Completion	Towards the end of the development, the units being tested are getting larger and more complex. The in-house specialist staff are kept on and the programmers who were hired-in, continue to other jobs. The major task to be completed at this stage is the documentation of the system.
Handover	The software is transported to the user's site and installed on the machines. The software specialists are on-hand to see that any problems can be resolved quickly. Staff are trained in the usage of the system and the MIS staff on its maintenance and support. Ongoing support is to be provided by the software house.
Check	The way in which each of the modules was developed is documented to provide a rich picture of the process. Mistakes and good practice are identified, and customer perceptions of the system canvassed. The results to the company in financial terms are compared with the proposal.
Act	Where deficiencies were highlighted, e.g. in the documentation of the system, the company put in place new procedures and practices that would ensure (a) that the problem for the customer was resolved in this case and (b) that it did not occur in the future.

by the potential customer) or terms of references and for the supplier to respond in the form of the proposal document. The scale of the project is not relevant to the degree of formality that occurs – but a general statement is that the larger the project, the higher the degree of formalisation will be.

The brief should be very precise. Any areas that are not so will need to be identified and clarified by the supplier prior to starting to prepare the proposal. However, it is becoming more common for the brief to describe the precise requirements of the output, but to leave the means of achieving this to the expertise of the supplier. Therefore, customers can often be guided as to the precise nature of their needs.

There are situations where leaving the brief as wide open as possible is essential. The Disney Corporation, for example, employs a large number of people who have the job of creating new ideas in entertainment – they are there to 'blue-sky' (a term which infers that they spend the day gazing skyward waiting for inspiration).

The brief is only the starting point. It is the responsibility of the project organisation to make the best interpretation of this. The conversion of the outline given in the brief into the proposal can be a major part of the planning process. Careful consideration is essential, as it is also going to set the criteria by which the outcome will be judged.

The proposal should be considered in the following light:

- who is the proposal for – the investment decision-maker or a third party?
- why is the proposal being requested?

The first part of the analysis in the proposal development should consider the potential customers for the work – are they internal to the organisation or external? In addition, are the customers, end-users, investment decision-makers or a third party acting on the behalf of one of these? The degree of formalisation will need to be tailored – a bid to an external organisation usually requiring a much higher degree of formality.

In addition, if the project is:

- for an internal customer, there needs to be the consistency with the organisation's stated goals or aims (usually included in the mission statement);
- for an external customer, the most basic requirement is that they will be able to pay for the work to be carried out. It is pointless generating detailed proposals only to find that the 'customer' is insolvent or the transaction cannot be completed for other reasons. During the 1980s many European engineering companies were generating proposals for countries such as Iraq – only to have export bans imposed when hostilities were declared. Where the customer is from overseas, it is worth investigating at a very early stage whether or not they are eligible for export credit guarantees, for example;
- going to be appraised by a set of people, it is useful to know their backgrounds. For example, where a client has a detailed knowledge of the subject

area, more detail of the nature of the work to be carried out should be included or, for an investment decision-maker, details of the cost-benefit analysis.

The reason for the proposal being requested should also be examined to ensure that the result is appropriate:

- if it is to be part of a full competitive bid for funding, then it is probably worth investing the time to prepare a detailed proposal;
- if it is to be a first examination of the possibilities of such a project, with the customer deciding to find out what would be involved if the project was undertaken, then an overview proposal should be submitted;
- if the proposal has been requested as part of organisational policy to consider more than one supplier for any product or service, it is worth finding out whether or not an existing supplier already has the contract, before investing your time. Providing a very rough proposal can be dangerous as the impression that is left with the customer may not favour you in the future. It may be worth in such a case declining to put in a proposal – though this again should be determined by the aims of the organisation.

Other scenarios where the supplier may decide not to submit a proposal (also called a 'bid') include when the capability (organisational capability), resource (e.g. if capital is already tied up in other projects) or the desirability (e.g. moving into direct competition with an existing customer) is questionable.

The process of preparing and submitting the proposal is the organisation's opportunity to sell itself to the potential customer. 'You only have one chance to make a good first impression', so basics like ensuring that the proposal document reaches the customer on time, presented in a way that demands attention, and is free from stupid mistakes (particularly spelling and grammatical errors) is essential. This is only part of the process. The pre-sell to the client can involve visits, informal discussions and general information gathering by both parties. The intention, as set out in describing the project environment, is to foster partnership relationships between the two parties. The focus is on long-term mutual benefit rather than short-term gain at the expense of the longer term.

The proposal itself should contain:

- an executive summary – provides the basic information in a few words – ideally one that can be read in one minute (Blanchard and Johnson, 1982);
- the main body of the report – diagrams and pictures convey information much better than reams of text. Modern word-processing packages put desk-top publishing quality graphics within the price range of the majority of businesses. In order to ensure that the presentation is consistent, a standard set of forms are often used which also makes it far more difficult to leave items out. Checklists are also of great value in compiling documents;
- appendices – any information that is summarised in the main report can be included in longer form here, along with supporting evidence for any major points made.

2.4 PROJECT ROLES

The most basic categorisation of the people within a project is shown in Fig. 2.4. The roles may not be explicitly stated, e.g. the project manager may have a different title. The conventional roles are provided to give a generic picture of the activities of the main people who have an interest in the project.

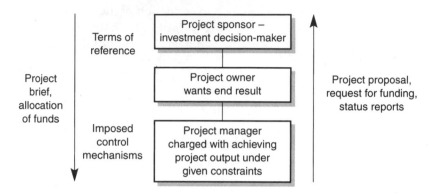

Figure 2.4 Project roles

The project sponsor is the investment decision-maker – the person who will give the final decision as to whether or not the project goes ahead. It is quite normal for medium–high complexity projects to have a project sponsor on the board of directors of the organisation (or equivalent in not-for-profit organisations). For projects of low complexity, a line manager or first-line supervisor may provide this role. The criterion for evaluating projects is discussed in Chapter 4. The sponsor will have to balance a portfolio of projects to ensure that the finances of the organisation are not overstretched, and will take a strategic overview of project progress.

The project owner is the person for whom the project is being carried out – they are interested in the end result being achieved and their need being met. Their role is more operational in nature, with the activities being related to the position in the project life-cycle. During the definition phase, for example, they will be involved in determining the terms of reference for the project manager and developing control mechanisms for the project activities.

The project manager/leader is the operational single point of responsibility for the planning, execution and review of project activities. They will have the largest input to establishing whether the project meets the criteria set for it in terms of time/cost/quality. Theirs is the day-to-day responsibility for feeding information to the sponsor and relaying needs to the project team. This interaction between the customer and the delivery process is vital to success.

The project team will have a variety of roles and responsibilities as allocated through the organisational structure and the work of the project manager. Where the project is a joint venture or involves collaboration between a number of organisations, the structure of Fig. 2.4 may be duplicated in each of the collaborating organisations.

It is becoming increasingly common for project management skills to be brought in to an organisation from an external source. This has occurred in the development of management information systems, and results in the structure shown in Fig. 2.5.

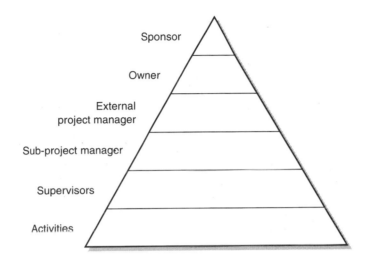

Figure 2.5 Project hierarchy

Overlapping roles

In smaller projects it is easy for the roles to become indistinct. Roles that can merge under such circumstances are those of the sponsor and owner. It is feasible for the person who is paying the bill also to be involved in the overseeing of the activities. Roles that must never be combined are those of project owner/ sponsor and project manager. This would cause a conflict of interests as the person paying for the project would also be the one with responsibility for delivering it. The arbiter of the quality of the project could then hardly be said to be impartial! In personal projects this is unlikely to matter, but where commercial interests are at stake, this would be inadvisable.

Projects which have a high degree of organisational complexity are likely to have more than one project manager. For example, in the introduction of a new banking service there were project managers in the subsidiary companies, a central (corporate) project manager who reported to a board level owner/ sponsor, and project managers in the regions who reported to the company project managers (see Fig. 2.6). This is a form of organisationally oriented work breakdown structure.

The categorisation shown in Fig. 2.6 is useful for definitional purposes, but the treatment and management of all those with any form of interest in the pro-

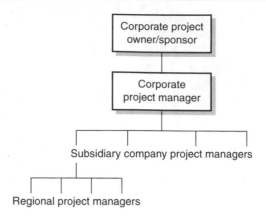

Figure 2.6 Organisationally oriented work breakdown structure in banking product development

ject process or outcome (called stakeholders) should also be considered. There are always two sets of teams involved in projects – the visible and the invisible team. The visible team is that group of people which is officially engaged in the project activities – the sponsor, owner, manager, team and any subcontractors. The invisible team includes anyone who is going to be affected by the outcome in any way – this may include the end-users of the project result. The stakeholders are further categorised as:

- outcome stakeholders – those who have an interest simply in the output and it being achieved within the three objectives of time, cost and quality. This view is the one usually attributed to accountants, and normally will be shared by clients, end-users and the project sponsor;
- process stakeholders – those who are involved in the core team, all direct and indirect contractors. The outcome for them is less important than the way they feel that they have benefited from the process – for example, in their levels of motivation and the learning and development opportunities. This group is vital in the new view of management and they are the people that a project manager is likely to have to work with in the future.

These are not necessarily exclusive groups as a client may be interested in the way that the process is carried out – in particular through the use of appropriate quality systems.

Obeng (1993) suggests that:

'The progress of projects can be largely visible or invisible. The level of visibility depends on the specific nature of the project activities. With a visible project, progress is obvious to all the stakeholders and progress is easily measurable. The stakeholders can therefore make up their own minds about how well it is going. To succeed, you must manage what your stakeholders observe to ensure that they are kept in balance.'

Project success will be defined by the stakeholders. Their expectations will need to be balanced with actual performance. The role of the project manager is then to ensure that the success is 'sold' to the various groups in the best way.

2.5 A SYSTEMS APPROACH TO PROJECT MANAGEMENT

The model of projects used in Chapter 1 (inputs, outputs, constraints and mechanisms) is a basic systems model. As suggested in the introduction, the complexity of a large entity is broken down systematically into smaller entities, making them manageable. There are other important characteristics of the systems approach:

- it considers the inter-relationships of:
  - the various parts of the system
  - the phases of the project
  - organisational functional components/departments
  - levels of hierarchy within the organisation;
- the approach is structured allowing logical assessment and analysis;
- both hard and soft elements are taken into account;
- the outcome of the systems study is a set of guides to the management decision-making process.

In order to build a full or 'rich' picture of all the elements of a project system, Checkland (1981) uses the CATWOE mnemonic. This is built up as follows:

C customers – those who will benefit from the project, e.g. end-users
A actors – the visible project team
T transformation process – the activity that satisfies the defined need or desire
W Weltanschauung or worldview – the point of view or range of possible points of view of someone interpreting the point or reason for the project
O owners – already defined as the owner, sponsor or project manager – the people who could destroy the project should they so wish
E environmental constraints – defined as constraint in the earlier model

Example – Developing a CATWOE statement for the widening of the M25 London orbital motorway, from three lanes to four lanes each way:

Customers – motor transport users, in particular those who live in the vicinity of London
Actors – the contracted companies who provide the miles of cones, vans with flashing lights and people who have perfected the art of standing gazing into holes
Transformation process – the digging up of verges, laying of base and surface, widening of bridges, upgrading of support services (drainage, lighting, etc.)
Worldview – the view that has been taken so far is that of a motorist who uses the road in question. Other worldviews include an environmentalist one (further

evidence of the destruction of the planet), a societal one (stimulating the economy through improvement of the infrastructure), and that of the residents of houses who are being affected by the project (do not build it in my back garden)

Owners – the Department of Transport, the contracting companies, the European Parliament

Environmental constraints – the existing road structures, work practices, etc.

Rather than just consider the practicality or feasibility of such a project, the formation of the CATWOE statement has increased the understanding of the possible views of the project. This formulation is vital if the goal of managing all the stakeholder perceptions is to be achieved.

The CATWOE statement is useful to help enrich the picture of the systems being studied. Once the picture has been enriched, the project manager needs a tool to handle the complexity of the work breakdown. It was noted that there was no technique that the project manager could use to unify the elements of the project into a cohesive whole. This was particularly true in the management of technology – particularly new product development. Boardman (1994) showed how the technique of preparing systemigrams (SYSTEMs dIaGRAM) could help. This approach helps the worldviews of many players, in a moderately complex project upwards, to be analysed and individual team members to see how their tactical role fits in with the overall strategy of the organisation in pursuing the project. Boardman also suggests that the implicit commitment of people to the project goals can be ensured as start and end points of activities are clearly defined. Figure 2.7 shows the use of a systemigram to describe the relationship between project sponsor, owner and manager.

A more complex example that looks in more detail at the process of new product development would be as shown in Fig. 2.8.

2.6 THE REQUIREMENTS OF A SUCCESSFUL PROJECT MANAGER (PM)

The role that the PM will play is determined by:

- the nature of the project – complexity, scale, position in hierarchy of projects;
- the nature of the organisation that it is being carried out in, e.g. sector, activities, organisational structure;
- the personality of the PM;
- the constraints under which they are working.

Trying to specify a generic list of characteristics for a successful project manager would be impossible. The list of characteristics that is presented below should be treated therefore as scales on which :

- initally projects should be rated to determine the requirements of the person for the job;
- individuals can be rated to determine their suitability for the job in hand.

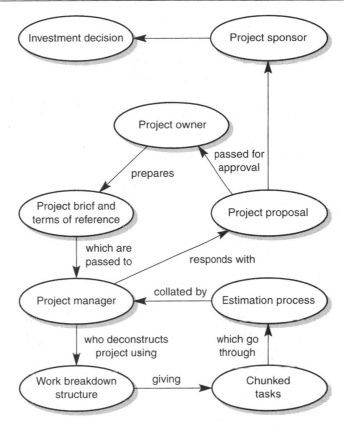

Figure 2.7 Project brief/proposal systemigram

The characteristics of individuals may be classified as either attitudes or skills. Attitudes are those characteristics which are determined by the way a person thinks about a particular issue and which are reflected in the intent of that person. The skills are those characteristics which a person has been trained in or has learned, and determines the tools available to that person regarding 'how' to handle a particular situation.

Attitudes which are desirable for project managers are:

- a desire not just to satisfy but to delight customers and stakeholders alike;
- accepting of both challenges and responsibility;
- being focused on action, rather than procrastination – getting the job done rather than avoiding critical or difficult issues;
- a desire to make the best use of all resources – minimise waste in all activities;
- does not lose sight of the light at the end of the tunnel – is goal focused;
- has personal integrity – people find it very difficult to respect and take the authority of a person who has low integrity;
- is flexible about the route that must be taken to achieve the stated end-goals;
- has personal goals that are consistent with those of the project organisation – the project team perceives that the PM and the organsiation are going the same way.

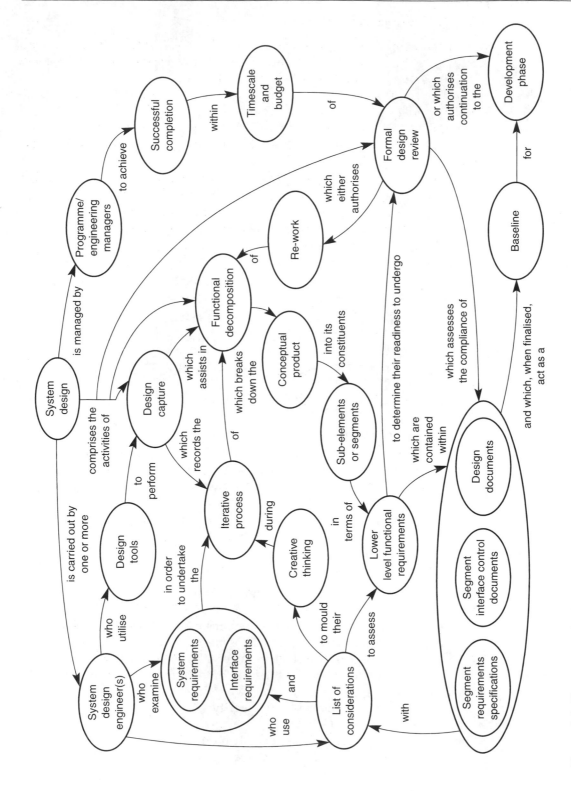

Figure 2.8 The system design process systemigram
(*Source:* Boardman, 1994, reproduced with permission)

Skills which are desirable include:

- ability to determine the real needs/desires of the customer. This is done through 'getting close' to the customer via visits and both formal and informal discussions, and asking the relevant questions;
- analytical skills to turn data into information and break down the project into comprehensible component parts;
- technical skills – the PM need not be a technical specialist, but must at least be capable of comprehending the work that is being carried out, and 'speaking the language' of the people involved;
- team skills (*see* Chapter 5) – many battles have been won against poor odds by the ability of individuals to motivate and enthuse a team;
- ability to delegate effectively – not try to do everything personally;
- ability to manage your own time (*see* Chapter 7) – you cannot expect to manage other people unless you can show that you can manage yourself;
- the balancing of stakeholder perceptions of project progress (otherwise known as being able to 'sell ideas');
- negotiating skills – resolve potential conflict situations so that all parties can be said to have 'won';
- problem-solving/facilitating problem-solving;
- question all assumptions made by stakeholder at all stages of activities.

and . . . if you can keep your head whilst all about you are losing theirs. . . .

The above are all internal factors of the person. Their role and the way that it is managed by the organisation are just as important. This consideration will centre around four factors:

- responsibility – the scope of the control of the PM as they perceive it;
- authority – the organisation's view as to the scope of control of the PM;
- accountability – the set of outcomes that are determined to be under the control of the PM;
- credibility – the organisation must stand behind the PM and back the decisions that are made. Not doing so removes the individual's credibility and hence authority.

The rules for balancing these roles are:

- no responsibility without authority – do not give a person the apparent responsibility for an area without giving them the authority to carry out their responsibilities;
- no authority without accountability – unless someone can be held to account for their decisions or actions, they should not have the authority to make those decisions.

One of the most common causes of stress amongst project managers is that they have apparent responsibility for an area, but not the authority to make the necessary changes in order for them to meet the requirements placed on them.

This is termed role ambiguity. It is common in organisations that are either only partly structured on project lines, or for whom the carrying out of project management in any formalised way is relatively novel. There are other stresses that befall project managers – most notably due to the need to constantly make deadlines and the ever-changing nature of the work. Kerzner (1987) suggests that a job advertisement for a project manager should read:

'WANTED – Project Manager – Facilities Planning and Development
Personable, well-educated, literate individual with degree in engineering to work for small firm. Long hours, no fringe benefits, no security, little chance for advancement are among the inducements offered. Job requires wide knowledge and experience in manufacturing, materials, construction techniques, economics, management and mathematics. Competence in the use of spoken and written English required. Must be willing to suffer personal indignities from clients, professional derision from peers in more conventional jobs and slanderous insults from colleagues.

Job involves frequent extended trips to inaccessible locations throughout the world, manual labour and extreme frustration from lack of data on which to base decisions.

Applicants must be willing to risk personal and professional future on decisions based on inadequate information and complete lack of control over acceptance of recommendations by clients. Responsibilities for work are unclear and little or no guidance offered. Authority commensurate with responsibility is not provided either by the firm or its clients.'

This is still the case in some companies, but many others have begun to recognise the specialism of project management. The career path of project managers can then be seen to be more than just a string of projects and some discernible progression – as for line managers – is defined. This has only occurred in organisations that have made the role of project management part of their corporate strategy.

2.7 THE USE OF PROJECT MANAGEMENT CONSULTANTS

There are many large and influential management consultancy firms (e.g. Coopers and Lybrand, McKinsey, Andersen Consulting – combined UK turnover in 1994 amounting to in excess of £1 billion) in addition to legions of individuals, but very little is written on their roles or how their skills can best be applied. The general role of consultants is in the provision of specific services – such as accountancy, strategic analysis, human resource development or information technology. The consultant within the project environment can have the following roles:

- an integrator – providing an overall project management service as a single point of contact for a customer. They arrange the allocation of tasks between subcontractors and are responsible for overseeing progress;
- as an honesty-broker – gaining an external 'independent' viewpoint on a situation can be immensely beneficial. As one consultant commented –

'Sometimes people get too close to the coal face to see the wood for the trees!' People working within the project organisation can be more inclined to accept the views of an outsider on changes, than to move from entrenched positions at the behest of a colleague. As importantly, such a solution may allow individuals to 'save face';

- as a change-agent – providing the focus for activities – whilst keeping an overview as to what is happening;
- as a knowledge provider in one or more specific areas or techniques;
- as a resource provider – to allow tasks to be carried out that people from within the organisation would claim that they do not have the time or capability to do (certain documentation activities or specialist technical knowledge);
- as a checker of the way in which the process is being carried out;
- as a trainer – rather than doing the job for the organisation, the knowledge is imparted to the members of the organisation through training. As one consultancy firm advertised – 'Your consultant says "Do this..." You do it. Your consultant says "Now do this...." You do it. Your consultant leaves. What do you do now?'

The first stage in employing consultants is to decide exactly what it is that they are being brought in to achieve. The means of achieving this must be determined, either through having the consultants do the job for you or through training. The evaluation of the suitability of one or other firm can be done through:

- membership of appropriate professional bodies;
- talking to previous clients;
- closely evaluating their capabilities;
- evaluating the costs for the job, in particular whether there is any financial incentive for them to finish the job in a given time, and whether their fee is linked to tangible benefits achieved from their work.

One encounter with a consulting company ended when the two consultants stated that nothing had been written on the area in question. The manager concerned had pre-prepared for the meeting by going to the local university library and locating two large tomes on the subject which he duly produced for the meeting. They did not get the assignment.

One of the challenges of employing consultants is how to evaluate the benefit of the service that they have provided. Many consultants in the field of total quality management treat it as heresy if a company employing them evaluates their impact in terms of financial cost and benefit. This may be condoned if there is going to be a definable longer-term benefit but the mechanisms need to be put in place to ensure that this is achieved. Many managers, when viewing the output of consulting assignments, have made the comment that '...if you give them your watch, they will tell you the time!' This does not mean that the findings had little value – getting someone impartial to state the obvious is as good a means as any of starting the debate on such issues.

One of the benefits of a consultant's study is that it is largely impartial. The allocation of tasks to consultants should be fully in the knowledge of any potential conflicts of interest, e.g. if they also do work for a major competitor or if they are employed at various stages in the project. A consultant may be employed to help in the evaluation of a project proposal. The same consultant could quite reasonably be brought in later in the project if it goes ahead – therefore they would have a vested interest in it going ahead!

In the future consultants are going to have an important role to play in the management of projects and in the provision of resources that companies do not have the size to have in-house. Their role will need intelligent purchasers of their services if it is to be successful. The lure of the consultant's patter can then be put to good use selling the necessary ideas to those for whom their activities will be value-adding in the longer term. The way that consultants charge for jobs may also be re-considered – the normal method is currently to work on the basis of a daily rate (one hundred up to several thousand pounds per day per consultant). This does not offer the consultant much incentive to get the job done at any particular speed.

PROJECT
MANAGEMENT
IN PRACTICE:
**THREE PROJECT
MANAGERS
WITH DISTINCT
ROLES**

1 The site manager of a housing development

'I am in charge of the construction of the buildings you see around you (he gestured with his hand to the mixture of partially and fully completed properties) and of making sure they go from this stage (he indicates a pile of drawings and building schedules) to the point where we can hand them over to the sales people to sell. Most of the work is supervisory, ensuring that orders are placed and materials arrive on time, people turn up, do the job properly and get paid for it at the end of the week. There are always arguments between the various tradespeople to resolve and problems just get dumped on the desk. Some of the toughest problems come with the people you have to work with. Some of them will do anything to try and get one over on you – they'll tell you a job is finished when you can see it is only half done. Unless you go and check it yourself you're in trouble. Also, they don't give a damn for my schedule. How do you get a roofer, at four o'clock in the afternoon when it is raining rather heavily (not the words actually used) when you know he has a long drive home, to get back on the roof and finish the job he is doing so that other jobs which rely on this being completed can start at eight o'clock the following morning? It wouldn't be the first time we had to block his car in with a pallet of bricks to stop him leaving.'

2 Implementing total quality management – the quality director

'The quality director was appointed with the brief to introduce total quality management (TQM) to the company. It was his responsibility to put the proposal as to how it could be done, and then to carry it out. As he described at the outset of the project '(this) is one of the most complex projects that we could undertake at this time'. The complexity came because the project would hopefully change the way that everyone in the company thought and worked (i.e. both attitude and procedures). This would have to be done through consultation, training and the demonstration through piloting small-scale improvement activities, that the move towards TQ was worth while. The initial phase as part of the proposal process was to carry out a companywide quality audit to determine attitudes, knowledge and current practice. The results paved the way for the carrying out of targeted efforts where needed most. The first phase of execution was to take the board of directors of the company on awareness training – showing them how working under a TQ environment would benefit them, and what changes would be needed. The next level of management were then trained and so on down the hierarchy until the middle management level. These managers then trained their own people – a process known as 'cascading'. The project to introduce the new philosophy to the company took several years, and has now moved on to become an accepted way of working. The quality director was initially involved in the management of the introduction process, where the employees and suppliers needed to be convinced that this was a good route for the company to take. His role then became one of project sponsor of a variety of improvement projects, which may be considered as sub-projects of the main one.'

3 Project manager in financial management system implementation

'The main roles of the job include:

- organisation – from the design of the system to determining support issues and providing training;
- anticipation of future requirements of the system;
- monitoring of progress of the implementation;
- communication and information – providing progress reports to local team members and national common-interest groups;
- audit – ensuring the housekeeping, procedures and system security are in order.

The initial system design work involved coordinating with external system designers, the providers of the software and the in-house IT group. Our local area network (LAN) needed upgrading to run the new system. Other organisational issues were the role that consultants would play in the system design and training of users and the allocation of the budget between activities.

Anticipation was required as the requirements of the system would change over its life. For example, higher level monthly indicators of financial performance would need to be provided where they had not been needed before. In addition, a management accounting system would be needed to provide budgetary controls.

The monitoring system we used for the project was PRINCE (*see* Chapter 1). This provided a basic set of planning tools, and we filled in the blanks on the planning sheets. A team was set up to monitor progress against the plan.

Training was one area where I was personally involved with the users, showing them how to use the system. People are very frightened of technology and do not always grasp immediately ideas you think are very simple. This is where the greatest attribute of the project manager was needed in plenty – patience.'

Case discussion

1 Identify the title which might be given to the project management role in each case.
2 Describe the role of the project manager in each of the cases.
3 Describe the desirable characteristics of each project manager using the set of skills and attributes as a starting point.
4 For each case, show why work breakdown structure would be essential to the comprehension of the case by the project manager.
5 Give examples of how consultants could be usefully employed in each of the cases and how their benefit might be assessed.

SUMMARY OF KEY POINTS

- work breakdown structure decomposes a complex whole into smaller parts that are more easily understood. This is done through creating a hierarchical series of activities from the one large one;
- the planning phase of the project may be broken down into conceptualisation, analysis, proposal, justification and agreement;
- the carrying out of the project activities may be categorised into start-up, execution, completion and handover;
- the brief is the document that defines the need of the customer/end-user of the outcome of the project and the proposal is the project organisation's way of showing how the requirements of the brief will be met;
- the project will have people occupying positions as sponsor, owner, manager and team – stakeholders are interested in both the outcome and the process, and need to have their needs satisfied by the activities if the project is to be a success;
- a systems approach has many benefits and can be aided by the construction of systemigrams;
- project managers will need to have a variety of attitudes and skills as required by the project, and must have the necessary responsibility, authority, accountability and credibility;
- project management will often require some form of input from consultants – this will need managing in the same way as the rest of the project activities.

KEY TERMS

work breakdown structure (WBS)	owner
chunking/unbundling	stakeholder
linked hierarchical series of activities	CATWOE
IDEF	systemigrams
proposal	skills/attitudes
brief	honesty-broker
sponsor	change-agent

REVIEW AND DISCUSSION QUESTIONS

1 Why is the use of work breakdown structure important to the project manager?

2 Define what is meant by 'a systems approach' to project management.

3 Who does the project manager have to 'sell' a proposal to?

4 When is it important for the brief to be highly precise and when should it be left as loose as possible?

5 Why is it important to know the customer for a proposal document?

6 Why should the project manager be concerned with satisfying not just the outcome stakeholders but all the stakeholders of a project?

7 How would the requirements for the project manager of a project with very high complexity differ from one where the complexity is very low?

8 Why might an organisation use consultants and what benefits can they bring to a project environment?

REFERENCES

Blanchard, K. and S. Johnson (1982) *The One Minute Manager*, Fontana

Boardman, J. T. (1994) 'A Process Model For Unifying Systems Engineering and Project Management', *Engineering Management Journal*, February.

Checkland, P. (1981) *Systems Thinking, Systems Practice*, Wiley.

Kerzner, H. (1987) 'In Search of Excellence in Project Management', *Journal of Systems Management Special Issue – Controlling the Project Development Cycle*, February.

Obeng, E. (1993) *All Change – The Project Leader's Secret Handbook*, Pitman Publishing Financial Times series.

FURTHER READING

Journal of Systems Management Special Issue – Controlling the Project Development Cycle, February 1987 (role of the project manager and requirements of that role)

Manufacturing Systems Design and Analysis, B. Wu, Chapman & Hall, 2nd edition, 1994, pp. 70–3, 77–9 (the deconstruction of a manufacturing activity), Chapter 2 (systems concepts).

CHAPTER 3

Project planning

'Even the longest journey begins with a single step.'

The purpose of this chapter is to outline the scope and applications of planning methods that address the fundamental question – what needs to happen and when? The planning methods are the basis of a formalised approach by which the project manager will show how the requirements set out in the project brief will be met. There are a number of specific graphical techniques which are greatly facilitated by the use of computers. It is important in the first instance for the project manager to understand what is being done behind the 'graphical user interface' before committing to the output. This understanding of the methods involved will facilitate the process of finding a suitable system (see Chapter 4). Much planning should take place away from the computer as there are equally important matters such as the manipulation of time constraints to be considered.

CONTENTS

3.1 PROJECT PLANNING AS A VALUE-ADDING ACTIVITY

The plan is the first step in providing the means of satisfying the requirements of the project owner or sponsor. It is the beginning of the project manager's input to ensuring that wherever possible, potential problems are identified and solved in advance. The plan is an explicit statement of the intended timing of project activities and the basis for estimating the resource requirements. Problem and error prevention, rather than rectification, is one of the main drivers of the planning process.

With the plethora of modern tools available through the medium of the computer, it is easy to forget the objectives of the plan, which are discussed here. Some of the basic techniques for establishing the logic and timing of activities are presented.

To call project planning a 'process' implies that there is a well defined route for the planner to take. This is not always clear, and a generic model of planning is difficult to construct.

Planning as a process involves the consumption of resources – it has costs associated with it. The project manager has to decide on the balance between the costs incurred in the process and the benefits that will reaped from it, as illustrated by Fig. 3.1. Costs associated with the planning process include:

- planned labour and associated expenses (travel, subsistence, etc.);
- planner's tools – may include computer assistance;
- cost of preparing the written plan – typing, binding, etc.;

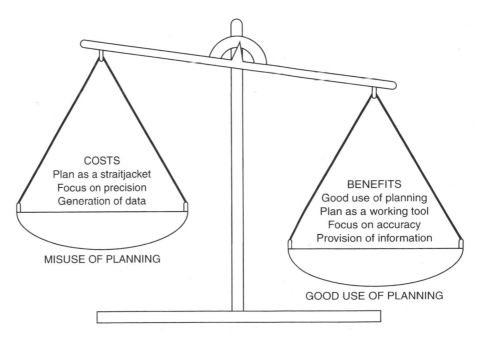

Figure 3.1 Balancing costs and benefits

- opportunity cost – what the planner and others drawn into the planning process could have been doing otherwise (e.g. working on an existing project).

In order for the planning process to be value-adding and not just cost-adding, the benefits of the activity have to be shown. These may be identified as:

- avoiding the costs of the chaos that would otherwise take place with an unplanned activity;
- providing a basis for a formalised evaluation process – filtering out projects that will provide a negative return;
- identifying problems in advance and being able to resolve them on paper.

The time that a planner spends preparing the plan should reflect the potential benefits of the activity. Figure 3.1 shows the positive and negative effects that the plan can have on project activities.

The plan as a working tool or organisational straitjacket

One of the paradoxes that the project manager has to address is whether the output of the planning process remains a working tool or becomes a form of organisational 'straitjacket'. As a working tool plans are used to help decision-making and guide future activities. A well-balanced plan will guide the actions of the project team, without the need to define to the absolute detail level what each person will do for every minute of every day. As the Prudential Corporation move case illustrates (*see* Project management in practice), project plans should change as circumstances change. People can get so involved in the plan that the project objectives are forgotten with the planning becoming an end in itself, rather than a means to an end. If the techniques that follow are applied intelligently, changed circumstances can be matched by a new course of action. The phrase 'because it says so in the plan' is the defence of a person who, wrongly, does not use the plan as a working tool.

Planning accuracy or precision?

A further argument which should be vocalised is the conflict between precision and accuracy – would you rather be roughly right or precisely wrong? The conflict is illustrated by 'The Sniper's Tale' below (Price, 1984):

'You are a sniper. You have a rifle with five rounds in the magazine. You spot your target; he is sitting under a tree leaning against its bole, his rifle resting across his knees. (He is a sniper as well, and he has got five rounds in his magazine.) You aim and fire five rapid shots. There are five thuds as each round bores into the tree trunk nine inches above your target's head. The holes they make are so tightly clustered you could cover them with a cigarette packet.

That is precision.

He jerks the muzzle of his gun and quickly fires his five bullets. The first hums past your ear, the second smacks into your thigh, the third clips your hair, the fourth smashes into your chest and the last drills into your head.

That is accuracy.'

Often, what is termed a 'quick and dirty' approach (with the objective of being as accurate as possible) may be far more beneficial than months of painstaking planning (with the objective of being as precise as possible). Precision, as Frank Price describes it, is pretty; accuracy is deadly.

There is clearly a role for detail planning, but not before an overview plan has been worked through. Evaluating the overview reveals fundamental flaws in assumptions. Until this level of plan satisfies basic criteria such as financial or technical feasibility, detailed plans are inappropriate.

Do plans provide information or just data?

One of the benefits of modern business systems is the ease and speed with which vast quantities of data can be generated. However, there is a tendency for managers to become overrun with data. Data is the numbers on the page. Information is the part or summary of that which can be usefully applied. The rest is just noise and clutters the thought and analysis process. One of the major roles of the project manager in projects, other than the smallest, will be to gather data from the relevant sources. Simply passing the data on is unlikely to be a value-adding activity. The project manager therefore needs to be not just a collector of data but a provider of information, usually in the form of management reports. The one page executive summary is one of the most beneficial of these in terms of information gleaned per time committed.

3.2 THE PROCESS OF PROJECT PLANNING – INPUTS, OUTPUTS AND THE PROCESS ITSELF

The process of project planning takes place at two levels. At one level, it has to be decided 'what' happens. This, the tactical level plan, then needs to be converted into a statement of 'how' it is going to be carried out (or operationalised) at the operational level. Figure 3.2 shows an activity model, as would be used to analyse systems of activity by considering the inputs, controls, outputs and mechanisms (ICOMs) for the activity (as discussed in Chapter 2). The inputs are the basis for what is going to be converted by the activity – in this case the project brief. The output is the project plan, or more specifically the project proposal. The controls provide the actuation, the constraints and the quality standards for the planning process in addition to its outputs and the mechanisms provide the means by which the process can happen.

At the operational level the way in which the proposal is generated should not be viewed as a one-off activity but should go through many cycles of suggestion and review before the 'final' document is produced. As Fig. 3.3 shows the first cycles are to provide the major revisions, where significant changes are made. Once these have been done and the project team are happy with the basic format, the last stages are those of refinement, where small adjustments are made.

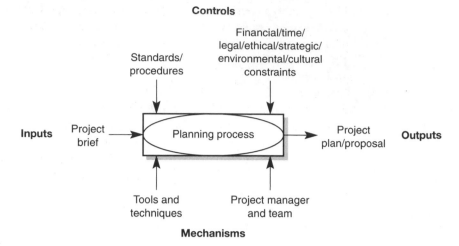

Figure 3.2 Activity model using ICOMs

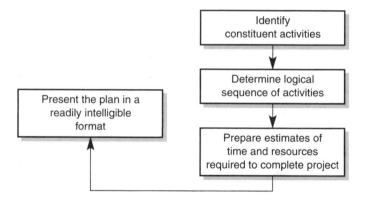

Figure 3.3 The project planning process

It is important for the overview to be verified first, before further effort is committed to planning at a detailed level – as discussed above. The life-cycle of planning shown in Fig. 3.3 shows the stages that the plan should go through. Cases such as the one given below are examples where the detail was considered before the major issues. As the example shows below, this is very wasteful of management time.

Example – the upside-down business plan

Business-plan meetings were serious affairs – they always were. The concept was quite attractive – to set-up an exclusive nursery school with an appealing teaching method in a smart area of the city. So far so good. This was, however, where the rough planning stopped and the group succumbed to the virus that plagues so many projects at this point – detailitus. The discussions were then waylaid by the need to have safety-tyres on the school minibus and on the detailed wording of the liability insurance. No matter that the lag between the money being spent on the buildings and equipment and any income from fees received would create interest payments that the company could never hope to meet ...

The revision/refinement process considers the necessary sub-projects (if any), the results of any numerical analysis (may be financial, resource, risk analysis or some form of mathematical simulation), the element of 'gut feel' (also referred to as the subconscious or back-of-the-mind element) as well as experience. The sponsor and other stakeholders will usually have some input to be considered in this process.

3.3 MANAGING THE PLANNING PROCESS

Most projects of low complexity will bias the ratio of planning : action heavily towards the action. As complexity increases, so does the necessity for a formalised plan. This is both a systematic analysis of the project (which provides its own set of benefits) and an opportunity to show that the project manager has been systematic in the planning process (by showing the level of consideration that the project manager has given to issues). 'Traceability' has become a major issue in many companies – allowing products to be traced back to records of their constituent parts. The same is required of a project plan. In the event of an unsatisfactory result, for whatever reason, a good plan can show that the planner took every possible precaution to ensure that the result was positive. Conversely, should the project go particularly well, you will have an assignable cause for this – namely your planning!

The benefits of using a systematic methodology in planning include:

- breaking down complex activites into manageable chunks (*see* work breakdown structure);
- determining logical sequences of activities;
- providing an input to subsequent project management processes, including estimating the time and resources required for the project;
- providing a logical basis for making decisions;
- showing effects on other systems;
- filtering frivolous ideas and activities;
- providing a framework for the assessment of programmes (the post-project review process relies on comparing the achieved result with the original plan, particularly for the purpose of improving the planning process);
- being essential for the revision/refinement process;
- allowing lessons to be learned from practice;
- facilitating communication of ideas in a logical form to others.

The process of revision and refinement can only take place if there is something to review or refine. The plan in this case provides a basis for making an objective judgement on the project, i.e. the plan should speak for itself. Drucker (1955) described a category of products for which there was unlikely ever to be a financial case for developing as 'investments in managerial ego'. This categorisation can be applied to projects – those which are not going to provide any direct benefit to the organisation but will get approved because of the personality involved. Forcing a systematic project plan to be produced can eliminate some of the more frivolous projects.

The above benefits of being systematic are clearly desirable, though the route to achieving them requires that a planning sequence is followed. This is illustrated by Fig. 3.4. The first step is the identification of the constituent activities of the project. These should initially be broken down in a logical form (as was required of the Channel Tunnel case in the previous chapter), selecting the main areas for further deconstruction. Guides to the relative size of the individual chunks vary, but are in the range of two to ten per cent of the total project time. Where a chunk makes up less than two per cent of the total project, it should be combined with other activities. Any activity which makes up more than ten per cent of the project should be broken down one further level, if possible.

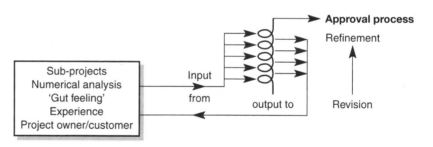

Figure 3.4 Planning sequence

It is human nature to tackle the easiest tasks first – sometimes only to find that an important step has been omitted. Any DIYer will happily recount stories of almost finishing a job, only to have to take it to pieces again because one of the first parts was missed out. The second stage is to determine the logical sequence of activities (e.g. close windows and remove aerial before driving car in to start car wash).

The third stage in the process involves the preparation of estimates for the time and resources required by the project. For small projects this may not be difficult, but where there are multiple projects with sub-projects, this can be a protracted and tortuous process. The techniques used for estimating are included in Chapter 4.

The fourth stage is the presentation of the plan. There are many techniques that can be used for presentation, some of which also facilitate analysis of the plans. The most popular ones are discussed in the following section.

It was stated at the start that the purpose of the project plan was to provide direction for the project. This is also the basis for assessing how the project is progressing. In the same way that a product or service may be judged in terms of its conformance to specification, a project is assessed as proceeding according to plan. The role that the plan plays in control is discussed in Chapter 6.

3.4 COMMUNICATING PROJECT PLANS – USING GRAPHICAL TECHNIQUES

Despite the diversity of projects being considered, one area of commonality between project managers is the use of various graphical techniques to:

- allow the construction of a comprehensive but comprehensible picture of the project activities;
- to communicate this with others.

The preference for graphical techniques is more than 'a picture telling a thousand words'. The whole revision/refinement process is built around people being able to understand what is going on. This is known as visibility, and is an essential feature of both the plan and the process.

The purpose of the graphical techniques is to illustrate the relationships between the activities and time. The simplest form is a horizontal bar chart, as in Fig. 3.5. This shows activity A represented by the shaded bar starting at time 1 and finishing at time 3. Multiple activities can be built up on the same chart, using the same timescale.

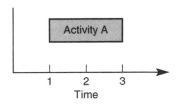

Figure 3.5 Horizontal bar chart: activity A starts at time 1 and finishes at time 3

A booking system for resources may use a similar format, as in Fig. 3.6. The shaded bars represent the amount of time that the resource is booked out for. It provides a readily interpreted record of who has booked the system and at which times.

Resource: AV system

	9–10	10–11	11–12	12–1	1–2
Mon	Dave Bg		Andy T		Sue B
Tues		Bill S			
Wed					
Thurs					
Fri					

Figure 3.6 Booking system

The following example involves a dissertation planning exercise. The student has a number of options as to how to present the information. The supervisor, being a busy person, has asked for the information to be presented in graphical form.

Planning a dissertation

The basic planning steps need to be followed here, namely:

- identify the constituent activities;
- determine their sequence;
- estimate the time and resources required;
- present the plan.

The time constraints are the start and end dates. The original statement looked as follows:

Activity	Time
Project start date	2/5
1 carry out literature review	2/5–20/6
2 arrange visits	20/6–4/7
3 prepare questionnaire	4/7–25/7
4 review questionnaire	25/7–8/8
5 deliver questionnaire	8/8–26/9
6 analyse results	26/9–2/11
7 write up	2/11–9/12
Hand-in date	9/12

The requirement to present the plan graphically is the next step. In this case, simply showing a week by a star is possible and requires nothing more than pen and paper or typewriter/wordprocessor, as shown in Fig 3.7. In this example, there was

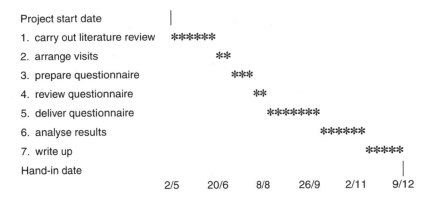

Figure 3.7 Project plan in graphical form

- a level of logic established and
- conventions used (time goes from left to right, activities are arranged top to bottom in order of their occurrence).

In addition the student has had to undertake two critical activities:

- forward schedule – started the activities at a given date and followed them forwards in time to determine the end date;
- backward schedule – looked at the time by which the project needed to be completed and worked the logic of activities backwards.

The tasks have had rough times allocated to see whether they meet the two constraints of start- and end-times. Where there was insufficient time, activities have been shortened. Any excess time (or slack) is used to lengthen activities.

Figure 3.8 shows an alternative presentation to the above. Logical links are indicated by the use of arrows. The head of the arrow points to an activity that cannot proceed until the activity at the tail of the arrow is completed. The diamond shapes on the chart are used to indicate 'milestones', i.e. important points in the life of the project – in this case the start and the hand-in dates.

Such a chart is often referred to as a Gantt or linked-bar chart as it is part of a family of techniques developed at the turn of the century by Henry Gantt. They were originally used in industrial planning.

Gantt charts, drawn by hand, are best suited to relatively simple projects, i.e.

- the number of activities and resources is low;
- the environment is fairly static;
- the time periods are relatively long – days and weeks rather than hours.

They do not make the link between time and cost and therefore do not provide a method for determining how resources should be optimally allocated, e.g. there are two activities, X and Y for which the times have been estimated and which use the same resource. If the resource could be shifted from activity X to activity Y, Y could be completed in a shorter time. X would obviously take longer, but how would this affect the project overall?

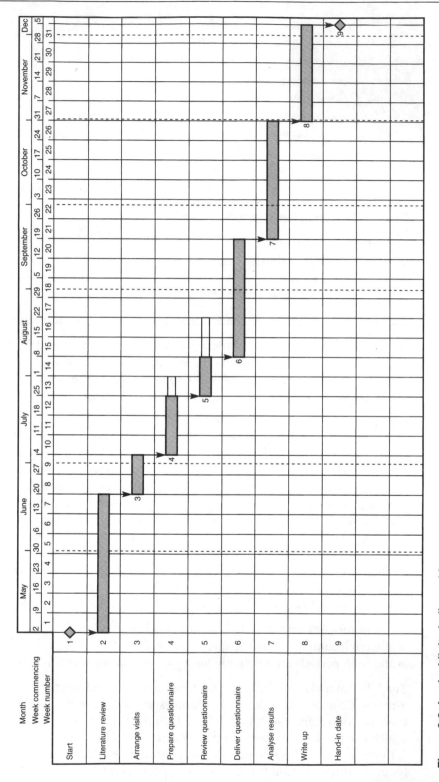

Figure 3.8 Logical links indicated by arrows

Gantt charts – summary

Good points	Limitations
● simple to draw and read ● good for static environments ● useful for providing overview of project activities ● very widely used ● the basis of the graphical interface for most PC software	● difficult to update where there are many changes – charts can quickly become obsolete and therefore discredited ● does not equate time with cost ● does not help in optimising resource allocation (*see* Chapter 4)

3.5 DEALING WITH INCREASED COMPLEXITY THROUGH NETWORK DIAGRAMS

Gantt charts are very useful at low levels of complexity. Many projects, however, require a higher degree of sophistication and a method which better lends itself to analysis. Rather than representing an activity as a bar on a bar chart, it can be represented as either:

● an arrow – method known as activity-on-arrow (A-o-A);
● a node – method known as activity-on-node (A-o-N).

The former will be discussed in some detail to illustrate the basics of planning. The type of analysis that can be applied is then demonstrated before the use of A-o-N is covered. Finally there is a summary of the debate as to which method should be used.

3.6 CONSTRUCTING AND ANALYSING ACTIVITY-ON-ARROW (A-o-A) DIAGRAMS

Under this convention the following 'rules' apply:

● the arrow runs from left to right indicating time running from left to right;
● the arrow starts and ends at an event (for the present this can simply be defined as a 'point in time');
● the events and activities should be given unique identifiers or labels;

e.g. Activity A on its own would be represented as running from event 1 to event 2 as in Fig. 3.9.

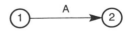

Figure 3.9 Activity-on-arrow diagram

The planning sequence identified above of:

- identify constituent activities;
- determine their sequence;
- estimate the times for each;

gives a verbal statement of the activities. This will now be converted into the A-o-A format for presentation, e.g. Fig. 3.10 shows two activities, A and B. B cannot start until A has finished and the times for A and B are five and seven days respectively. This logic is known as dependency and can be expanded as shown in Figs. 3.11 and 3.12. Here, more than one activity is dependent on another, in this case B, C and D cannot start until A has been completed. Likewise, H cannot start until all of E, F and G are finished.

Figure 3.10

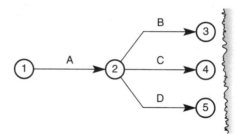

Figure 3.11

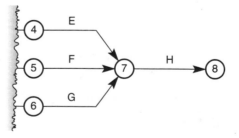

Figure 3.12

Essential to this convention, where all but the simplest projects are being described, is the addition of 'dummy' activities where:

- the logic of the activities' sequence needs to be preserved;
- the dummy will clarify the diagram;

e.g. taking the verbal statement that 'activity L is dependent on activity J but activity M is dependent on both activities J and K' would lead to Fig. 3.13. Simply writing it like this would add an extra logic dependency however – namely that of activity L on K. In this case a dummy is added to preserve the logic. It is written as a dotted arrow and in essence is an activity with zero duration, as in Fig. 3.14.

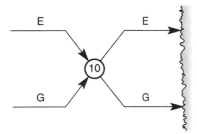

Figure 3.13

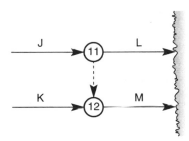

Figure 3.14

Clarification should be added where two activities have the same start and end events. Figure 3.15 should be expressed as Fig. 3.16.

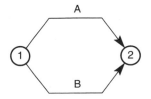

Figure 3.15

Figure 3.16

3.7 ANALYSING THE NETWORK – CRITICAL PATH ANALYSIS (CPA)

In order to provide a consistent format for the analytical phase, the convention for the symbols being used will be in accordance with BS6046:Part 2:1992, and are as Fig. 3.17. In order to facilitate the revision of diagrams, the event labels will now go up in tens or fives – allowing interim events to be added without modifying the labels to all subsequent events.

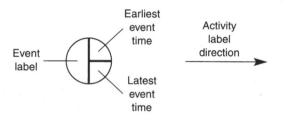

Figure 3.17

There are two new terms to be introduced to the diagrams:

- earliest event time (EET) – determined by the activities preceding the event and is the earliest time at which any subsequent activities can start;
- latest event time (LET) – is the same or later than the EET and is the latest time at which all the previous activities need to have been completed to prevent the whole network being held up.

Figure 3.18 shows the simplest case with a single activity.

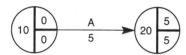

Figure 3.18

Figure 3.19 will be used as the basis for the calculation of the EET and LETs – please complete these on the page. The calculation of the two times is split into two processes.

1 Forward pass to determine the EET

The first event is assumed to start at time 0 for the purposes of this exercise. The forward pass starts at the first event (10) – the EET in this case is 0. Moving left to right, the subsequent activity time is added to this EET to give the EET for event 20,

i.e.:

EET at 20= [EET at 10] + [activity A duration]
$$= 0 + 5$$
$$= 5$$

This can now be added to the diagram. Event 20 should now look as in Fig. 3.19.

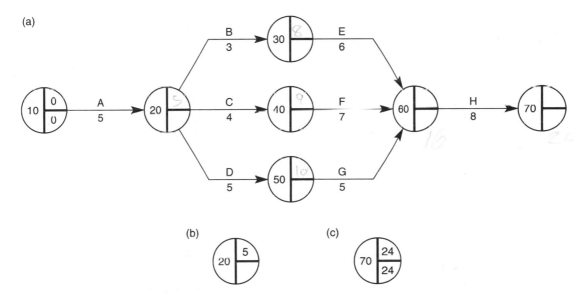

(a)

(b)

(c)

Figure 3.19

The same process can be repeated for events 30, 40 and 50. At event 30,

EET = [EET at 20] + [duration of connecting event (activity B)]
$$= 5 + 3$$
$$= 8$$

Add this to the diagram as before and do the EETs for 40 and 50.

The first logic snag occurs at event 60. As a reminder, the event cannot happen until all the preceding activities have been completed. In this case there are three possible EETs as shown:

[EET at 30] + [activity E duration] = 8 + 6 = 14
[EET at 40] + [activity F duration] = 9 + 7 = 16
[EET at 50] + [activity G duration] = 10 + 5 = 15

In this case the earliest that all the preceding activities will have been completed is 16 and therefore this is the EET at 60. Enter this on the diagram and calculate the EET for event 70.

The EET for the last event is the earliest time that the project can be completed, with the times and precedence given. Assuming that the project is required to be completed in the shortest possible time, this figure provides the basis for the next step.

2 Reverse pass to determine the LET

As the name suggests, the analysis begins on the right-hand side of the diagram at the last event. If the assumption that the project is required to be completed in the shortest possible time is correct, the LET of the final event is the same as its EET. Enter the LET for event 70 so that it looks like Fig. 3.19C.

Working backwards from the end, the next activity is 60, and the LET for 60 is calculated by:

LET at 60 = [LET at 70] − [activity H duration]
          = 24 − 8
          = 16

Do the same calculations for events 30, 40 and 50 and note that in two cases the EETs and LETs of those events are different. Enter these on the diagram. A logic challenge now occurs when trying to calculate the LET for event 20, similar to that in the forward pass. There are three possible LETs as shown:

[LET at 30] − [activity B duration] = 10 − 3 = 7
[LET at 40] − [activity C duration] = 9 − 4 = 5
[LET at 50] − [activity D duration] = 11 − 5 = 6

In making the choice we again check the logic definition of the LET as the time at which all previous activities (in this case, activity A) will have to be completed to prevent the whole network being held up. Here the LET is 5 – if it occurs any later than this, the whole project will be set back. Fill in the diagram and satisfy yourself that the original LET for event 10 still holds.

Having completed the network diagram, it is now possible to identify the critical path, which we define as:

that sequence of activities which begin and end in events where the EET = LET

You should now be able to identify this from the diagram. Marking the critical path activities should be done using one of the methods shown in Fig. 3.20.

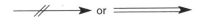

Figure 3.20 Marks used for critical path activities

We define *float* or *slack* as follows:

Float or slack = LET − EET

The critical path is that sequence of activities which have no float or slack. In the example, the path B–E has some slack which is evident at event 30. The slack is 10–8 = 2. Either of these events could:

● start late;
● take longer than expected;

or

● there could be a gap between E finishing and H starting;

and provided that the total of these deviations does not add up to more than two, the project will not be held up due to these activities.

The completed network is shown in Fig. 3.21.

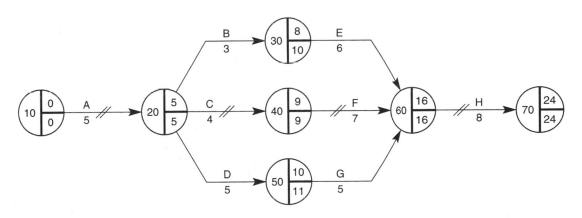

Figure 3.21 Completed network

Origin of CPA

The 'invention' of the techniques that have been described here as CPA, are variously attributed depending on the particular book you read. The time of first use, 1957/8, is less debated. The first users/developers are credited as being:

- the Catalytic Construction Company for the planning and control of a construction project for Du Pont Corporation;
- Du Pont Consulting;
- J. Kelly of Remington-Rand and M. Walker of Du Pont.

Whoever instigated its usage, the applications are now far and wide – it is only a shame that unlike products such as the ring-pull on cans, such methods cannot be patented. If they were given just 0.1p every time a company had produced a CPA diagram....

3.8 ACTIVITY-ON-NODE (A-o-N) DIAGRAMMING

This technique is included here because some project managers and their customers prefer it as a convention of project planning. The relative advantages and disadvantages of each method are included later in the chapter.

The most common way of representing the activity-on-node is as Fig. 3.22.

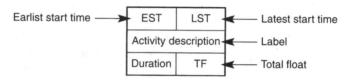

Figure 3.22 Activity-on-node diagram

Rather than talking about EETs and LETs, the method considers the activities directly and records the earliest start times and latest start times directly on the diagram as shown. The activities are linked in a similar way, but there are four ways in which activities can link (*see* Fig. 3.23). Precedence is indicated by arrows going from:

- the start of an activity (top left-hand or bottom left-hand corner of the box);
- the finish of an activity (middle of right-hand edge of box);

to:

- the start of an activity (middle of left-hand edge of box);
- the finish of an activity (top right-hand or bottom right-hand corner of the box).

The four ways in which activities can link are:

- finish-to-start – the second activity cannot start until the first has finished;
- start-to-start – the second activity cannot start until the first has started;
- finish-to-finish – the second activity cannot finish until the first has finished;
- start-to-finish – the second activity cannot finish until the first has started.

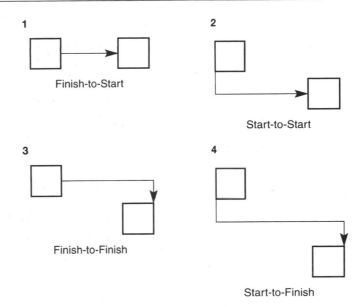

Figure 3.23 Four ways to link A-o-N activities

The arrows represent a potential time lag in the logic, e.g. if there was a figure, say 2 on the arrow in the start-to-finish case, the second activity could not finish until 2 time units after the first had started.

The way in which activities are built up into projects is very similar to that already discussed for A-o-A diagrams – with the exception that dummies are not required for clarification or maintaining logic flow.

3.9 ACTIVITY-ON-ARROW VERSUS ACTIVITY-ON-NODE METHOD

There is a preference for A-o-A diagrams amongst people who use such tools regularly. Whether this is because they were taught this technique first and have stayed with it or through conscious choice is debatable. There are many project managers who will not have A-o-A diagrams used in the planning of their projects. The debate can be roughly summarised as follows:

A-o-A
- easier to prepare and modify
- non-experts have a better change of understanding the network
- milestone events are easily marked
- where there are multiple predence relationships, (*see* Fig. 3.24) this is much more clearly illustrated

A-o-N
- easier to show complex relationships, e.g. start-to-finish precedence with time lag (complex with A-o-A)
- no dummy activities – keeps the number of activities the same as in the verbal statement (except when showing milestones)
- all the information about the activities is contained within the box – easier to ensure the right numbers are associated with the right activity

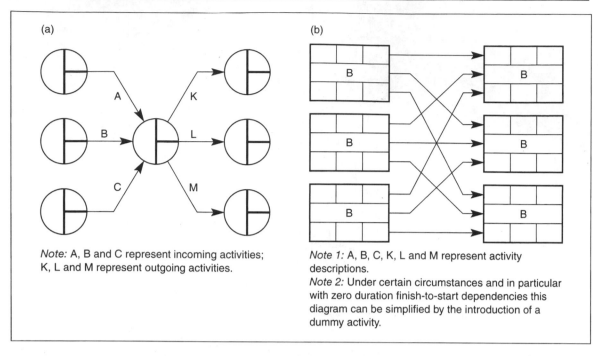

Note: A, B and C represent incoming activities; K, L and M represent outgoing activities.

Note 1: A, B, C, K, L and M represent activity descriptions.
Note 2: Under certain circumstances and in particular with zero duration finish-to-start dependencies this diagram can be simplified by the introduction of a dummy activity.

Figure 3.24 Comparison of network drawing modes (a) activity-on-arrow (b) activity-on-node

Example – planning the marketing of a new product

In Fig. 3.25 all the principles so far discussed are used to plan the launch of a new food product. It is possible through examining the EETs and LETs to determine which activities are on the critical path. The triangles are included to show milestones in the project, i.e. go-ahead, artwork go-ahead, production starts and sell-in starts. Trying to convey this volume of information through a verbal statement would clearly be a nightmare for both the planner and the reader, and would not lend itself to the kind of analysis that could be done with this diagram. Figure 3.25 was prepared using a computer program that would allow the information to be quickly displayed and altered as the situation changed.

3.10 DEALING WITH UNCERTAINTY – PROGRAMME EVALUATION AND REVIEW TECHNIQUE (PERT)

Programme evaluation and review technique (PERT) was developed for use in the Polaris project in the USA in 1958. Due to the success of the technique in this case, it was for a long time held up as the model that everyone should work to in planning projects. The technique is intended to deal with the likeli-

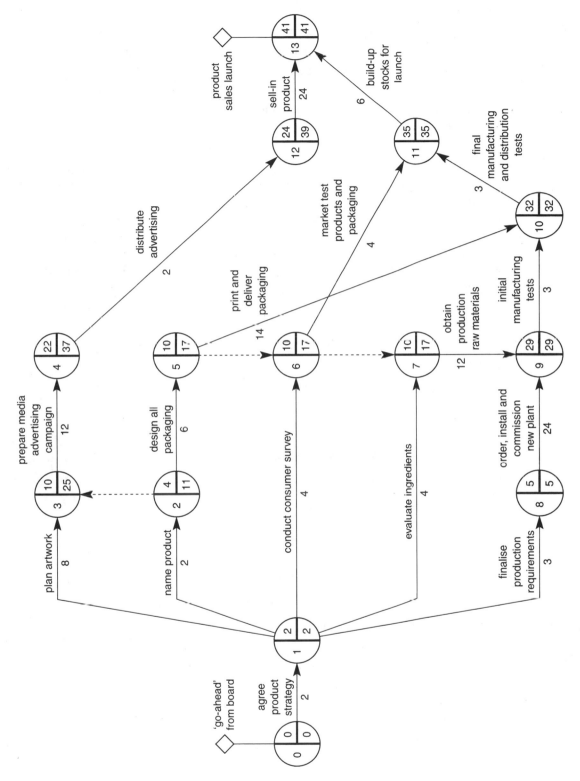

Figure 3.25 Planning the launch of a new food product

hood that the single value given as the estimated time for completion of activities, is going to have a degree of error associated with it. Instead of taking a single time, three time estimates for each activity are required:

- optimistic time – how long the activity would take if the conditions were ideal;
- most probable time – time if conditions were 'normal';
- pessimistic time – how long the activity would take if a significant proportion of the things that could go wrong, did go wrong.

There are an infinite number of possibilities as to how this range is distributed, e.g. optimistic and most probable times may be close together with the pessimistic time considerably different from the other two, or all three may be very close together. This flexibility in the distribution that is applied is one of the major appeals of the technique. The analysis that can be applied can be very simple or go into complex statistics that require the use of a computer. The following example can be done without the need for this. The project that was planned in the critical path analysis section (Section 3.7) was further examined, and the times estimated for each of the activities expanded to include an optimistic and a pessimistic element. The result is shown in Fig. 3.26.

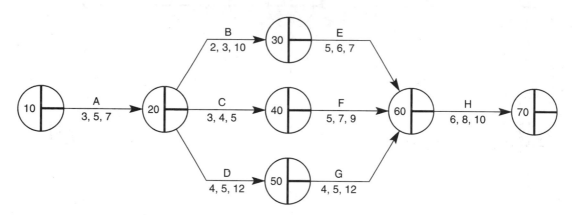

Figure 3.26 Network diagram showing optimistic, most probable, and pessimistic times

The activity arrows now have three figures associated with each in the order: optimistic, most likely, pessimistic, e.g. for activity A:

optimistic time = o = 3
most likely time = m = 5
pessimistic time = p = 7

In order to schedule these activities, it is necessary to calculate the *expected* time for each activity. This is done by calculating:

expected time = [o + 4m + p] / 6

In the case of activity A, the expected time = [3 + [4 x 5] + 7] / 6 = 5.

For activity B, the expected time = [2 + [4 x 3] + 10] /6 = 4.

This distribution can be represented by Fig. 3.27.

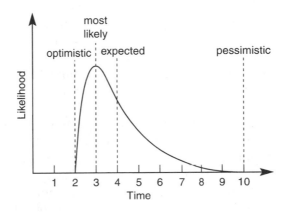

Figure 3.27 Distribution of estimated times for an activity

The example is now completed using the expected times shown in Table 3.1 instead of the most likely times and a critical path analysis carried out. Putting these figures into the network diagram and carrying out the forward pass gives a project expected duration of 25 days. This is not considerably different from the 24 days that the original analysis revealed. The reverse pass reveals that the critical path has changed. Originally it was ACFH, but with the consideration of the ranges of times, it is now ADGH.

Table 3.1

Activity	Optimistic time 0	Most likely time m	Pessimistic time p	Expected time
A	3	5	7	5
B	2	3	10	4
C	3	4	5	4
D	4	5	12	6
E	5	6	7	6
F	5	7	9	7
G	4	5	12	6
H	6	8	10	8

In order to save drawing the distribution each time, it is possible to compare activities in terms of a variance measure. This is calculated as follows:

variance of activity time = $[[p - o] / 6]^2$

Explanation

The standard deviation of each activity's time is approximated to one sixth of the difference between the optimistic and pessimistic times. The variance = [standard deviation]^2. The standard deviation is the normal measure of spread in a set of numbers, and is represented by the Greek symbol σ or sigma. It is a characteristic of a normal distribution, that 99.7 per cent of the numbers being analysed (called the 'population') fall within $+/- 3\sigma$ of the mean (the average of the population).

In this case, the extremes of the distribution are represented by the optimistic and pessimistic times. The normal distribution is applied and the approximation is made that between these two values, 99.7 per cent (practically all) of other values will lie. The upper limit (mean + 3σ) and the lower limit (mean – 3σ) are equated to the pessimistic and optimistic times respectively.

The distribution which is being considered is the beta distribution, a generic form of which the normal distribution is a special case. Unlike the normal distribution (represented by a bell-shaped curve) the beta distribution need not be symmetrical about the mean, i.e. it can be skewed. It therefore encompasses the effects of one of the values of o and p being further from m than the other.

Applying this to the example

variance for activity B = $[[10 - 2] / 6]^2 = 1.78$
for activity A = $[[7 - 3] / 6]^2 = 0.44$

Thus we have a mathematical measure for what can be seen from the figures, that the variance (as a measure of uncertainty with this activity) is much higher for activity B than for A, i.e. there is more uncertainty in the completion of B than A.

Figures, such as the variance, are of greatest practical use in estimating the likelihood that a set of activities will be completed within a certain time. The steps involved are:

1 Calculate the variance for each activity.
2 Calculate the variance for each path (a sequence of activities that will take you from the first event to the last – there are generally many paths through networks) in the network diagram. This is done by summing the variances of all the activities on the path.
3 Calculate the standard deviation for that path:
    σ_{path} = square root of the variance.
4 Identify the time within which you wish to complete the activities.
5 Calculate the value for z determined by:
    z = [specified time – expected time]$/\sigma_{path}$.

Table 3.2(a) Areas under the standardised normal curve from $-\infty$ to $-z$

.09	.08	.07	.06	.05	.04	.03	.02	.01	.00	z
.0002	.0003	.0003	.0003	.0003	.0003	.0003	.0003	.0003	.0003	−3.4
.0003	.0004	.0004	.0004	.0004	.0004	.0004	.0005	.0005	.0005	−3.3
.0005	.0005	.0005	.0006	.0006	.0006	.0006	.0006	.0007	.0007	−3.2
.0007	.0007	.0008	.0008	.0008	.0008	.0009	.0009	.0009	.0010	−3.1
.0010	.0010	.0011	.0011	.0011	.0012	.0012	.0013	.0013	.0013	−3.0
.0014	.0014	.0015	.0015	.0016	.0016	.0017	.0018	.0018	.0019	−2.9
.0019	.0020	.0021	.0021	.0022	.0023	.0023	.0024	.0025	.0026	−2.8
.0026	.0027	.0028	.0029	.0030	.0031	.0032	.0033	.0034	.0035	−2.7
.0036	.0037	.0038	.0039	.0040	.0041	.0043	.0044	.0045	.0047	−2.6
.0048	.0049	.0051	.0052	.0054	.0055	.0057	.0059	.0060	.0062	−2.5
.0064	.0066	.0068	.0069	.0071	.0073	.0075	.0078	.0080	.0082	−2.4
.0084	.0087	.0089	.0091	.0094	.0096	.0099	.0102	.0104	.0107	−2.3
.0110	.0113	.0116	.0119	.0122	.0125	.0129	.0132	.0136	.0139	−2.2
.0143	.0146	.0150	.0154	.0158	.0162	.0166	.0170	.0174	.0179	−2.1
.0183	.0188	.0192	.0197	.0202	.0207	.0212	.0217	.0222	.0228	−2.0
.0233	.0239	.0244	.0250	.0256	.0262	.0268	.0274	.0281	.0287	−1.9
.0294	.0301	.0307	.0314	.0322	.0329	.0336	.0344	.0351	.0359	−1.8
.0367	.0375	.0384	.0392	.0401	.0409	.0418	.0427	.0436	.0446	−1.7
.0455	.0465	.0475	.0485	.0495	.0505	.0516	.0526	.0537	.0548	−1.6
.0559	.0571	.0582	.0594	.0606	.0618	.0630	.0643	.0655	.0668	−1.5
.0681	.0694	.0708	.0721	.0735	.0749	.0764	.0778	.0793	.0808	−1.4
.0823	.0838	.0853	.0869	.0885	.0901	.0918	.0934	.0951	.0968	−1.3
.0985	.1003	.1020	.1038	.1056	.1075	.1093	.1112	.1131	.1151	−1.2
.1170	.1190	.1210	.1230	.1251	.1271	.1292	.1314	.1335	.1357	−1.1
.1379	.1401	.1423	.1446	.1469	.1492	.1515	.1539	.1562	.1587	−1.0
.1611	.1635	.1660	.1685	.1711	.1736	.1762	.1788	.1814	.1841	−0.9
.1867	.1894	.1922	.1949	.1977	.2005	.2033	.2061	.2090	.2119	−0.8
.2148	.2177	.2206	.2236	.2266	.2296	.2327	.2358	.2389	.2420	−0.7
.2451	.2483	.2514	.2546	.2578	.2611	.2643	.2676	.2709	.2743	−0.6
.2776	.2810	.2843	.2877	.2912	.2946	.2981	.3015	.3050	.3085	−0.5
.3121	.3156	.3192	.3228	.3264	.3300	.3336	.3372	.3409	.3446	−0.4
.3483	.3520	.3557	.3594	.3632	.3669	.3707	.3745	.3783	.3821	−0.3
.3859	.3897	.3936	.3974	.4013	.4052	.4090	.4129	.4168	.4207	−0.2
.4247	.4286	.4325	.4364	.4404	.4443	.4483	.4522	.4562	.4602	−0.1
.4641	.4681	.4721	.4761	.4801	.4840	.4880	.4920	.4960	.5000	−0.0

6 Refer to Table 3.2 – the value of z corresponds to a probability (expressed between 0 and 1). This is the probability that the activity path will be completed within the time identified in 4.
7 The probability that all the paths that have been considered will be finished in the given time, is found by multiplying the probabilities for each of the paths together.

Table 3.2(b) Areas under the standardised normal curve from $-\infty$ to $+z$

z	.00	.01	.02	.03	.04	.05	.06	.07	.08	.09
.0	.5000	.5040	.5080	.5120	.5160	.5199	.5239	.5279	.5319	.5359
.1	.5398	.5438	.5478	.5517	.5557	.5596	.5636	.5675	.5714	.5753
.2	.5793	.5832	.5871	.5910	.5948	.5987	.6026	.6064	.6103	.6141
.3	.6179	.6217	.6255	.6293	.6331	.6368	.6406	.6443	.6480	.6517
.4	.6554	.6591	.6628	.6664	.6700	.6736	.6772	.6808	.6844	.6879
.5	.6915	.6950	.6985	.7019	.7054	.7088	.7123	.7157	.7190	.7224
.6	.7257	.7291	.7324	.7357	.7389	.7422	.7454	.7486	.7517	.7549
.7	.7580	.7611	.7642	.7673	.7703	.7734	.7764	.7794	.7823	.7852
.8	.7881	.7910	.7939	.7967	.7995	.8023	.8051	.8078	.8106	.8133
.9	.8159	.8186	.8212	.8238	.8264	.8289	.8315	.8340	.8365	.8389
1.0	.8413	.8438	.8461	.8485	.8508	.8531	.8554	.8577	.8599	.8621
1.1	.8643	.8665	.8686	.8708	.8729	.8749	.8770	.8790	.8810	.8830
1.2	.8849	.8869	.8888	.8907	.8925	.8944	.8962	.8980	.8997	.9015
1.3	.9032	.9049	.9066	.9082	.9099	.9115	.9131	.9147	.9162	.9177
1.4	.9192	.9207	.9222	.9236	.9251	.9265	.9279	.9292	.9306	.9319
1.5	.9332	.9345	.9357	.9370	.9382	.9394	.9406	.9418	.9429	.9441
1.6	.9452	.9463	.9474	.9484	.9495	.9505	.9515	.9525	.9535	.9545
1.7	.9554	.9564	.9573	.9582	.9591	.9599	.9608	.9616	.9625	.9633
1.8	.9641	.9649	.9656	.9664	.9671	.9678	.9686	.9693	.9699	.9706
1.9	.9713	.9719	.9726	.9732	.9738	.9744	.9750	.9756	.9761	.9767
2.0	.9772	.9778	.9783	.9788	.9793	.9798	.9803	.9808	.9812	.9817
2.1	.9821	.9826	.9830	.9834	.9838	.9842	.9846	.9850	.9854	.9857
2.2	.9861	.9864	.9868	.9871	.9875	.9878	.9881	.9884	.9887	.9890
2.3	.9893	.9896	.9898	.9901	.9904	.9906	.9909	.9911	.9913	.9916
2.4	.9918	.9920	.9922	.9925	.9927	.9929	.9931	.9932	.9934	.9936
2.5	.9938	.9940	.9941	.9943	.9945	.9946	.9948	.9949	.9951	.9952
2.6	.9953	.9955	.9956	.9957	.9959	.9960	.9961	.9962	.9963	.9964
2.7	.9965	.9966	.9967	.9968	.9969	.9970	.9971	.9972	.9973	.9974
2.8	.9974	.9975	.9976	.9977	.9977	.9978	.9979	.9979	.9980	.9981
2.9	.9981	.9982	.9982	.9983	.9984	.9984	.9985	.9985	.9986	.9986
3.0	.9987	.9987	.9987	.9988	.9988	.9989	.9989	.9989	.9990	.9990
3.1	.9990	.9991	.9991	.9991	.9991	.9992	.9992	.9992	.9993	.9993
3.2	.9993	.9993	.9994	.9994	.9994	.9994	.9994	.9995	.9995	.9995
3.3	.9995	.9995	.9995	.9996	.9996	.9996	.9996	.9996	.9996	.9997
3.4	.9997	.9997	.9997	.9997	.9997	.9997	.9997	.9997	.9997	.9998

This method is best illustrated by an example. If the middle section of the previous example is used, and the events 20-60 considered, the steps are as follows:

1 Calculate the variance for each activity (shown in Table 3.3).
2 Now it is necessary to identify the paths. There are several rules regarding the selection of paths for this process:

Table 3.3

Activity	Optimistic time o	Most likely time m	Pessimistic time p	Variance
B	2	3	10	1.78
C	3	4	5	0.11
D	4	5	12	1.78
E	5	6	7	0.11
F	5	7	9	0.44
G	4	5	12	1.78

- each activity must be on only one path – where activities are shared between several paths, the one that is the critical path should be used;
- activities on different paths need to be independent – there should be no unwritten logic relationship between activities on different paths.

With these in mind the three paths that need to be considered here are:

B – E
C – F
D – G

The following steps are calculated in Table 3.4. The variances are then summed for each path.

Table 3.4

Path	Path variance	Standard deviation	z	Probability of completion in 11 days
B – E	1.78+0.11 = 1.89	1.37	[11–10]/1.37 = 0.73	0.7673
C – F	0.11+0.44 = 0.55	0.74	[11–11]/0.74 = 0.0	0.5000
D – G	1.78+1.78 = 3.56	1.87	[11–12]/1.87 = –0.53	0.2981

3 The standard deviations are then calculated.
4 The time required for completion is arbitrarily 11 days.
5 The z values are added.
6 The probabilities are derived from Table 3.2 (pp. 69–70).
7 The probability of each of these times being achieved is clearly highest where the expected time was less than the time required for completion (path B–E). These values are now required to find the probability that all three paths will be completed in 11 days. This is achieved through the multiplication of the three probabilities. In this case, the probability that the three paths will all be completed in 11 days is:

$$0.7673 \times 0.5000 \times 0.2981 = 0.1143$$

i.e. there is less than a 12 per cent chance that this part of the project will be completed in 11 days.

Many authors choose to use PERT as the generic title for network techniques. This is perfectly valid – the original CPA that was carried out using a single value for the estimated time can be taken as a special case of PERT, where the most likely = optimistic = pessimistic time.

The use of PERT in practice

As mentioned at the start, PERT was very popular in the 1960s. It appears to be less well used today as many project managers feel that the additional complexity is not justified by the return in the accuracy of the plans produced. Also, it was suggested that in organisations where this kind of planning is prevalent, the use of PERT can encourage people to be less accurate in their forecasting.

3.11 PLANNING WITH STANDARDS – FOUR FIELDS MAPPING

A related graphical technique, used in Japan and finding favour elsewhere, is that of four fields mapping. As shown in Fig. 3.28, it is a way of relating four information fields:

- the team members;
- the logical phases of an activity;
- tasks to be performed including decisions made;
- the standards that apply for each task.

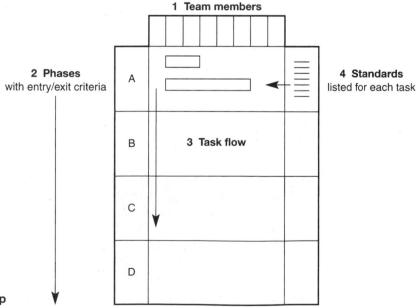

Figure 3.28 Four fields map
(*Source:* Dimancescu, 1992)

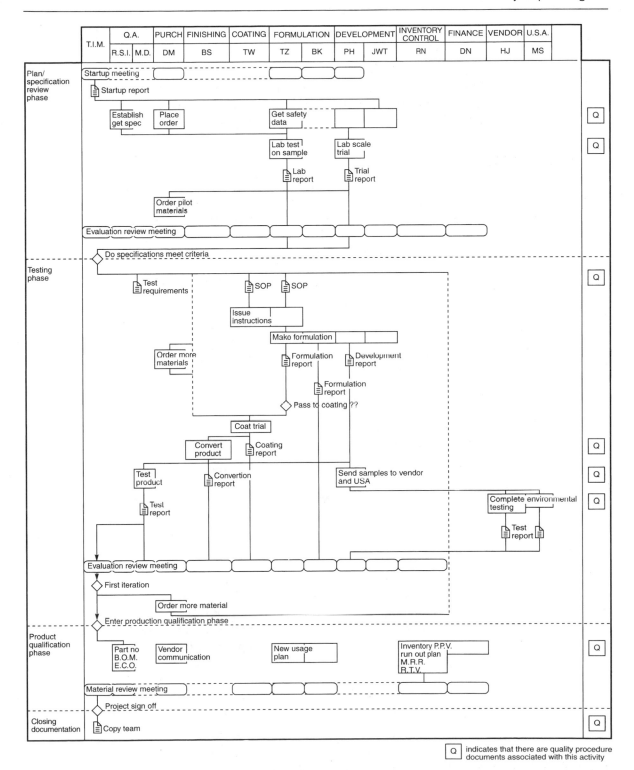

Figure 3.29 The use of four fields mapping in planning the introduction of a new coating material

By incorporating the standards element into the plan, not only is the time and activity planned in detail, but the controls also specified so that the sharing of information across an organisation needed to make the project work can take place.

Figure 3.29 shows the use of the technique in the selection of a replacement coating product used in the manufacture of computer disks. The entry and exit criteria at each phase ensure that the project does not move on without the team having met certain criteria at that point. For example, at the end of the first phase, the outcome must be that the specifications meet the criteria set. No phase can be completed until all errors have been corrected and the causes identified. This, as can be seen, does not sit terribly comfortably with the conventional ideas of project planning where activites just proceed at some stated point in time, regardless.

PROJECT
MANAGEMENT
IN PRACTICE:
**ADOPTING A
STANDARD FOR
PROJECT
PLANNING –
USEFUL
DISCIPLINE OR
UNNECESSARY
CONSTRAINT?**

Should all the project plans produced in an organisation conform to a particular set of rules as to how they should be constructed such as:

- the notation used in diagrams;
- the use of time-scaled axes (the left-to-right scale where distance on the diagram is proportional to time);
- the units to be used;
- who can construct the diagrams;
- what procedure, if any, should be used for checking the plans prior to their issue;
- the filing, storage and control of plans to ensure that only the current version is being worked to;
- the format of reports;

... or is this just creating unnecessary bureaucracy?

The role of such working practices in organisations will be covered in Chapter 6. There was a clear divide amongst the project managers who were questioned on this issue, which can be summarised in the following composite cases.

Example 1 – Makesure Electronics

There are very tight controls as to how project plans may be drawn up. The bureaucracy of the company is considered necessary to ensure that the end-customers of the projects are kept happy (generally military procurement agencies). The correct paperwork is essential to the project and would be returned to the originator if all the boxes on the accompanying forms are not fully completed. It is generally felt that the process prevents any dynamic activity taking place, but that is appropriate for the market they are in.

Example 2 – internal consultancy in a public service industry

The role of the consultancy is one of a team that moves in to help a department solve a particular problem before moving on to the next. The team is required to be dynamic and respond quickly to changes. Plans are mainly for the use of the team in structuring how they tackle the problem. No particular convention is adhered to and there are no rules which the team believe would constrain the problem-solving process. This often causes problems with their 'customers' many of whom believe in the benefits of the more formalised approach but who nonetheless are generally satisfied with the results of their work.

The arguments for and against using a highly formalised approach may be summarised as follows:

For formalisation
- ensures that everyone is working to the same standard – gives the best chance that the plans are universally understood
- imposes a degree of discipline into the process
- can be used as a marketing feature for the project organisation
- is a requirement for some markets, e.g. some construction tenders, government contracts
- covers your back

Against formalisation
- restricts creative activity
- standardisation is to some extent taken care of by the use of a common project planning software package
- can mask problems of disorder
- costly to implement and maintain systems
- it is very unusual for two organisations to work to the same standard or set of rules – does not improve inter-organisational communication

PROJECT MANAGEMENT IN PRACTICE: PRUDENTIAL CORPORATION ON THE MOVE

The corporation left its ancestral home, 142 Holborn Bars, London, in 1988 in anticipation that the building would re-emerge after restoration and modernisation, stripped of its more arcane features, but retaining its Gothic fenestrated charm and tradition. Despite many false dawns, we have not been disappointed.

A successful move is built on a monument of planning activity. Equally true, as we have learned, this monument must be constructed like Lego, so that as expectations change or deadlines shift it can be quickly re-assembled in a different configuration.

Our planning process was based upon a top-level committee which contemplated an enormous variety of seriously important issues ranging from the colour of the carpet to the shape of the dining chairs and the location of the coffee machines. The committee was served by a professional project manager with the backing of a full-time team. However mundane each decision may appear, coordinating them is a task to rank with re-designing the space shuttle for complexity.

Clearly a move on this scale risked dislocating our business operations completely. We could scarcely close down our investment operations for a day to move the furniture or tell our customers their maturity cheques must wait until we found the crate containing the file.

Finally, it is worth remembering that however detailed the plans, some elements will inevitably escape, just as some carefully chosen furniture will look uncomfortable in its new home.

(*Source*: adapted from 'Tip from the Top: What about the Carpet Colour', Newmarch, M., Financial Times 22 November 1995 p. 11)

**SUMMARY OF
KEY POINTS**

- the planning process must be managed as for other phases of project activity to maximise the value added by the process, and ensure that it does not become an organisational straitjacket, become hampered by over-attention to precision or overloaded with data;
- the purpose of the plan is to be both systematic and to be seen to be systematic;
- the planning process involves identifying activities, determining their logical sequence, estimating times and presenting the plan;
- the use of graphical techniques helps in the presentation of the plan and facilitates its review and revision;
- Gantt charts are a time-scaled graphical planning tool which give a static representation of the relationship between activities and their duration;
- network techniques provide a graphical means of expressing more complex projects and include activity-on-arrow (A-o-A) and activity-on-node (A-o-N) methods of representation of the verbal statement of activities;
- A-o-A activities move from left to right, and start and finish at an event with the arrow representing the activity;
- dummies are used to clarify the logic and preserve precedence relationships;
- critical path analysis allows determination of the path of activities, where, if there is any delay, the whole project will be delayed. The critical path should therefore be the initial focus for management attention;
- the critical path is determined by carrying out a forward pass through the diagram to establish the earliest event time (EET), then a reverse pass to establish the latest event time (LET);
- A-o-N facilitates the display of relationships other than simple precedence;
- PERT is a method which assesses the uncertainty of timing data and evaluates the optimistic, most likely and pessimistic times and allows a range or distribution of values to be considered;
- four field mapping is a technique which ensures that the relevant people are involved in the planning of activities, and places emphasis on managing information.

KEY TERMS

value-adding	networks
precision and accuracy	activity-on-arrow/activity-on-node
data and information	dependency
tactical	dummies
operational	critical path
systematic	earliest/latest event times
revision/refinement	forward/reverse pass
forward/backward schedule	slack
Gantt or linked bar chart	PERT
visibility	four fields mapping

REVIEW AND DISCUSSION QUESTIONS

1 Discuss the advantages to be gained from a well-balanced project plan.

2 Why should the plan be viewed as a value-adding activity?

3 Identify the costs and potential negative effects of the mis-use of plans.

4 You have been put in charge of organising a group trip to visit a company in Japan which has expertise that you and your group are interested in finding out more about. Identify the constituent activities, their sequence and estimate the times that each of the activities will take. Show how you have used forward and backward scheduling to achieve this. Display your plan as using a bar chart or similar method.

5 Discuss why graphical techniques for displaying plans are superior to verbal statements.

6 Describe what is meant by 'precedence' and illustrate your answer with an appropriate example.

7 Show the dissertation case example (Fig. 3.8) as an activity-on-arrow diagram.

8 Illustrate the differences between A-o-A and A-o-N methods.

9 Show the information given in Table 3.5 about a project activity as an A-o-A diagram.

Table 3.5

Activity	Description	Duration (weeks)	Preceding activity
A	Select software	4	–
B	Select hardware	3	A
C	Install hardware	6	B
D	Install software	2	C
E	Test software	3	D
F	Train staff	5	E
G	System run-up	1	F

(a) From your diagram identify the total project duration.

(b) Show which activities you feel could be run alongside others (in parallel, rather than sequentially). Redraw the network diagram and calculate the new project duration.

(c) What further benefits may arise from using parallel activities, rather than sequential?

10 Show the information given in Table 3.6 about project activities as an A-o-A diagram, using the notation of Fig 3.17.

Table 3.6

Activity	Description	Duration (weeks)	Preceding activity
A	Select software	4	–
B	Upgrade office network	3	A
C	Install hardware	6	A
D	Test software	2	B
E	Structure database	3	B
F	Train staff	5	C, D
G	System run-up	1	E, F

(a) From your diagram, do the forward pass and calculate the minimum project duration.
(b) Do the reverse pass and calculate the latest event times.
(c) Show the critical path activities using the notation suggested.
(d) Assuming that the completion time is critical, identify which activities you would suggest should be the focus for management attention.

11 Table 3.7 considers the development of a short-course in project management. From the information, construct the A-o-A diagram.

Table 3.7

Activity	Description	Duration (weeks)	Preceding activity
A	Design course overview and publicity	4	–
B	Identify potential staff to teach on course	2	–
C	Construct detailed syllabus	6	–
D	Send out publicity and application forms	10	A
E	Confirm staff availability	2	B
F	Select staff to teach on course	1	C, E
G	Acknowledge student applications	3	D
H	Identify course written material	2	F
J	Preparation of teaching material	20	G, H
K	Prepare room for the course	1	G

(a) Determine the ESTs, the LSTs, the project duration and the critical path activities.
(b) Show the slack for each activity.
(c) What further factors should be considered in order to give a better view of the realistic timescale for the organisation of the course?

12 The above network can be supplemented by further information. The coordinator has also prepared optimistic and pessimistic times. These are as shown in Table 3.8.

Table 3.8

Activity	Optimisic time	Most likely time	Pessimistic time
A	3	4	11
B	1	2	3
C	3	10	11
D	8	10	18
E	1	2	3
F	1	3	5
G	2	3	4
H	2	6	10
J	16	20	30
K	1	1	1

(a) Calculate the expected times for completion of each activity.
(b) Calculate the expected project duration.
(c) Show the critical path and comment on any differences with the original plan.

13 Considering the critical path alone for the above project, calculate the activity variances and the total variance of the critical path. From this, calculate the standard deviation. Determine the probability of the project being completed within the following times:

(a) 30 days.
(b) 40 days.
(c) 42 days.

14 A construction project requires five major pieces of work which are independent to be completed. These five paths have variances as given in Table 3.9.

Table 3.9

Path	Expected duration (weeks)	Variance
A	10	1.21
B	8	2.00
C	12	1.00
D	15	2.89
E	14	1.44

Determine the probability that the project will be completed within:

(a) 18 weeks.
(b) 16 weeks.
(c) 13 weeks.

15 You are in charge of a new product launch. This will be a formal press launch, where the product is introduced by your managing director and the press and major customers have the opportunity to see the product for the first time. The formalities are to be proceded by a buffet. Before hiring the catering service it is necessary to identify the guest list and invite them, to determine numbers. Because of tied arrangements between certain venues and the caterers, you will have to select the venue, then select the caterers. The launch publicity materials will need to be designed, and artwork carried out before brochures can be printed. These must be available on the day. The promotional boards to be placed around the launch room should be constructed once the publicity materials have been designed. No artwork is required for these. A sound system is required and must be hired once the venue has been identified.

The activities are included in Table 3.10, together with the best estimates for optimistic, pessimistic and most likely times. The MD has asked you to set the launch date (all times are in weeks). Show the criteria that you have used, and include the network diagram.

Table 3.10

Activity	Description	Optimistic time	Most likely	Pessimistic time
A	Select launch venue	1	2	3
B	Design launch publicity	2	3	4
C	Have artwork prepared	2	3	5
D	Print brochures	1	2	4
E	Construct promotion stand	1	2	3
F	Order sound system	0.5	1	1.5
F	Select caterers	1	2	3
H	Develop invite list	1	1	1
J	Invite and get replies	2	3	5

REFERENCES   British Standards Institute:

BS 6046 : Part 1 : 1984, 'The Use of Network Techniques in Project Management: Guide to the Use of Management, Planning, Review and Reporting Procedures'.

BS 6046 : Part 2 : 1992, 'The Use of Network Techniques in Project Management: Guide to the Use of Graphical and Estimating Techniques'.

BS 6046 : Part 3 : 1992, 'The Use of Network Techniques in Project Management: Guide to the Use of Computers'.

BS 6046 : Part 4 : 1992, 'The Use of Network Techniques in Project Management: Guide to Resource Analysis and Cost Control'.

Dimancescu, D. (1992) *The Seamless Enterprise: Making Cross Functional Management Work*, HarperCollins.

Drucker, P., (1955), Management, Butterworth-Heinemann.

Price, F. (1984) *Right First Time*, Gower.

FURTHER READING   Badiru, A.B.   (1993) *Quantitative Models for Project Planning, Scheduling and Control*, Quorum.

Lockyer, K. and J. Gordon (1991) *Critical Path Analysis and Other Network Techniques*, 5th edition Pitman Publishing.

Randolf, W.A. and B.Z. Posner (1988) *Effective Planning & Management: Getting the Job Done*, Prentice Hall.

Reiss, G. (1992) *Project Management Demystified: Today's Tools and Techniques*, Chapman & Hall.

Sapolsky, H.M. (1972) *The Polaris System Development: Bureaucratic & Programmatic Success in Government*, Harvard University Press.

CHAPTER 4

Estimation, resource analysis, justification and evaluation

An organisation will wish to pursue a portfolio of projects that will yield the greatest benefits, and so requires systematic methods for assessing proposals. These methods should be reflected in the preparation of proposals.

Much of the assessment of proposals used to be carried out by specialists, especially financial justification. Twenty years ago, engineers, for example, would not have been expected to be able to complete the financial elements of a proposal. Project management skills today should include the ability to speak the language of the financial analyst. Proposals can be produced and amended with this financial element in mind.

This chapter considers the basic skills required in such analysis. Strategic investment decisions are identified as an area in which the normal rules of appraisal do not apply and where new methods are being sought.

CONTENTS

4.1 INTRODUCTION TO ESTIMATING

In Chapter 3, the basic methods of planning time were considered. In this chapter the role and nature of estimates will be examined, with the purpose of providing realistic cost-benefit analysis. The methods of equating time to cost and the evaluation of benefits will be considered. The changing role of project evaluation techniques and methods for incorporating both risk and potential soft (unquantifiable or strategic) benefits into proposals are included.

The motivation for carrying out an activity is that there will be some kind of benefit: in the case of a construction project, a building, or, in manufacturing industry, time saved or quality improvement. In medium and high complexity activities, the process of planning will be ongoing throughout the life of the project and provide the basis for control actions (*see* Chapter 6). Changes in the project environment arise and the plan will need to enhance the flexibility to change schedules accordingly.

The further into the future a set of events, the more difficult they are to estimate. There will be a higher degree of uncertainty, and more inputs to the estimates have to be treated as variable rather than constants. The changes that have the greatest effects can be discussed in terms of the systems model of project activities, presented in Chapter 1. The nature of the changes are as follows:

- inputs – the project brief can be changed by the customer; the longer the project duration, the more likely there are to be significant changes;
- constraints – any of the list provide a degree of uncertainty, e.g. planning for five years hence will have to take account of different financial conditions (interest rates, availability of cash, investor confidence);
- mechanisms – the availability of people and the state of technology are notoriously difficult to predict.

The project manager's role in the estimation process will vary from the collection of estimates from other people in the preparation of the proposal, to the provision of detailed financial cost : benefit analysis. It is imperative that this function does not operate in a vacuum – that the feedback from previous plans and estimates is used to guide the process. Estimation is an activity which continues during the project life-cycle. As the project nears completion, the manager will have more certainty of the final times, resources, and therefore costs. The accuracy of the estimates is therefore going to get better. The types of estimates, their nature, role and accuracies are shown in Table 4.1.

4.2 COSTING PROPOSALS

There are two basic approaches to the preparation of costing information:

- ground-up costing – the estimates of each level in the work breakdown structure are compiled and added together by each level of supervision in the project hierarchy;

Table 4.1 The nature, role and accuracy of estimate types

Name	Nature	Role	Accuracy (per cent)
Rough/finger-in-the-air/ballpark	Much uncertainty as to what is involved	Early check on feasibility of brief	± 25
As-buts	As was carried out previously, but with the following amendments – some quantitative data exists	With an appropriate contingency factor – can be used for proposals	± 15
Detailed estimates	Some initial work is carried out to determine what the likely problems are going to be	Proposals	± 10
... to finish	Much of the project is completed and additional funding is needed to complete the tasks	Additional funds request	± 5

- top-down costing – you are allocated a certain amount of money to complete the project activities and this has to be split between the sub-projects. The allocation is either based on senior management estimates or through the use of target costing (*see* below).

The two systems are illustrated in Fig. 4.1. The advantage of ground-up costing is that the estimates are prepared by the people who will carry out the activities or their supervisor. This gives some notion of commitment to achieving these figures, if the costs are accepted unmodified by the project manager. Where it is common for costing proposals to be cut by project managers, the

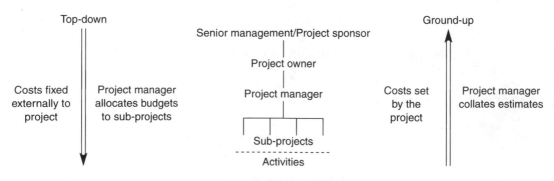

Figure 4.1 Top-down and ground-up approaches to costing

activity level costs generally become artificially inflated, as staff try to remove the effect of such cuts. The process consequently loses credibility. This method is not particularly good at generating accurate estimates. Top-down costing involves the allocation of the costs to the sub-activities. This creates a degree of competition between the supervisors of the activities which many view as being beneficial.

Activity level costs

The major elements of cost are:

- time – the direct input of labour into activities;
- materials – consumables and other items used in the process;
- capital equipment – the purchase of the means of providing the conversion process, or part of its cost, maintenance, running and depreciation offset against activities;
- indirect expenses – e.g. transportation, training;
- overheads – provision of an office, financial and legal support, managers and other non-direct staff.

To determine the time input to a project, there are a number of techniques that can be employed:

- direct work measurement of the time input – timesheets are completed by individuals showing which activities they spent what time working on. These are then aggregated and the total costs charged against project budgets by the accounting system;
- work sampling – random samples are taken of what individuals are doing over a period of time, usually several days. This data is representative of how the individual proportionally spends their entire time. From this proportion the input of that individual to a project can be estimated and fed into the costing system as for direct work measurements;
- synthetic estimation – the times for people to carry out certain activities can be analysed to provide a generic set of actions and consequent timings. New activities can be deconstructed into these generic actions and the timings added accordingly. Little or no direct measurement of the workplace needs subsequently to be carried out;
- learning curve calculations (*see* Section 4.6).

Materials can be included in the costings, either at the cost to the company or with a margin added. Capital equipment may have to be purchased specially, in which case its entire cost, or part of it will need to be offset against the project. Where the equipment will have potential further use after the project has finished with it, it may attract a residual value. Indirect expenses are those not directly related to the value-adding activities, but which are considered necessary to support the project. Overheads are carried by all organisations and include the runnning of the headquarters and the provision of central services.

The elements of cost are added as shown in Fig. 4.2.

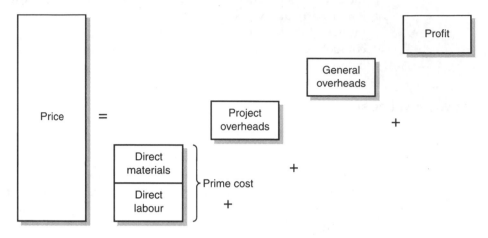

Figure 4.2 Elements of cost

Example

The following case considers the process of determining the costs of running a commercial training course. The course coordinator wishes to advertise the course, but needs to know how much will have to be charged in order to make a profit.

The time estimates are made based on the proposed course length – determined by first considering what it could usefully achieve in given times. These are correlated with the necessary labour input to ascertain the direct cost. The programme requires a consultant to do three days' training which costs £250 per day, which will be supported by an administrator, whose time is costed at £90 per day. The direct costs (fixed, i.e. regardless of how many delegates attend) are therefore £1020. The course requires the provision of printed materials and stationery, which are a variable cost (the more delegates, the greater the cost) of £60 per delegate. Assuming the course is fully subscribed and can accommodate 15 delegates, a further £900 needs to be added to the estimate. The total of these is the prime cost. Indirect labour and materials include administrative time arranging the course (say eight days at £90 per day), and general overheads would be the ongoing 'fixed costs' of providing the building, heating, lighting and functions such as finance to provide the funds, and procurement in raising the necessary purchase orders. The overhead is added to the total cost at a rate of 60 per cent.

The cost build-up is as Fig. 4.3. This does not include the profit for the organisation. The minimum rate per delegate should be the total cost (£4224) divided by the number of delegates (15). This gives £281.60. To this should be added a profit margin and a contingency figure, in case the course is under-subscribed.

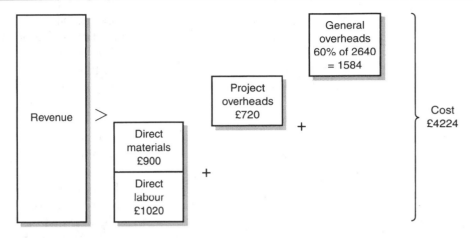

Figure 4.3 Cost build-up

The reliance on this form of allocating overheads does cause anomalies in costing, which are very damaging to the profitability of the organisation as a whole (e.g. Waldron and Galloway (1988)). These anomalies cast doubts on the merits of conventional cost accounting, though it is still the most used system. Where, for example, new methods are introduced which speed the flow of tasks through a department, the revenue for that area falls – it is doing the same work only faster, but revenue depends on hours spent on 'doing'. The improved methods therefore generate less revenue for that department, which is unlikely to encourage improvement.

4.3 BUDGETS

Collins English Dictionary defines a budget as:

> **'a written statement of money: where it is drawn from, its amount, how it is to be spent'**

Most operations require managers to perform budgetary analysis at least annually and project managers are in a perpetual cycle of seeking approval and then allocating funds. Management according to budgets is the key tool of cost control.

The following are categories generally found in budget applications/grants. They are more explicit statements of the categories of costs identified above:

- labour;
- materials;
- consumables;
- cap-ex (capital expenditure);
- travel;
- subsistence.

In developing ground-up costs, these are the basic elements that should be considered. Further elements should be added as appropriate. In addition, it is usual for these to provide headings within project codes which activities can draw against. The example at the end of this section questions whether this kind of artificial division of resources really helps progress or project monitoring and control, or simply makes the accounting system neater.

Budgets in public sector environments can be allocated using 'zero-base' budgeting. Where activities are ongoing but are reviewed on an annual or similar basis, this approach takes into account previous performance. Where progress can be demonstrated, funding may be made available. Where progress is deemed to be unsatisfactory, either the remaining activities may be denied funding altogether or may be cut. This has been the case where stipulations of attracting private funding to supplement government grants have been made.

The discussion of budgeting would not be complete without looking at how costs are tracked as the project progresses. In the majority of industries, direct labour and materials would be allocated and costs tracked through a job-costing system. For the purpose of accounting, the job could be issued a code against which charges are made. When costs are incurred, they are noted against these codes. The construction and defence industries use this method extensively. There is usually a budget holder (often the PM) who periodically checks that what has been recorded is an accurate record.

In considering the value added by the budgetary system, there are two problems which frequently arise:

- what should happen to funds left in a budget at the end at a project or accounting period?
- what should happen when one category of expenditure is exhausted, but project activities still need funding in that category?

Residual funds at the ends of projects or accounting periods are often spent to prevent them being 'lost' back into the accounting system. This results in unnecessary purchases or in acquisitions being rushed through, to beat deadlines. This is unlikely to encourage good use of resources. Underspend through cost efficiency goes unrewarded under conventional systems of budgeting. Alternatives to this include the reward of cost efficiency through greater allocations of funds in the future.

The imposition of constraints, concerning the movement of funds between budget categories, causes anomalies and can result in wasted money (*see* example below).

Example

Four senior engineers working on the development of a new motor system, required a face-to-face meeting with colleagues in Switzerland. This was a reasonable request, but it was pointed out that the budget for air travel had been exhausted. Normally, they could have flown out and back in the same day, but that was not possible. There was, however, money left in the accommodation budget and travel by road could be subsidised from general funds. The four hired a car, drove to the ferry and to Switzerland, ovenighting on both out and return journeys, with the round-trip taking three days. Flights would have cost in the region of £800, and used four person-days of time. The total, including accommodation and subsistence for the three day trip was also £800. The time used, however, was 12 person-days – which represented a considerable additional, but hidden, cost. Adhering to the rules of a budgeting system, which was designed to help cost control, caused considerable unnecessary additional costs to be incurred.

4.4 RESOURCE ANALYSIS

Having prepared initial estimates, part of the review process of plans is to make changes that will ensure that the constraints of time and cost are met. This is achieved through:

- crashing – shortening one or more project activities;
- resource allocation and smoothing.

Crashing

As part of the analysis of the time and resource plan you have prepared, the issue frequently arises as to how all or part of the project could be carrried out in less time. There are few projects of any scale that have the benefit of significant slack. Even if they do have slack as the project proceeds, unforeseen challenges arise and time needs to be clawed back from a subsequent activity.

There are a number of ways that activities can be shortened:

- provide an incentive for the work to be completed early – this has been done to great effect on contracts for road repair on major motorways;
- add additional resources such as extra people or machine capacity, provide overtime, additional contracts, etc.;
- parallel activities – reduce the risk of over-run by providing parallel means of obtaining an output;
- reduce the level of technological change – use existing technology.

Clearly, there is a decision to be made here – either to compromise the output in terms of time or specification, or to commit extra resources. Good project managers often find ways of circumventing such challenges, e.g. through:

- personal supervision of one or more activities, which can ensure an early completion;
- meeting with the project sponsor to find the time at which the output was required in reality (the absolute latest time) as opposed to what had been given in the brief;
- discussion with the members of the project to find areas that have been conservatively estimated and therefore provide scope for shortening.

Any of these can be achieved, usually at minimal visible cost. Where there is a formalised solution required, the addition of further resources will be needed to crash the project. There is a limit with most activities as to how much they can be crashed as physical limits are reached, e.g. drying time of concrete in construction projects or the number of people who can work on one activity at any one time.

The trade-off between cost and time should be balanced such that the minimum cost schedule is achieved, i.e. the activities are crashed in a systematic way – the ones that cost the least being the first to be crashed. The following sequence should be followed once the critical path has been established:

1 The following data will be needed for calculating the minimum cost schedule:

Normal time	t_n
Normal cost	C_n
Crashed time	t_c (the shortest possible time an activity can take)
Crashed cost	C_c (the cost to achieve the shortest possible time)

2 Calculate the cost per unit time to crash each activity (the relationship between cost and time will be assumed to be linear)

$$= \frac{C_c}{t_n - t_c}$$

3 Select those activities on the critical path as the first to be crashed.
4 Select the one with the lowest costs per unit time (beware parallel paths!).
5 Reduce this by one time unit.
6 Re-calculate the critical path.
7 If total time needs shortening further, go to step 3.

Table 4.2 shows the way in which sequential crashing of activities can be achieved. The network diagram is shown in Fig. 4.4, along with the critical path calculated from the normal times.

The project duration with the normal activity times is 17 days. Table 4.3 shows the optimal route for taking one day at a time out of the schedule, following the seven-step method given above to achieve the minimum cost

Table 4.2

Activity	Normal time t_n (days)	Normal cost C_n	Crashed time t_c (days)	Crashed cost C_c	Crash cost per day
A	5	300	3	600	150
B	6	700	5	775	75
C	7	500	4	650	50
D	5	400	3	600	100
E	4	700	3	1000	300

schedule. The activities cannot now be crashed any further – the absolute minimum time that the project could take is 11 days.

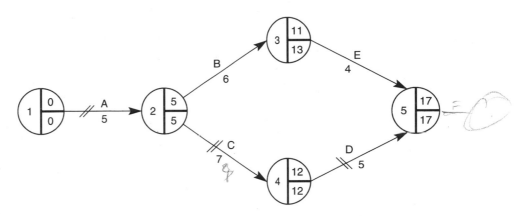

Figure 4.4 Network diagram

Table 4.3

Project duration	Crashed activities	Marginal crash cost	Total crash cost	New critical path	Notes
17	None	–		ACD	1
16	C–1	50	50	ACD	2
15	C–2	50	100	ABCDE	3
14	C–3, B–1	125	225	ABCDE	
13	C–3, B–1, A–1	150	375	ABCDE	4
12	A–2, C–3, B–1	150	525	ABCDE	
11	A–2, B–1, C–3, D–1, E–1	400	925	ABCDE	5

Notes:

(1) + (2) The cheapest of the critical path activities to crash is C, therefore crash this one.

(3) All the activities now lie on the critical path and so to take one unit out of the system either take one day out of A or one day out of B–E and C–D. Costs are:

Option 1: A – 150
Option 2: B–E (cheapest is B) – £75; C–D (cheapest is C) – £50 = £125
therefore option 2 is cheaper at £125.

(4) Cannot be shortened any further – neither can B. Option now is

   one unit out of A – cost £150

or

   one unit out of E *and* one out of D – cost £100 + £300 = £400.

(5) A cannot now be crashed further therefore take one unit out of E and one from D – cost £400.

Resource allocation and smoothing

In the ideal world, when a project was planned, the plan would result in all resources being uniformly utilised. However, projects are generally like the proverbial no. 9 bus – nothing for ages, then three come along together. The result is that time is wasted when resources are under-utilised, and projects run late because the resource is needed by three projects simultaneously. The project manager does have a degree of control over this by considering loadings on each resource throughout a period. This would ordinarily be a laborious task but has been considerably eased by the use of project management software.

The allocation of tasks to a project team can be eased by the use of a responsibility matrix. Where there are clear skills requirements for tasks, these should be met first, with the less constrained resources matched to the remaining tasks. A responsibility matrix is shown in Fig 4.5.

Person \ Activity	1	2	3	4
A		●	○	○
B	●		○	
C	○	○	○	○
D		●	●	
E	○			○
F		○		●

● High level of involvement
○ Some involvement

Figure 4.5 Responsibility matrix

Having allocated resources, not just people to tasks, the loading on those resources should then be analysed. This can be done as an extension to the responsibility matrix, by allocating the time estimates for the activity to those resources. The effect is as shown in Fig. 4.6. The resources are equated to four weeks' work – with a high level of involvement representing the input of two weeks and a low level representing one week. These are then added and the results displayed on the right-hand side of the chart. As can be seen, the resources D and E are under-utilised, whilst B is considerably over-utilised. Levelling would involved the transfer of tasks from B to D, for example. All resources would be fully-utilised over the period being considered.

Resource-levelling through re-allocating activities has the benefit of improving the efficiency of usage of resources. It is quite normal for this to result in the project taking a longer time, however, as the levelled plans (those produced after the levelling exercise) will often be in conflict with the minimum-time plans produced first. The project manager has to consider the costs and benefits of each position before resolving which course of action to take.

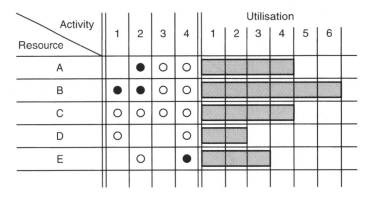

Figure 4.6 Responsibility matrix with resource loading

4.5 PRICING PROJECTS

The basic method of determining price according to costs plus a profit margin was discussed in Section 4.2. The basic relationship between price, cost and profit can be expressed in a number of ways:

$$\left.\begin{array}{l}\textbf{cost + profit = price} \\ \textbf{price – profit = cost} \\ \textbf{price – cost\ \ = profit}\end{array}\right\} \text{same equation – different meaning}$$

Which one applied depends on whether price, cost or profit is fixed first. These differences can be explained as follows:

- in the first case, the price is fixed through legislation, for example, or in the case of a target costing system, through market analysis;
- in the second the cost is fixed, generally through contract purchase which guarantees that goods will be supplied to you at a particular price. This fixes your costs, whilst your selling price and profits can be varied;
- some agreements state the profit that a company is allowed to make through the system known as 'cost-plus' pricing.

Target pricing is being used increasingly in the automotive industry. The target price for a vehicle is established that will give it cost competitiveness in the intended market. The intended profit margin is then established and designers work back from the remaining figures. The main implication is for component suppliers, who are subsequently set target costs to achieve on their components. This system is described in more detail by Monden (1992).

It was normal in the defence industry, until a few years ago, for everyone to work on a cost-plus basis. This required very detailed time and material cost estimates for a project to be submitted to the purchaser for vetting. Should a supplier be awarded a contract it would be on the basis of direct costs plus a percentage towards overheads and profit. The procedures were lengthy, involved massive bureaucracy, and, most importantly, did not encourage suppliers to improve their performance. If costs over-ran, they would still be paid. The changes in the relationships between the Ministry of Defence (MOD) and its suppliers mean that contracts are now awarded on the basis of competitive tendering (only one per cent of contracts in 1994 were cost-plus). The supplier knows how much they will be paid if awarded the contracts, and has a vested interest in ensuring costs are minimised.

Not everyone welcomed the demise of cost-plus – as one veteran of the era said: 'When we worked to cost-plus, you would do the job properly and know you'd get paid for doing a proper job. Now we have to watch every bean. Previously, the engineers had control over these projects, now its the accountants.'

4.6 TIME ESTIMATION – LEARNING CURVE EFFECTS

Watching a skilled craftsperson at work shows how a highly intricate task can be learned and carried out so that it is made to look easy. Gaining such a level of skill requires years of training and practice (and many mistakes). A project rarely has such an opportunity to gain advantage through repetition. There will, however, be repetitive elements to any activity, particularly during the execution phase. Where this occurs, the time taken each time the task is carried out will decrease as the person becomes familiar with the methods. Subsequent improvements in speed are seen to become smaller over time. This can be quantified using the following formula:

$$Y_x = Kx^n$$

where:

x = the number of times the task has been carried out
Y_x = time taken to carry out the task the xth time
K = time taken to carry out the task the first time
n = log b/log2 where b = learning rate

Example

A team is set up to carry out a quality audit of ten departments. The first audit takes four days as the auditors are unfamiliar with the procedures. The second audit takes three. After a period of time, the minimum audit time is reached, and very little further improvement is seen. We can plot this progression as shown in Fig. 4.7.

If we wish to find out how long the eighth audit will take, we need to calculate the learning rate, b. The following values can be assigned from the above information:

x = the number of times the task has been carried out = 2
Y_x = time taken to carry out the task the xth time = 3
K = time taken to carry out the task the first time = 4
n can be calculated

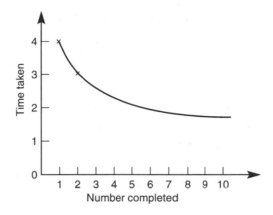

Figure 4.7 Learning curve effect on time taken

Putting these values in:

$$3 = 4(2)^n$$
$$2^n = 3/4$$
$$n.\log2 = \log(3/4)$$
$$n = -0.1249/0.4149$$

$$n = \log b/\log2 = -0.4149$$
$$\log b = -0.1249$$
$$b = 0.75$$

From this we can say that the project has a 75 per cent learning curve.

This can also be seen intuitively, as another way of expressing the learning curve is to say that every time the total number of audits completed doubles, the time taken for the last audit will be the learning percentage multiplied by the original time. In this case as the number of audits doubled from 1 to 2, the time decreased from 4 to 3. The percentage is therefore 3/4 = 75 per cent. As the number of times the audit is done increases, the times taken will decrease as shown in Table 4.4.

Table 4.4

Audit no.	Time taken (days)
1	4
2	3
3	2.54
4	2.25
5	2.05
6	1.90
7	1.78
8	1.69

4.7 PROJECT JUSTIFICATION AND EVALUATION

The financial appraisal of project proposals will consider the potential rewards for carrying out a project against the predicted costs. The form of this evaluation will depend on:

- the size of the project being considered;
- the timespan over which the costs and benefits are going to be spread.

Once the cost of completing the project has been determined from the WBS (ground-up) or senior management (top-down) system, the justification is that the return will at least exceed the amount spent. This return or payback can be analysed in a number of ways to determine feasibility or net benefit:

- payback analysis – simply considers the cash flow of costs and benefits;
- discounted cash flow – considers the 'time value' of cash flows;
- internal rates of return – set basic return criteria on time value of money.

Payback

The most basic method of financial evaluation is simply to compare the income that will be generated with the initial investment. From this a payback period can be determined, i.e. the amount of time the revenue will need to be generated to cancel out the investment. For instance, an initial investment of £30m will be paid back in five years if the revenue generated is £6 million per year. Many companies set this time period as a hurdle for projects. Some examples of payback times for various items are as follows:

manufacturing company (Western) production hardware	5 years
manufacturing company (Japanese) production hardware	10 years
manufacturing company computer facilities	3 years
McDonalds franchise burger production	12 years

Whilst this method has inherent simplicity it ignores:

- the total life-cycle cost of an item and only considers costs within the payback period (if there are major items outside this period to be considered, e.g. high disposal or decommissioning costs, the analysis does not provide a good financial model of reality);
- the time value of money (*see* below).

Discounted cash flow

Where the timespan extends over more than one finanical period and certainly where it is over many years, this 'time value of money' will need to be taken into account, through techniques known as *discounting*. The basis of the technique is the comparison between the value of the return on an investment and the value of the same sum of money, had it been deposited in a bank account at a given rate of interest for the same period. The technique therefore considers the opportunity cost of the project (i.e. the cost of *not* doing something else with the resources).

Example

A project proposal aims to spend £100 000 on information technology and £20 000 a year to maintain it for four years. The return is £50 000 per year in terms of labour savings and extra revenue generated. Would the project be worth pursuing or should other options be considered?

The payback model shows that the project would generate £200 000 in revenue from an expenditure of £180 000, and so looks plausible. However, if the money was deposited in a bank account, at say seven per cent interest p.a., the account would show a balance of £ 226 120 at the end of year 4 (see later work for how the calculation was carried out). It is clearly better to leave the money in the bank rather than risk it on this project.

The concept of discounting is applied to the cash flows (not just profits) to determine whether or not the projected costs and benefits are going to yield the necessary results and is called discounted cash flow.

Compound interest or 'to those that have shall be given...'

When a sum of money is left on deposit in a bank account, it accrues interest. If the interest is paid into the account, then in the following period there will be interest paid on the original amount plus interest on the first period's interest. As time progresses the amount on which interest is being paid grows, hence in the following period more interest is paid, and so on. This phenomenon is known as compound interest and was described by Einstein as the eighth wonder of the modern world! If you are in a situation where you have money in the bank it is a great invention. Of course, the converse is also true, that if you borrow money, you will accrue interest charges not only on the capital amount but also on the unpaid interest levied on the amount.

Discounting is the opposite of compounding. All values are considered in today's terms – called the present value (PV). We can calculate the value of the sum that would have to be deposited at a given rate of interest for a certain period to yield a stated end value.

Example

If you wanted to have a final value of £2012 in 12 years' time with a rate of return (called the discount rate) of six per cent, the present value (the amount that would have to be deposited) is £1000. The calculation is done through

$$PV = \frac{C_n}{(1+i)^n}$$

where

C_n = future value of the investment n years hence
i = discounting rate

(Check the above example by putting $C_n = 2012$, $i = 0.06$ and $n = 12$.)

This basic calculation is applied to the benefits, which must then be offset against the costs. This figure is called the net present value (NPV).

Net present value = present value of benefits – present value of costs

Example

If a project requires the expenditure of £100 000 now, and will yield £200 000 in six years, how will the manager evaluate whether or not this is viable (assuming a ten per cent discount rate)?

$$\text{The PV of the benefits} = \frac{200\,000}{(1+i)^n}$$

$$= \frac{200\,000}{(1+0.1)^6}$$

$$= 112\,800$$

The PV of the costs = 100 000

$$\therefore \text{ the NPV} = 112\,800 - 100\,000$$
$$= 12\,800$$

The minimum criteria for project selection is that the NPV ≥ 0 at a given discounting rate. The project therefore meets this basic criterion and could be allowed to proceed.

The discounting rate can be taken as the interest rate which could be earned from a bank. It is more usual for the rate to be stated according to the type of project and allied to the cost of borrowing that money. A consequently higher rate than the normal bank rates is set, e.g. one manufacturing company had a discounting rate of 20 per cent. The effect was that it was correspondingly harder for projects to meet the minimum criteria of having an NPV of zero.

It is usual for the revenues and costs to be occurring over a period of years. More complex examples such as the following can be evaluated.

Example

You have been asked to evaluate the following proposal. Apply the technique of discounted cash flow to the figures to show whether or not this is worth pursuing. The applicable discount rate is 12 per cent.

	Now	Year 1	Year 2	Year 3
Start-up costs	£50 000			
Running costs (rent, rates, staffing, etc.)		£30 000	£45 000	£45 000
Revenues		£40 000	£50 000	£60 000
Sale of business				£70 000

$$\text{NPV(project)} = \text{NPV(year 1)} + \text{NPV(year 2)} + \text{NPV(year 3)}$$

$$= (-50\,000) + \frac{(-30\,000 + 40\,000)}{(1+0.12)^1} + \frac{(-45\,000 + 50\,000)}{(1+0.12)^2} + \frac{(-45\,000 + 60\,000 + 70\,000)}{(1+0.12)^3}$$

$$= -50\ 000 + 8928 + 3986 + 60\ 501$$

$$= \pounds23\ 415$$

The project on this basis is worth pursuing.

Future value (FV)

The future value of an investment is the value of that money C if deposited for n years at an interest rate of i and is given by:

$$\textbf{FV} = \textbf{C(1+}\textit{i}\textbf{)}\textit{n}$$

Rule of 72

There is a 'rule of thumb' called the 'rule of 72'. If you invest at a per cent for b years, where $a{\times}b = 72$, your money will roughly double, e.g . if you invest £1000 at a fixed rate of 6 per cent for 12 years, the balance at the end of the 12th year (6x12=72) will be roughly £2000 (actually £2012), and if the rate was 18 per cent and the term four years the balance would be the same (actually £1938).

The internal rate of return (IRR)

A related technique is to calculate the IRR of a project, i.e. the discount rate for which the NPV = 0. This can be done mathematically involving a number of iterations (working out the NPV with a variety of discount rates and gradually getting to the point where NV = 0), or graphically. This does depend on the problem to solve being limited.

Example

£100 000 is invested over six years with a potential yield of £200 000 at the end of the sixth year. What is the IRR of the project? As a starting point, an arbitrary rate of ten per cent is chosen.

$$\text{NPV}_{10\%} = \frac{200\ 000 - 100\ 000}{(1 + 0.1)^6}$$

$$= 112\ 895 - 100\ 000$$
$$= 12\ 895$$

The discount rate in this case is clearly too low (the PV of the benefits is too high), try 14 per cent:

$$\text{NPV}_{14\%} = \frac{200\ 000 - 100\ 000}{(1+0.14)^6}$$

$$= -8883$$

This rate is too high (the PV of the benefits is too low). Having two points for the NPV, each on either side of the zero NPV target, the value must be somewhere between the two. This is shown graphically in Fig. 4.8. As can be seen, the relationship within small changes in the discount rate can often be approximated to linear. Over a larger range, the change is as shown in Fig. 4.9. As the number of benefit points and payout points increases, there will be multiple IRRs. This is shown in Fig. 4.10, there being one change in direction of the curve (point of inflection) for each change in the sign (+ to −, or − to +) in the NPV analysis. To make analysis of proposals easier, a program is included which can be run in 'basic' to carry out IRR analysis.

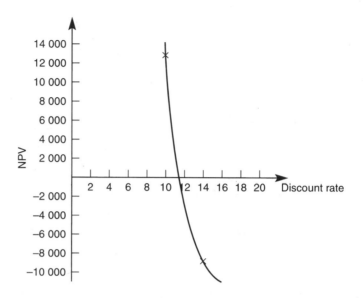

Figure 4.8 NPV profile

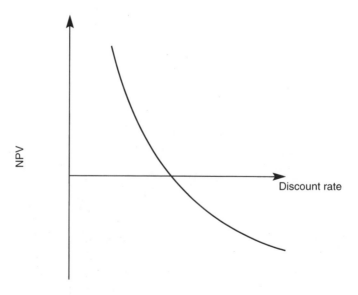

Figure 4.9

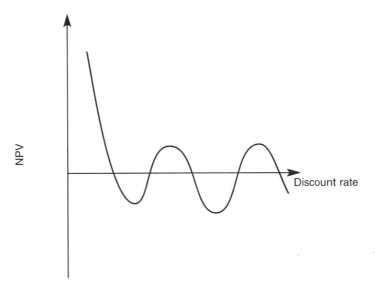

Figure 4.10

Using IRR

Using the percentage rate from an IRR calculation has a certain appeal. It also gets over the need to choose a discount rate for a project, which can save considerable debate. On the other hand, two projects may have the same IRR, but yield very different NPVs, e.g. two proposals having the same IRR but one has a much higher NPV – the one with the high NPV is clearly preferable (risk and availability of funds allowing). The IRR also cannot cope with changes in the discount rate over time. This would have been particularly problematic over the last ten years when bank rates have varied by as much as ten per cent.

Using discounted cash flow (DCF)

Originally it was only accountants who would be given the knowledge for the use and application of DCF, and would be the ones to accept/reject projects. Its use is now widespread and built into most financial appraisal systems. Anyone can run a project through the financial constraints without needing to submit a project plan formally. This has numerous benefits to the project manager, as they can build not only time-based models of the project, but also financial ones. The use of financial models has similar benefits to written project plans:

- the model can be interpreted by a non-financial expert to make changes where necessary to components of the model and evaluate the impact of those changes;
- no third-party intervention is necessary until a well developed plan has been constructed.

It does have certain limitations however:

- how to determine the interest rate to use – as the late 1980s showed, just about anything can happen where this is concerned. In four years, interest rates have fluctuated by as much as ten per cent;
- the process of forecasting cash flow years into the future involves a high degree of uncertainty;
- defining the cash flows – they are different to the data generally presented in a balance sheet – write-off values, for example, are treated very differently.

Determining cash-flow figures for DCR and IRR calculations

In order to present the most accurate picture of the financial health or otherwise of the proposal, the following rules should be applied (Hogg, 1994):

- cash flows, not profit figures, should be used;
- sunk costs (those already incurred) should be ignored;
- only costs arising directly from the project should be included (fixed costs, which would be incurred whether or not the project goes ahead, should be excluded);
- opportunity costs must be taken into account (developing one area of a business to the detriment of another).

Determining the discount rate

It is more usual for the project manager to have discount rates set as part of organisational policy. There are a number of methods for obtaining values for the discount rate – this one determines the risk adjusted discount rate (RADR). There are three factors which determine the discount rate:

(a) = the rate charged for the use of the capital
(b) = the rate due to inflation (so that the purchasing power is not reduced)
(c) = a premium factor due to the fact that the investor is taking a risk that the capital amount may never be repaid

These are selected as follows:

(overall rate) = $(1+a)(1+b)(1+c)$

4.8 PROJECT RISK ANALYSIS

An evaluation of potential risks can show at an early stage whether or not a proposal is worth pursuing. The risks can be categorised as follows:

- project will fail completely;
- project will be compromised on time, cost or both.

Part of the role of the project manager is to evaluate the likelihood of one or both of the above happening. This can be done through examining the individual tasks or sub-tasks to be performed and calculating:

- the likelihood of a particular undesirable event or events happening;
- the severity of the effect on the project of each of these events:
  critical – will cause the total failure of one or more parts of a project;
  major – will hold up or increase costs in one or more areas;
  minor – will cause inconvenience but not set the project back financially or in time;
- the probability of detection of that undesirable event occurring – problems that only show up over a longer period of time are particularly bad in this case, as remedial action cannot be taken to remedy the problem.

It is not possible to envisage every possible action or turn that the project might take but some evaluation of the top 20 per cent of risks (those that are likely to cause 80 per cent of the delays or overrun) is going to be beneficial. When a significant risk is encountered, it is normal for some form of contingency plan to be put in place for that eventuality. Such plans should form part of the project proposal.

Formal use of risk analysis techniques may be required by:

- company policy;
- clients (especially for defence contracts).

The benefits are considered to be:

- providing a vehicle for improving project plans and better reflecting reality;
- highlighting areas for attention and contingency planning at the planning stage;
- attempting to remove much of the 'gut-feel element' of risk assessment and putting it on a more scientific footing;
- allowing the quantification of risk to build up experience in a structured way and allowing this factor to be traced historically for future benefit in other projects.

As for planning, risk analysis is an attempt to provide a mathematical model of the scenario, in an attempt to allow the brain to comprehend the effect of a large number of variables on the outcome. Other quantitative risk evaluation techniques include:

- PERT (as previous chapter);
- catastrophe theory;
- game theory;
- decision trees (*see* Chapter 8);
- multiple-criteria decision-making models;
- expected value;
- sensitivity analysis;
- Monte-Carlo simulation.

Of these, PERT is the most widely accepted, with expected value, sensitivity analysis and Monte-Carlo simulation also being widely used.

Expected value

The expected value of an event is the possible outcome times the probability of its occurrence, e.g. if a project has a 50 per cent chance of yielding a profit of £30 million, the expected value is 0.5 x 30m = £15m. This provides a basic tool for evaluating different project proposals as an investment decision-maker. Two projects require funding – one has a potential return of £200 million and the other a return of £150 million. The first has a 50 per cent chance of yielding this, whilst the second has a 70 per cent chance. The expected value calculations yield £100 million for the first and £105 million for the second – on this basis the second is more attractive.

Sensitivity analysis

This works similarly to PERT analysis – an expected value for the main inputs to the project is put into the calculations of the outcome as well as an optimistic (in this case $+n$ per cent) and pessimisic ($-n$ per cent) value (value of n is often 10). This will show the effect on the outcome of a change in the variable considered and can show where management control attention should be focused.

The price of materials and labour for a project is likely to fluctuate. As the contract price needs to be fixed in advance, the project manager needs to see the effect of fluctuations on bottom-line performance. The material is one of the major contributors to the cost of the project. Overheads are calculated on the basis of 175 per cent of direct labour.

Costs:
materials – £0.60m
direct labour – £0.20m
contribution to overheads – £0.35m

Revenues: fixed at £1.2m

The calculations are carried out in Table 4.5 as follows:

revenue
– material costs
– combined labour and overhead costs
= profit

As can be seen, the effect of the changes in costs means that although on initial inspection this looks viable, the figures indicate that should materials increase by ten per cent, unless there is a drop in the labour costs of the project, it will make a loss.

Table 4.5

		Materials		
		−10%	*expected*	*+10%*
Labour + overheads	*−10%*	1.2 − 0.54 − 0.495 0.165	1.2 − 0.6 − 0.495 + 0.105	1.2 − 0.66 − 0.495 + 0.045
	expected	1.2 − 0.54 − 0.55 + 0.11	1.2 − 0.6 − 0.55 + 0.05	1.2 − 0.66 − 0.55 − 0.01
	+10%	1.2 − 0.54 − 0.605 + 0.055	1.2 − 0.6 − 0.605 − 0.005	1.2 − 0.66 − 0.605 − 0.065

Monte-Carlo simulation

This method requires the use of a computer to be practicable, and uses a range of values or distribution, rather than single values, for time, cost and other estimates, and then shows the effect on the finances or other critical project factor.

Monte-Carlo simulation is available as an extension to most popular spreadsheet packages (including LOTUS and EXCEL), allowing the planner the option of modelling from a spreadsheet without having to use a dedicated piece of software.

4.9 CASH-FLOW CONSIDERATIONS

The rejection or deferral of a project proposal may have nothing to do with its intrinsic merit. The decision will be based on the availability or otherwise of the necessary cash. A project is almost certain to be competing against others for scarce resources, and as the project manager will have to balance the trade-offs inherent in a project, so will the project sponsor have to balance the cost-benefit trade-offs of a number of proposals.

In large projects, the timing of payments may be critical for both the project organisation and their customers. For this reason it is necessary for both to know when expenditures are going to be made. In order to ease cash flow, projects may involve stage payments. This is common both in construction and large-scale engineering. Whilst all the necessary credit checks can and should be carried out, it is still a matter of risk for both parties when large contracts are entered into.

4.10 STRATEGIC INVESTMENT DECISIONS

The previous section was concerned with conventional theoretical approaches to the appraisal of projects. The case of the National Lottery (Project management in practice) shows how it would be almost impossible to justify some projects by conventional means. These include;

- where there is no guaranteed return;
- where the benefit is made in terms of reduction of labour – some companies do not see this as being in line with their philosophy;
- where the project is considered to be 'strategic' in nature.

A good example of these is in new manufacturing technology. Very often the justification will be made in terms of increased flexibility or capability – both of which are very difficult to assign a monetary value to.

Similarly for a service industry, a new computer system may help speed the transfer of information and encourage the organisation to become more integrated, but will be challenged to show a cash return.

Other countries, particularly Germany and Japan appear to have less demanding payback criteria set. As Charles Handy (1994) commented:

'...the Japanese put long-term growth above short- or even medium-term profits, indeed the profitability calculations hardly figure in some of their strategic decisions. To keep IBM at bay, Fujitsu won the computer contract for the water-distribution system of Hiroshima City with a bid of just one yen. The required rate of return for a 10 year R&D (research and development) project averages 8.7 per cent in Japan compared with 20.3 per cent in the US and 23.7 per cent in the UK. As a result, there is more investment in the future in Japan than in other countries.'

Some projects do have to have a 'leap of faith' attached to them – the founder of the Kentucky Fried Chicken fast-food chain presented a proposal that was not an attractive proposition to hundreds of banks (over 600 said 'no'). There are many other pieces of business folklore that initially did not meet the conventional criteria. Indeed, as companies strive to find competitive advantage, conventional solutions are less likely to provide them. This is far more likely to be provided by ones that challenge the limits of appraisal systems.

PROJECT
MANAGEMENT
IN PRACTICE:
**BIDDING FOR
THE CONTRACT
TO RUN THE UK
NATIONAL
LOTTERY**

The UK National Lottery was set up with the intention of providing a fund-raising tool for culture and the arts. The government put out an open invitation to tender for the contract to run the £5 billion-a-year business. With costs allowed, it would be worth in the region of £700 million in profit per annum to the winning bidder.

The bidders were consortia of companies – the project was simply too big and required too wide a range of skills (and political lobbying!) for one company. The idea was for people to be able to select their own lottery numbers, enter them at £1 a time in a range of retail stores, and for the winning number to be drawn on prime-time TV once a week. The winner could receive between £1 and £10 million.

The bids (or tenders) were submitted in February and on Wednesday 25 May 1994, the contestants were informed of the outcome simultaneously by fax. The

Camelot consortium would be awarded the contract. The main players in the consortium were:

Racal	– to provide electronics expertise
G.Tech	– an American lottery organiser
De La Rue	– to provide printing and security expertise
ICL	– to provide the computing expertise
Cadbury Schweppes	– to provide consumer marketing expertise
Saatchi & Saatchi	– the advertising agency

By nature, the bids were speculative – this was one project for which there was no guaranteed return for the competing consortia, but as David Rigg, Director of Communications, stated 'We knew it was a risk, but in this race there were no prizes for coming second'. They had spent in the region of £5 million on the bid – and it was commented that many people felt that this level of commitment is what had swung the decision in their favour. They had played as if they expected to win, and had a system in place that could be fully operational only six months after the contracts were awarded. Much of the operational infrastructure was either in place or planned. This had taken three years to prepare, and would be almost impossible to justify under conventional accounting practice. Yet by sharing their risks and by presenting the best project plan, the profits for all concerned would be considerable.

Case discussion

1 Considering the techniques discussed in this chapter, how could expenditure on such a project be justified?

2 Why did it make more sense for a consortium to be assembled for the bid, rather than one company doing the entire project in-house?

SUMMARY OF KEY POINTS

- estimates become more uncertain the further ahead in time the situation being considered;
- estimates range from rough (+/– 25 per cent) to-finish (+/– 5 per cent);
- cost assessment drives the estimation process and can be top-down or ground-up;
- estimates of times can be through direct work measurement, work sampling, synthetic estimation, or via learning-curve calculations;
- total costs include elements of direct time and materials, indirect time and materials, project overheads, and organisational overheads;
- budgets are a request for funds or an allocation of funds, and will be given over a number of separate categories;
- budgeting systems do not always provide the best form of financial management;
- resource analysis can be carried out through the application of crashing techniques (to determine the least-cost schedule for shortening projects) and allocation of resources (via the responsibility matrix). Resource levelling is often needed but can increase project duration;
- pricing policies include target costing and 'cost-plus' though the latter is rarely used today;

- learning curves show quantitatively how, when activities are repeated, their cycle times reduce;
- project justification can be carried out using payback methods or those involving the time value of money – including discounted cash flow (NPV and IRR);
- project risk analysis is a range of techniques which includes PERT, expected value, sensitivity analysis and Monte-Carlo simulation;
- part of the project evaluation process is the effect that project cash flows will have on the organisation;
- strategic projects provide problems for the conventional justification techniques outlined in this chapter.

KEY TERMS		
cost:benefit analysis	payback
ground-up/top-down costing	discounting
overheads	internal rates of return (IRR)
work measurement	opportunity cost
work sampling	compound interest
synthetic timing	net present value
learning curves	risk adjusted discount rate
budgets	expected value
crashing	sensitivity analysis
minimum cost schedule	Monte-Carlo analysis
resource smoothing/levelling	stage payments
target costing	cost-plus

REVIEW AND DISCUSSION QUESTIONS

1 Discuss the different levels of accuracy required of estimates at different stages in the planning process. Why is accuracy considered to be important to the process?

2 Show how feedback on actual performance of previous plans, compared to estimates, could improve the estimating process.

3 In costing proposals, discuss the differences between top-down and ground-up approaches.

4 Describe the major elements of cost in a proposal to:
   (a) implement a new computer system for the administration of a college or university.
   (b) construct a new theme park.
   (c) introduce a new range of non-paracetamol headache tablets.

5 Discuss the relative merits of each of the methods for determining the time content of activities.

6 Identify the benefits and potential disadvantages of a budget system

7 Show qualitatively how activities can be shortened or 'crashed'.

8 Draw the network diagram for the project given in Table 4.6.

Table 4.6

Activity	Predecessor	Normal time (days)	Crash time (days)	Normal cost £	Crash cost £
A	–	3	1	900	1700
B	–	6	3	2000	4000
C	A	2	1	500	1000
D	B, C	5	3	1800	2400
E	D	4	3	1500	1850
F	E	3	1	3000	3900
G	B, C	9	4	8000	9800
H	F, G	3	2	1000	2000

(a) Calculate the critical path, the project duration and the total normal cost.

(b) The project has to be completed in 16 days. Calculate the minimum total additional cost (the minimum cost schedule) of this crash.

(c) Calculate the minimum time for completing the project. What is the marginal cost over the original costs calculated in (a)?

9 From the network diagram shown in Fig. 4.11, identify the critical path and show the project duration.

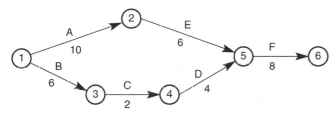

Figure 4.11 Network diagram

Table 4.7

Activity	Normal time (days)	Crash-cost per day	Crash time (days)
A	10	50	6
B	6	30	3
C	2	–	2
D	4	40	2
E	6	80	4
F	8	100	5

In Table 4.7 the crash cost per day is given along with the crash time. Use the information to show the sponsor of this project the most economical way of taking two days out of the plan. You should explain all the terms used.

10 In the development of the Sinclair C5 (a recumbent, electrically-assisted tri-cycle), there was the opportunity to develop both new power supplies and new motors, but both required additional development time. The decision was taken to proceed with existing technology – in this case a conventional car battery and the motor from a truck engine cooling fan. Intended performance was significantly compromised as a result.

Evaluate the risks that the company ran by pursuing this course of action and suggest alternative means by which a better technical result might have been achieved.

11 Describe how a 'responsibility matrix' may help in the allocation of work tasks and subsequent smoothing/levelling activities.

12 'Evans the Steam' has set up a new business and secured a contract to build 32 locomotives for mountain railways which are being reopened as tourist attractions. The order is to be fulfilled in two batches of 16. The first locomotive takes 30 days to assemble with seven people working full time on it. The daily rate for a locomotive fitter is £80 and the overheads are estimated to be 50 per cent on top of the labour rate. Evans is confident that an 80 per cent learning curve is possible. The first batch has been priced with a labour estimate of £16 000 per locomotive and the last 16 with a labour cost of £10 000. Comment on the pricing of the labour content and show whether the rates per locomotive are sufficient to cover the likely actual costs.

13 Evaluate, using discounting techniques, which option, lease or buy, is most financially beneficial in the scenario given in Table 4.8. You should consider the discount rate to be 10 per cent and the period of consideration to be five years.

Table 4.8

	Buy	Lease
Purchase/lease cost	£50 000	£10 000 per year
Annual operating cost	£4000 per year	£4000 per year
Maintenance cost	£2000 per year	maintained by leasing co.
Salvage value at the end of five years	£20 000	not applicable

14 The purchase of new office furniture for a boardroom has caused conflict between two factions within a company. One faction argues that the company should buy modern furniture, which will cost £12 000, and can be scrapped (replaced with zero salvage costs) in six years' time. The other favours the purchase of antique furniture which costs £30 000, but can be sold for £30 000 in six years' time. The modern furniture will cost £500 in maintenance, and the antique £1000. You have been asked to arbitrate the decision and resolve the conflict using financial methods (calculate the net present value of each scheme, using the company discount rate of 12 per cent).

15 Discuss the three main pricing strategies and indicate which one you feel provides the greatest benefits to customers and which to suppliers.

DISCOUNTING TABLES

Discounting tables are given in Table 4.9.

Table 4.9 Present value of £1

Year	1%	2%	3%	4%	5%	Discount rate 6%	7%	8%	9%	10%	12%	14%	15%
1	.990	.980	.971	.962	.952	.943	.935	.926	.917	.909	.893	.877	.870
2	.980	.961	.943	.925	.907	.890	.873	.857	.842	.826	.797	.769	.756
3	.971	.942	.915	.889	.864	.840	.816	.794	.772	.751	.712	.675	.658
4	.961	.924	.889	.855	.823	.792	.763	.735	.708	.683	.636	.592	.572
5	.951	.906	.863	.822	.784	.747	.713	.681	.650	.621	.567	.519	.497
6	.942	.888	.838	.790	.746	.705	.666	.630	.596	.564	.507	.456	.432
7	.933	.871	.813	.760	.711	.665	.623	.583	.547	.513	.452	.400	.376
8	.923	.853	.789	.731	.677	.627	.582	.540	.502	.467	.404	.351	.327
9	.914	.837	.766	.703	.645	.592	.544	.500	.460	.424	.361	.308	.284
10	.905	.820	.744	.676	.614	.558	.508	.463	.422	.386	.322	.270	.247
11	.896	.804	.722	.650	.585	.527	.475	.429	.388	.350	.287	.237	.215
12	.887	.788	.701	.625	.557	.497	.444	.397	.356	.319	.257	.208	.187
13	.879	.773	.681	.601	.530	.469	.415	.368	.326	.290	.229	.182	.163
14	.870	.758	.661	.577	.505	.442	.388	.340	.299	.263	.205	.160	.141
15	.861	.743	.642	.555	.481	.417	.362	.315	.275	.239	.183	.140	.123
16	.853	.728	.623	.534	.458	.394	.339	.292	.252	.218	.163	.123	.107
17	.844	.714	.605	.513	.436	.371	.317	.270	.231	.198	.146	.108	.093
18	.836	.700	.587	.494	.416	.350	.296	.250	.212	.180	.130	.095	.081
19	.828	.686	.570	.475	.396	.331	.276	.232	.194	.164	.116	.083	.070
20	.820	.673	.554	.456	.377	.312	.258	.215	.178	.149	.104	.073	.061
25	.780	.610	.478	.375	.295	.233	.184	.146	.116	.092	.059	.038	.030
30	.742	.552	.412	.308	.231	.174	.131	.099	.075	.057	.033	.020	.015

Year	16%	18%	20%	24%	28%	Discount rate 32%	36%	40%	50%	60%	70%	80%	90%
1	.862	.847	.833	.806	.781	.758	.735	.714	.667	.625	.588	.556	.526
2	.743	.718	.694	.650	.610	.574	.541	.510	.444	.391	.346	.309	.277
3	.641	.609	.579	.524	.477	.435	.398	.364	.296	.244	.204	.171	.146
4	.552	.516	.482	.423	.373	.329	.292	.260	.198	.153	.120	.095	.077
5	.476	.437	.402	.341	.291	.250	.215	.186	.132	.095	.070	.053	.040
6	.410	.370	.335	.275	.227	.189	.158	.133	.088	.060	.041	.029	.021
7	.354	.314	.279	.222	.178	.143	.116	.095	.059	.037	.024	.016	.011
8	.305	.266	.233	.179	.139	.108	.085	.068	.039	.023	.014	.009	.006
9	.263	.226	.194	.144	.108	.082	.063	.048	.026	.015	.008	.005	.003
10	.227	.191	.162	.116	.085	.062	.046	.035	.017	.009	.005	.003	.002
11	.195	.162	.135	.094	.066	.047	.034	.025	.012	.006	.003	.002	.001
12	.168	.137	.112	.076	.052	.036	.025	.018	.008	.004	.002	.001	.001
13	.145	.116	.093	.061	.040	.027	.018	.013	.005	.002	.001	.001	.000
14	.125	.099	.078	.049	.032	.021	.014	.009	.003	.001	.001	.000	.000
15	.108	.084	.065	.040	.025	.016	.010	.006	.002	.001	.000	.000	.000
16	.093	.071	.054	.032	.019	.012	.007	.005	.002	.001	.000	.000	
17	.080	.060	.045	.026	.015	.009	.005	.003	.001	.000	.000		
18	.069	.051	.038	.021	.012	.007	.004	.002	.001	.000	.000		
19	.060	.043	.031	.017	.009	.005	.003	.002	.000	.000			
20	.051	.037	.026	.014	.007	.004	.002	.001	.000	.000			
25	0.24	.016	.010	.005	.002	.001	.000	.000					
30	0.12	.007	.004	.002	.001	.000	.000						

NPV CALCULATION PROGRAM LISTING	

This program may be typed into a basic or turbo-basic shell. The REM statements may be omitted when entering the program.

```
100    REM
110    REM  NPV PROFILE PROGRAM
120    REM    BY MARK GOODE & HELENA SNEE
130    REM
140    REM    THIS PROGRAM WILL CALCULATE ALL THE NPV VALUES
150    REM    VALUES BETWEEN A AND B INTEREST RATES IN STEPS
160    REM    OF C. RESULTS ARE WRITTEN TO TEST FOR INPUT
170    REM    INTO A SPREADSHEET OR TO BE PRINTED.
180    REM
190    REM    LIMITS ON PROGRAM. 1) LENGTH OF PROJECT IS 100 YEARS.,
200    REM                       2) INTEREST RATES ARE IN INTEGER STEPS.
210    REM
220    REM    PROGRAM IS WRITTEN IN TURBO BASIC
230    REM    DATE 24/11/94
240    REM
250    DIM VA(100),NPV(100)
260    INPUT"WHAT IS THE LENGTH OF THE PROJECT";NG : LNG=NG+1
270    FOR I=1 TO LNG
280       PRINT"PLEASE INPUT THE CASH FLOW FOR YEAR"I-1:INPUT;VL
290       PRINT
300       VA(I)=VL
310    NEXT I
320    INPUT"PLEASE ENTER THE STARTING VALUE FOR THE INTEREST RATE";A
330    PRINT
340    INPUT"PLEASE ENTER THE END VALUE FOR THE INTEREST RATE";B
350    PRINT
360    INPUT"PLEASE ENTER THE STEP VALUE";C
370    PRINT
380    REM
390    REM CALCULATE NPV
400    REM
410    FOR I=A TO B STEP C
420    SUM=0 : CT=0
430    FOR J=1 TO LNG
440       DIS=1/(1+(I/100))^CT
450       SUM=SUM+VA(J)*DIS
460       CT=CT+1
470    NEXT J
480    NPV(I)=SUM
490    NEXT I
500    F1$="TEST"
510    OPEN F1$ FOR OUTPUT AS #3
```

```
520    FOR I=A TO B STEP C
530       PRINT# 3,I,NPV(I)
540    NEXT I
550    CLOSE #3
560    PRINT"END OF CALCULATION"
570    STOP
```

For a project of a given duration, the program will carry out the calculations for the NPV within the discounting range you specify. In order to calculate the IRR, put in a range of values for the NPV within which the IRR is likely to lie. The more values you choose, the longer the program will take to run. The output from the program is stored in a file 'test.prn' and can be printed directly (type 'print test.prn') or imported into any spreadsheet to produce graphical output.

Test the program with any of the examples from this chapter or Table 4.10. The numbers represent the cash flows for each of the years over a three year period. Use the printout to estimate the IRR for each of the projects.

Table 4.10

	Year 0	1	2	3
Project 1	−1000	3600	−4310	1716
Project 2	−6696	3430	3430	3430
Project 3	−10776	5520	5520	5520

REFERENCES

Handy, C. (1994) *The Empty Raincoat*, Hutchinson.

Hogg, N., (1994) *Business Forecasting Using Financial Models*, Financial Times/Pitman Publishing.

Monden, Y. (1992) *Cost Management in the New Manufacturing Age*, Productivity Press.

Waldron, D. and D. Galloway, (1988), 'Accounting – The Need for a New Language for Manufacturing', *Management Accounting*, Vol. 66, No. 10, November pp 34–35.

FURTHER READING

Kaplen, R.S. and A.A. Atkinson (1989) *Advanced Management Accounting*, 2nd edition, Prentice Hall.

Lumby, S. (1991) *Investment Appraisal & Financial Decisions*, 4th edition, Chapman & Hall.

CHAPTER 5

Teams and organisation

The gathering together of individuals with the aim of making them a cohesive whole and ensuring the benefit of all stakeholders, is a fundamental role of most project managers. This is at best likely to be a very hit-and-miss process (very few will naturally achieve both good social interaction and commercial success) and at worst, financially disastrous. There have been many attempts to describe the best mixture of personalities that will ensure that the group dynamics are right and some of these will be discussed here. These are project issues. A strategic issue is how the project management structure fits in with the structure of the organisation as a whole. The ideas of the various forms of matrix are discussed along with the emegence of concurrency.

5.1 THE ROLE OF TEAMS

The organisation of people into *ad hoc* groups takes advantage of bringing together individuals from different specialisms (marketing, engineering, etc.) as needed for a project task. It is notable that as organisational size increases, the degree of specialism of individuals is increased. Since the days of Henry Ford, large organisations have been organised by functional specialism into 'chimneys' (*see* Fig. 5.1). The notion is that by grouping all the specialisms together, the arrangement is very efficient as when you need that function performing, there is an obvious resource to draw upon. Quite reasonably, from the point of view of the individual, career paths are well defined, and basic administration systems are geared to this way of working. Give a group the task of setting-up and running their own business and, 99 per cent of the time, the first task they set themselves is to allocate roles as heads of the various line functions. This is typically the case in many traditional industries, but has been shown to be detrimental to the creativity of individuals and the responsiveness of the organisation to changing market needs.

However, as discussed in Chapter 1, one single function will rarely provide a customer's entire need or want. To do this requires cross-functional activity, i.e. the linking of the activities of more than one functional area. Functional arrangements tend to lead individual managers to build their own empires by creating work for themselves – regardless of whether this is value-adding for the organisation as a whole. Departmental head-count is considered to be a measure of the status of the individual manager and the importance of their function.

The conventional management hierarchy or pyramid (*see* Fig. 5.2) has provided the basis on which the majority of organisations are ordered. The style is militaristic and there may be 11 or more layers in the chain of command (foot soldier to top-ranking general). Other structures include organisation by:

- product group;
- customer type (e.g. military/civil);
- geographical area (of their operations or the customers they serve);
- the function they perform.

It is common to see a mixture of these forms of organisation being employed – depending on the nature of the business and the degree of vertical integration in the supply stream (how many of the suppliers/customers are owned by the same organisation).

Where a project can be defined as having more than one function involved (which systems and strategy projects are almost bound to have) it is emerging as one of the roles of the project management specialist to define possible organisational forms. Many authors note that project managers themselves

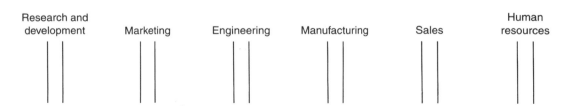

Figure 5.1 Management chimneys

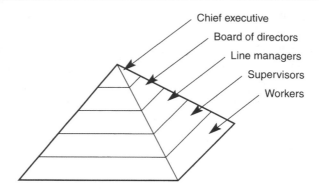

Figure 5.2 Hierarchical pyramid

rarely have the choice about how the project organisation is arranged and, consequently, have to use what are often inappropriate structures. The emerging strategic importance of the project manager means that they are likely to have more input in determining the structures within which they work in the future.

The nature of the work organisation is important as it:

- defines responsibility and authority;
- outlines reporting arrangements;
- determines the management overhead (costs);
- sets the structure behind the organisational culture;
- determines one group of stakeholders in project activities.

As organisations have expanded, so the functions have often become less integrated by, for example, geographical separation. Walls, both literal and metaphorical, are constructed around them. In order to try and enforce communication between departments, many organisations use 'dotted-line responsibility'. Here an individual may have a responsibility to one functional manager, with a dotted-line responsibility to another. This device has been used frequently to ensure that certain individuals do not engage in empire-building. In manufacturing industry, this was done by manufacturing directors who wanted to ensure that they retained responsibility for the running of the entire manufacturing operation. Consequently, when it became fashionable to employ a quality manager, they were not given any direct staff, but inspection and other quality staff would work for the manufacturing manager, whilst given a dotted-line responsibility to the quality manager (indicating that they were linked to the goals of this part of the operation). It did still leave power in the hands of the manufacturing people....

In addition to the dotted-line responsibility, detailed administrative procedures are introduced to ensure that some form of integration takes place. Often involving interminable meetings and mountains of bureaucracy, they are an attempt to make the organisation perform acts which it is not designed to do, i.e. integrate. Sloan's General Motors in the US of the 1930s was run using considerable command-and-control structures – based on the premise that 'whoever holds the purse strings, commands'.

5.2 THE PURE PROJECT ORGANISATION

To move away from the functional chimneys to the project-based organisation is a major step. It is a structure that predominates in the construction industry (*see* Fig. 5.3). At the highest levels in the organisation there are staff posts – senior managers, directors, administrative staff, etc. (called the 'project board'). The next level down is a series of project managers who have control over one or more projects at a time. The constitution of the project team depends on the stage in the life-cycle of the project, e.g. at the planning stage, there will be architects, structural engineers, quantity surveyors, and various other technical specialities such as ground water engineers and legal advisers. These will be replaced by various contractors who are brought in to carry out specific tasks (such as steel fixers, electricians and heating/ventilation engineers) as the project moves through the operational phase. Once the particular task is completed, the team in each case is disbanded. The project manager may be retained to move on to other projects.

The advantages of such an arrangement are that:

- the labour force is highly flexible – labour can generally be attracted as and when required, without providing a labour burden or overhead for the rest of the time;
- the main company only have to administer the employment of their own staff – saving on the costs of directly employing others.

The disadvantages are significant:

- the project team is only temporary and so these people have no commitment to its success. The pay on a piece-rate basis may encourage the speed of work, but does little to ensure high quality or solve problems ahead of time. Paying on a time rate only encourages people to drag jobs out over a longer period of time. The only one who has an interest in the achievement of cost:quality:time objectives is the project manager;

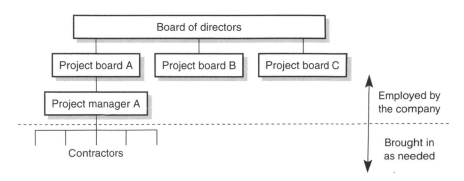

Figure 5.3 Project organisation

- when there is a boom in a particular area in an industry, there is a shortage of labour, increasing labour rates and making hiring of the necessary resources problematic;
- where there are significant events occurring in a project, it is very hard for the lessons of these to be passed on to future projects as the people who have carried out the 'do' part of the project are not around for the 'review' and 'act' parts. They cannot benefit therefore from the review process. Progress in improving work methods is likely to be slower.

5.3 MATRIX MANAGEMENT

Matrix management was invented as a way of achieving some of the benefits of the project organisation without the disadvantages. Mullins (1993) suggests three situations where a matrix management structure is appropriate:

- where there is more than one orientation to the activities of the operation, e.g. multiple customers or geographical differences in markets served;
- where there is the need to process simultaneously large amounts of information;
- where there is the need to share resources – one function or project cannot justify the expenditure on a dedicated resource.

Davis and Lawrence (1977) define matrix organisation as:

matrix structure + matrix systems + matrix culture + matrix behaviour

The matrix structure and the variations on the theme are included below. Matrix systems include the activities of management in planning, organising, directing, controlling and motivating within the structure. The culture requires acceptance of the system by the people who have to work within it, and the behaviour required is the ability to understand and work with overlapping boundaries.

The organisation of the matrix follows one of three models (Knight, 1977).

1 The coordination model

In this arrangement the project manager acts as a coordinator of the work of the project and chairs meetings of the representatives of all the departments involved. Responsibility is shared for the success of the project between the departments. This is regarded as being the weakest form of matrix structure as there is little commitment to project success from anyone and the project manager is relatively impotent compared to the functional managers. The project meetings can be either led off-course or totally discredited by the inclusion of people of too high/low levels of authority respectively in the group.

2 The overlay model

This is an attempt to balance the power of the project manager with that of the line manager. The administration of the organisation is such that the line manager needs the activities of the project manager to balance their resources, i.e. the project provides a means of securing part of the income of that function. The emergence of a second line of command – the project and the line manager – over any member of the team is the crucial drawback of this model. The person will have project responsibilities in addition to their line responsibilities.

3 The secondment model

Functional departments have the role of providing resources through seconding people on a full-time basis to the project team. On completion of the project, they return to the line function. In this way it is possible to have the resources available to bring in technical specialists without the project being saddled with their cost on a continuous basis. Such an arrangement is feasible where the project is of vital importance to the organisation. Drawbacks include the discontinuity of tasks for the individual and the resident department.

The success of application of the above models depends on:

- the training given to both managers and team members on working in such environments;
- the support systems – administrative, informational and career-wise;
- the nature of the individual – in particular, their tolerance level for role ambiguity. Working in the uncertain environment of the project, and with career progression allied to the department rather than the project, means that there are often conflicting priorities.

There is much evidence to suggest that although matrix models are still widely employed, their contribution to project success is very mixed. Early research into the role of matrix management (quoted in Knight, 1977) compares the performance of 38 US military defence contracts. Those that were delivered by organisations which had team-based structures (not necessarily matrix) showed superior performance in terms of time and cost. Those organisations that used matrix structures generally succeeded in delivering a higher level of quality (technical specification).

The result of research carried out by Bartlett and Ghoshal (1990), and the anecdotal evidence of Peters (1987 and 1992) amongst others, is that matrix management is unwieldy and practically unworkable. This is based on the fact that in the most used case (the use of the overlay model), people have to report to two bosses. Peters (1992) comments that 'matrices become hopelessly complicated bureaucracies and gut the emotional energy and ownership of those closest to the marketplace'. The dual command leads to power struggles where one functional manager may 'win' but the organisation as a whole loses out. Davis and Lawrence (1977) cite the following additional problems:

- anarchy – people perceive that as soon as we get something working, we change it;
- groupitis – decision-making is removed from the individual who will not take a decision without group approval;
- overhead that is imposed is excessively costly;
- decision-strangling – so much time is spent trying to get consensus that any individual flair is stifled and the group becomes a barrier to any rapid progress.

Having stated all these potential problems it is understandable that many organisations avoid the matrix form. There are, however, others who use it to good effect, proving that there is not one single way of managing a project that is applicable in all situations. The model that is chosen must be on a contingent basis, i.e. responds to the needs of the organisation at that moment in time.

5.4 THE SEAMLESS ENTERPRISE

Dimancescu (1992) stated:

> 'A new management agenda lies ahead ... one piece of that agenda [is] the weaving together of companywide teams that gather strength by understanding the whole endeavour to which they are connected. This frees them to function independently of the artificial labels and boundaries constructed around them. It also frees them to tap the collective genius of the group, rather than simply cementing individually conceived parts into a lesser whole.'

Having observed the best Japanese companies' management practices, Dimancescu's view is that the future for project management is to encourage cross-function teaming and communication. Unlike matrix management there is none of the 'two-boss structure' and whole processes of integrating your own operation, your suppliers and customers in one supply chain are considered. This is the operationalising of the view stated above – that to do anything in an organisation which meets a customer's need involves many functions.

The cross-function teams that Dimancescu studied, consisted of members from all functions regardless of seniority. The tasks would typically be meeting customer quality requirements, controlling costs or ensuring that deadlines were met (*see* Fig. 5.4).

The use of traditional planning tools such as CPA or PERT do not state information requirements that are very often met informally through impromptu corridor meetings, for example. The promise of information technology to overcome this deficiency (in identifying information requirements) has not been realised in the majority of organisations. Information provision is frequently hampered by different departments working on different hardware and software, with compatibility between the two being non-existent. Better solutions look to come from improved use of people rather than any increase in the use of technology.

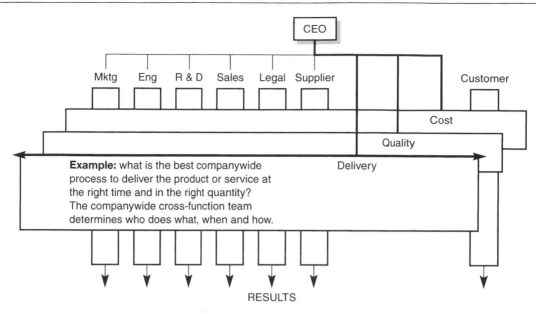

Figure 5.4 Cross-function 'process teams'
(*Source:* Dimancescu, [1992])

Four fields mapping, as discussed in Chapter 3, is part of the toolkit that can enable the management of cross-functional teams. It is decided at the planning stage who needs information and to be involved at the various stages in a project. This is by nature an integrator – a tool that can be used to keep the overall objectives in view. It can also point to the kind of structure that will be appropriate during the different phases. Cross-function teams may be appropriate for all phases – whereas matrix or project organisations are only really useful during the 'doing' phase.

5.5 TEAMWORK

The distinction between the terms 'team' and 'group' is made to indicate the differences in operating characteristics of each. A group is simply a collection of people. A team meets the following criteria:

- the output of the group is greater than the sum of the outputs of the individuals, e.g. a team can engage in creative processes (idea generation) far more effectively than a collection of individuals;
- a greater range of options can be considered by exploiting differences in individual thought processes;
- decision-making by the team is likely to be better (*see* Chapter 8).

The purpose of studying the role of teamwork in the project environment is:

- to help the project manager in the design and selection of the workgroup;
- to enable the monitoring of the degree to which the team is functioning effectively;
- to provide feedback to the team to help improve effectiveness.

The above assumes that in the first instance the project manager has the luxury of a free hand in the selection of who should form their project team. In reality, the team or group is more likely to be 'inherited' rather than designed. The study of teamworking will raise awareness of what is possible through teaming and the symptoms and consequences of the process not being managed to best effect.

Other characteristics of teams include:

- more openness to taking risks as the risk is shared between the team rather than carried by one individual;
- higher overall level of motivation as there is an inherent responsibility to others in the team and a desire not to let them down;
- better support for the individuals within the team who are more likely to be included in a greater range of activities than they would normally be exposed to, but without them having to work alone.

Typically a team consists of 2 to 20 people, though most managers recognise that effectiveness will decrease once the numbers go above 10.

5.6 LIFE-CYCLES OF TEAMS

Teams, like projects can be seen as having various stages of development. These can broadly be defined as collection, entrenchment, resolution/accomodation and synergy followed almost inevitably by decline. At some point, the team will be disbanded because either they have reached a point at which it is no longer feasible for them to carry on working together, or the task they are working on has been accomplished. The characteristics of each phase are shown in Table 5.1 and the effectiveness profile during the life-cycle is shown in Fig. 5.5.

Using this knowledge, the project manager can identify the stage at which their team is operating, ensuring that the decline phase is held back for as long as possible. This may be done through changing the composition of the team to take the development back a little or expanding the range or scope of the tasks being undertaken to add a new challenge. The important point is, though, that teams do have a natural life-cycle and this should be recognised and used to advantage.

Table 5.1 Team life-cycle

Stage	Characteristics
Collection	The bringing together of individuals into a group with a collective task or problem to solve. The participants have a degree of eagerness and initial enthusiasm and generally rely on the authority and hierarchy to provide a degree of certainty in this uncertain environment. They will use this initial phase to establish themselves and find what is expected of them.
Entrenchment	As the group starts work they begin to find out where each other stands on various issues. The entrenchment comes when people arrive with preconceived ideas as to how the project should be proceeding and are unwilling to be persuaded of the merits of allowing the group to decide on the course of action. This phase can be very destructive and is generally fairly unproductive. The reasons for this unproductiveness are issues such as disillusionment with the goals of the project, competition for power or attention within the group, or general confusion as the work being under taken bears little relationship to the goals of the project.
Resolution/ accomodation	The disagreements begin to be resolved, and characteristics such as mutual trust, harmony, self-esteem and confidence are seen. This is where the team starts to put the negative social effects aside and move to being more productive.
Synergy	Based on Ansoff (1969), synergy is defined as when the output of the whole is greater than what would be obtained from the component parts, otherwise stated as 2+2=5. This is the peak of effectiveness of the team, leadership is shared, and there is a new motivation to complete the tasks at hand.
Decline	At some point the team will hit an event when their effectiveness starts to decline – this can be through the nature of the task being undertaken not changing or the focus of the activities being allowed to move towards a social group.
Break-up	If this occurs naturally before the task is finished, there can be problems in getting a new team to take up the remaining work. They will be expected to get 'up to speed' very quickly and have an additional pressure on them. Where the group finishes its task and it is during one of the earlier stages of development, either in resolution or synergy, the effects on future projects can be highly beneficial as the participants go away with good memories of the work they have done.

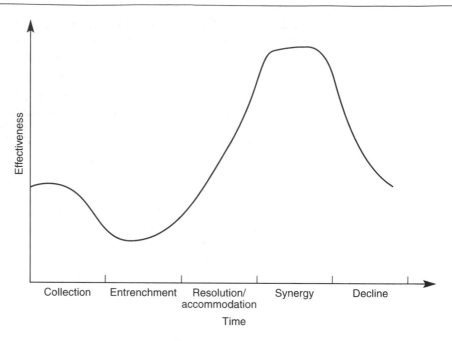

Figure 5.5 Effectiveness profile of team life-cycle

Example

Quality circles have been a very popular management tool for encouraging people from all parts of organisations to work together to solve problems. They are a move to get people who only previously had maintenance responsibilities to use their natural creativity and have the opportunity to innovate. The idea was promoted very heavily during the 1980s by the UK's Department of Trade and Industry for use in all organisations. The frequently quoted example was that of a trade delegation to Japan who were amazed to find the extent of the use of quality circles in industry, and even more to find it in service industries – including a restaurant where the waiters had formed their own quality circle.

The initiative was taken up by a large number of companies. Quality circle meetings would often take place in the workers' own time, though generally they were given worktime at the start to set the circles up. It was notable that within a very short period (often less than 12 months), these project teams were being disbanded and the idea of quality circles discontinued. Initial results were generally found to be excellent – the biggest problems were tackled first by the newly integrated groups and considerable savings were made. Then they started to decline. As Lawler and Mohrman (1985) found:

'During this period, groups meet less often, they become less productive, and the resources committed to the program dwindle. The main reason the groups continue at all is because of the social satisfaction and pleasure the members experience rather than the group's problem-solving effectiveness. As managers begin to recognise this they cut back further on resources. As a result, the program shrinks. The people who all along have resisted the program recognise that it is less powerful than it once was, and they openly reject and resist the ideas it generates.'

The idea of using quality circles over an extended timeframe neglects to take account of the natural life-cycles of teams. The alternatives are:

1 Have the team assembled for the purpose of solving one single problem, then to be disbanded once it has been solved.
2 Provide a path for the development of the role of the team from solving one or a small number of low-level problems into semi-autonomous workgroups. This will require other changes (in management reporting arrangements, for example) and considerable development of the team through education and training.

5.7 MANAGING PERSONALITIES IN TEAMS

It is stated above that the project manager can benefit from an understanding of the ways in which individuals behave in group situations. The understanding of the processes that are taking place (known as 'group dynamics') can be assisted through the study of the work of such authors as Berne (1967). The understanding of what is happening and managing the process are very separate items. Managing the process is discussed in the following section whilst here it is useful to consider the role of the individual.

In order to determine the character of an individual (the 'personality profile'), there are hundreds of commercially available psychometric tests that can be used. Two of the more popular are the Watson-Glazier (to assess critical thinking) and the 16PF (Cattell – which provides a description of the nature of the person's natural roles in groups). Many claim to be the 'definitive and only possible test you will need to find that ideal candidate for your team', but most can be bluffed by an intelligent candidate and few are totally applicable to people other than graduates (Donkin, 1995). They can also be expensive to administrate and often require expert guidance to interpret the results. The interview, though maligned, is still the normal mode for recruiting.

In designing your team there are certain basic requirements you may wish key players to have, e.g. qualifications or relevant experience. These determine their eligibility for the job. The suitability can be determined through assessing how they are likely to fit in with the rest of the team, and whether or not the team has a balanced portfolio of characteristics relative to the task being undertaken. Belbin (1993) has shown that a structure based on a greater number of classifications than those given above can prove useful in both the selection and ongoing management of the project. The characteristics that Belbin identifies are shown in Fig. 5.6.

	Roles and descriptions – team-role contribution	Allowable weaknesses
	Plant: creative, imaginative, unorthodox. Solves difficult problems.	Ignores details. Too pre-occupied to communicate effectively.
	Resource investigator: extrovert, enthusiastic, communicative. Explores opportunities. Develops contacts.	Overoptimistic. Loses interest once initial enthusiasm has passed.
	Coordinator: mature confident, a good chairperson. Clarifies goals, promotes decision-making, delegates well.	Can be seen as manipulative. Delegates personal work.
	Shaper: challenging, dynamic, thrives on pressure. Has the drive and courage to overcome obstacles.	Can provoke others. Hurts people's feelings.
	Monitor evaluator: sober, strategic and discerning. Sees all options. Judges accurately.	Lacks drive and ability to inspire others. Overly critical.
	Teamworker: cooperative, mild, perceptive and diplomatic. Listens, builds, averts friction, calms the waters.	Indecisive in crunch situations. Can be easily influenced.
	Implementer: disciplined, reliable, conservative and efficient. Turns ideas into practical actions.	Somewhat inflexible. Slow to respond to new possibilities.
	Completer: painstaking, conscientious, anxious. Searches out errors and omissions. Delivers on time.	Inclined to worry unduly. Reluctant to delegate. Can be a nit-picker.
	Specialist: single-minded, self-starting, dedicated. Provides knowledge and skills in rare supply.	Contributes on only a narrow front. Dwells on technicalities. Overlooks the 'big picture'.

Strength of contribution in any one of the roles is commonly associated with particular weaknesses. These are called allowable weaknesses.
Executives are seldom strong in all nine team roles.

Figure 5.6 The nine team roles

(*Source:* Belbin, 1993, reproduced with permission)

Having categorised the individual's personalities, it is worth while considering the effect this has on their behaviour. Belbin cites this as consisting of six factors:

- personality – as determined through testing;
- mental abilities – e.g. critical reasoning;
- current values and motivations (determined by all sorts of personal factors – the weather, family situation, how well the blues did on Saturday, etc.);
- field constraints – those rules and procedures that impact on behaviour from the environment in which you are working;
- experience – prior events which have left varying degrees of impression on the individual;
- role-learning – the ease with which an individual can take on one of the roles listed in Fig. 5.6, but which is not their natural role – this increases their role versatility.

The effects on the design of the team are that there can be a degree of scientific method applied to the selection of individuals. There is no substitute for personal selection however. At the newly built Triumph Motorcycle factory at Hinckley (UK), teams working in the assembly area are given the final say on the suitability of new team members. This is assessed through a try-out period where the prospective employee joins the team prior to being formally taken on. The team then has a veto if the person does not fit in.

5.8 EFFECTIVE TEAMWORK

Larson and LaFasto (1989) identify eight characteristics, most of which are under the control of the project manager, which can help ensure that project success, at least as far as can be managed through the team, is achieved. These are:

- a clear, elevating goal – a sense of mission must be created through the development of an objective which is understood, important, worth while and personally or collectively challenging;
- provide a results-driven structure – the structure and composition of the team should be commensurate with the task being undertaken (*see* below);
- competent team members – need to balance personal with technical competence;
- unified commitment – create the environment of 'doing what has to be done to succeed';
- foster a collaborative climate – encourage reliance on others within the team;
- standards of excellence – through individual standards, team pressure, knowledge of the consequences of failure;
- external support and recognition – where good work is performed, recognise it. It is likely to be absent from the other stakeholders, so will be the responsibility of the project manager to provide it;
- institute principled leadership – *see* Chapter 7.

The first point is stated in virtually every consideration of this subject. Indeed many go as far as to say that demanding performance which is challenging is an integral part of the way to creating a team. In addition, the first tasks that the team carries out will set the scene for the entire project, in particular through the definition of roles and rules of behaviour.

The structure of the team and its composition is broken down into three basic categories – creative, tactical and problem-resolution (Larson and LaFasto, 1989). The use of each can be related to the appropriate or most likely phase in the project life-cycle. The requirements of the structure of each are shown in Table 5.2.

Table 5.2 Requirements of team structure

Category	Likely phase of project life-cycle	Characteristics of team structure
Creative	Planning	Needs to have a high degree of autonomy in order to explore the widest range of possibilities and alternatives. Needs to be independent of systems and procedures and requires independent thinkers and people who are self-starters.
Tactical	Doing	Needs a well-defined plan, hence unambiguous role definitions and clarity of objectives for the individual members. The team members should have loyalty and a sense of urgency.
Problem-solving	Doing (when problems arise)	Will focus on problem-resolution rather than any pre-determined conclusions – these must be eliminated. The desirable characteristic of the people involved is that they are intelligent and have people sensitivity.

How teams/groups work can be seen in Fig. 5.7. At one end of the spectrum is the disintegrated group, where there is no agreement between the team members and complete breakdown of the decision-making processes. At the other end is the integrated team, which has complete consensus on all matters, but which has 'gone over the edge' in terms of effectiveness. Their processes can be categorised by what is termed group-think, otherwise described by 'they've beaten the defence, but no one can bang the ball into the back of the net without discussing it with the group first'. Generally this results in ludicrous decisions being made – the ill-fated Charge of the Light Brigade resulted from a group of generals who sat around and agreed with each other, rather than upset the working of the group by disagreeing with the decision!

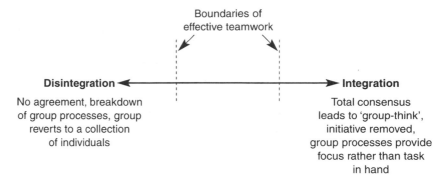

Figure 5.7 Spectrum of team/group performance

5.9 MANAGING THE TEAM – RUNNING EFFECTIVE MEETINGS

The project manager will often have to chair meetings, so a discussion of the theory of how they should be run is very relevant. This is an exceptional management skill, yet it is so basic that most people assume that they know how to do it. In practice, this is rarely the case and meetings often break up without any progress being made. This short section is only intended to provide a few guidance notes as to what constitutes good practice.

1 Confirm the purpose of the meeting – there has to be a reason why you need to bring people together – this should be very specific so as to help eliminate spurious issues which can take away from the main purpose.
2 Deciding who should be invited with the minimum requirement of including anyone who would be offended if they were left out. It is often worth checking by asking the individual concerned if you are in doubt.
3 The pre-meeting preparation – the location and timing, agenda, and any reports providing background information on the topic under discussion should be circulated in advance.
4 Running the meeting – provide a forum for constructive debate whilst limiting the scope of discussion to the matter in hand. Do not allow repetition of points or any one member to dominate the discussions. Regularly summarise progress and ask for conclusions to be drawn based on the discussions. The project manager should have in mind that the level of attention of most people declines rapidly after the first 20 minutes, and after two hours there is unlikely to be any constructive progress. People will often agree to anything at this point simply to get out of the meeting. Obtaining consensus is an art which the skilful chair of a meeting will aim for. This ensures that the entire meeting has 'bought-in' to a decision and makes carrying it out far easier than with a number of dissenters.
5 Post-meeting follow-up – send copies of the minutes with action points and who should carry them out listed against each. Most meetings can have their conclusions and action points stated on one side of A4 paper – they have a

high chance of being read in this form, rather than 'filed'. These minutes and action points must then form the basis of the next meeting's early discussions, ensuring that whoever said they would carry out a task has a natural responsibility to the meeting to do it. They also know that should they fail to carry out an action, this will be identified at the next meeting.

There are many excellent management skills courses which develop the above ideas, including some of the more complex aspects such as conflict resolution, and aspiring project managers should avail themselves of these. The further reading section at the end of this chapter contains several texts which provide an expansion of the subject.

5.10 CONCURRENCY IN PROJECTS

Due to the need to get products to market faster, functional barriers need to be broken down to facilitate the passing of information. This multi-disciplinary teaming approach to new product development is known as 'concurrent engineering'. No discussion of teaming and organisations would be complete without considering this. These ideas are applicable across all sectors as they can be treated as a special case of the use of cross-function management.

The conventional life-cycle for a new product development (NPD) project is shown in Fig. 5.8. This suffers from two major drawbacks:

- the message or customer specification is interpreted by different people at each stage of the process. The information that reaches the manufacturing people telling them what to make is potentially very different from what goes in at the start of the process ('Chinese-whispers' syndrome – Fig. 5.9);
- due to the constant process-revision that is required, engineering changes are often made very late in the development process. These cause enormous disruption, in particular delay. A recent survey (Nichols et al, 1993) showed that product development programs overran their planned times by an average of 27 per cent.

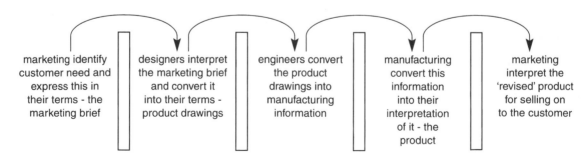

Figure 5.8 Conventional approach to new product development

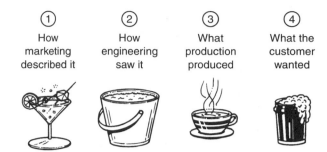

① How marketing described it ② How engineering saw it ③ What production produced ④ What the customer wanted

Figure 5.9 Effect of 'Chinese-whispers' syndrome on new product development

It was seen by many who visited Japan and investigated their automotive industry, that the level of design changes and engineering activity had a very different profile. The Japanese model was focused on getting the product 'right first time' with the result as shown in Fig. 5.10. As can be seen, the amount of activity declines as the product nears production. The importance of time-to-market has been shown recently to be responsible for over 30 per cent of the total profit to be made from a product during its life-cycle. The reduction in long-term costs has also been shown to be significant if concurrent engineering is used.

The arrangement of product development into a process stream, with all the necessary parties involved at all stages to prevent the cycle of work and re-work of ideas, has the natural effect of allowing activities to run alongside one another (concurrently) as opposed to one after the other (sequentially). This is shown in Fig. 5.11.

The advantages of a concurrent engineering approach are shown by the ability of the Japanese automotive producers to bring new vehicles to market every three to four years, whilst western manufacturers have been taking five to seven years. The electronics sector is typified in this way by Sony, who introduce new

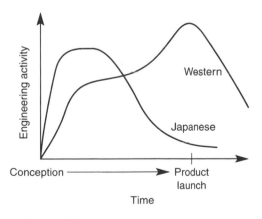

Figure 5.10 Engineering activity

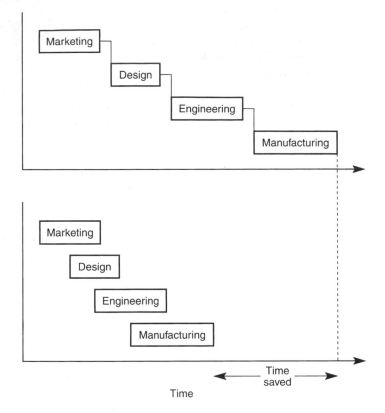

Figure 5.11 Sequential versus concurrent models of new product development

versions of the Walkman almost on a weekly basis. The benefits can be summarised as potential for:

- reduced product time-to-market;
- reduced engineering costs – due to the reduction in re-working new designs;
- better responsiveness to market needs.

The disadvantages of applying this method of working include:

- increased overheads – as the teams require their own administration support;
- costs of co-location – people being re-located away from their functions to be with the team with which they are working;
- cultural resistance;
- inappropriate application – it is no panacea for product development problems – a poor conceptual design will not be improved by using concurrent methods.

The role of concurrency should be used to induce cooperation during planning (not necessarily involving co-location), high levels of communication and simultaneous activities during the activity phases. If used in this way it can secure the benefits without incurring the disadvantages.

PROJECT MANAGEMENT IN PRACTICE: MATRIX MANAGEMENT AT CARDIFF BAY DEVELOPMENT CORPORATION

As a government-funded body, the corporation is one of a number of UK regional development corporations charged with the regeneration of specific areas. It is a predominantly project-based organisation – the life-span of the corporation generally being fixed at its inception. Its roles include the promotion of the area and the bringing in of business, housing and the necessary infrastructural changes necessary to make it all work. Aside from London's Docklands development, the Cardiff Bay development is one of the most ambitious schemes currently running. It includes the construction of a barrage across the estuaries of the rivers Taff and Ely, which will form a freshwater lagoon when completed. The 2200 acres of land that will be directly adjacent to the lagoon are in the control of a number of owners, with around 60 per cent of it being under contract or negotiation for re-development.

When founded in 1987, the corporation was divided into functional groups – engineering, commercial, finance and administration, each under the control of a director. As the work of the corporation grew, it was decided that this was becoming unwieldy and that in order to simplify matters, a matrix (overlay) structure would be adopted. The directors maintained overall charge and the team members were drawn in as needed. The overlay consisted of eight horizontal functions, divided into geographical areas.

As the engineering director commented,

'This proved to be too complicated as people found themselves on too many teams. They lost sight of the corporate objectives – the teams ended up competing against each other for developers to take plots of land, regardless of who was most suitable for that site. What we needed to do was to maintain that competitive spirit, but channel it more constructively. The sale of sites was also problematic as the revenue generated would technically be earned by the teams, but would go back into a central pot for use by all.'

The experiment with this form of matrix management was abandoned. The current structure keeps the power of the functions intact but looks at four key areas through the business processes that are carried out in those areas. In this way, it now more closely follows the seamless ideas than those of the conventional matrix.

PROJECT MANAGEMENT IN PRACTICE: SEMCO

Semco is an unusual company. Based in Brazil, it has gone through the worst of Brazil's economic mayhem, survived (800 per cent plus inflation, the government seizing large proportions of available cash, and at times an almost non-existent home market for its goods) and still grown. It has done this through the evolution of a new management structure – known as the satellite or networked organisation. The case is an example of taking the project management organisation to an extreme.

Semco was a traditional hierarchically-oriented manufacturing business which was run by its founder. When the business passed to his son, the changes started. The recession in Brazil meant that there would have to be major redundancies or the firm would close. This presented a unique opportunity to the company. Employment legislation in Brazil meant that severance pay was very high. Their services would still be required, however, in some measure, particularly those of the direct employees. By selecting the workers who could handle the break, the company helped these people set themselves up in their own businesses, providing the company (and any others who might wish to use their services) with the service they had previously provided as employees. Often this would be on the very hardware that they had used previously, but which was now leased or owned by them. This idea was applied to all areas of their operations – legal, accountancy as well as some manufacturing. No guarantees were given on either side, a strategy which was intended to make sure that both parties could remain competitive and flexible. The structure is shown in Fig. 5.12.

Treating people who were previously employees as contractors had the necessary effect of reducing the fixed labour overhead. In addition, people treat problems differently when working for themselves. Too often project managers would be left with other people's problems because they had no stake in solving them. Now they have the same interest in the achievement of an end-result as the project manager. Encouraging people to take control of their working lives through self-employment is a major break – a person is now paid for what they do, rather than what their job title is worth.

What Semco has done is to hive off much of the line-management responsibility and become purely project focused – removing the constraints of processes and procedures. Its core business is a small amount of assembly work with the coordination of innovation being the central aim of the core. This is an example of what Handy (1989) calls the 'Shamrock Organisation', and does away with conventional structures in favour of something far less easily comprehended, but which meets the needs of the modern business in achieving the necessary strategic flexibility. Such a form is clearly the ultimate expression of that current management buzzword – empowerment.

Figure 5.12 Satellite organisation

SUMMARY OF KEY POINTS

- the conventional approach to designing organisations is to have the key functions arranged into 'chimneys' with people who perform a similar set of tasks grouped together with their own hierarchies;

- other forms include organisation by the nature of the market being supplied or by the customer served;

- the pure project organisation is possibly the most flexible and far removed from the conventional approach to management – people are brought in on a contract basis for the project and no other task. The hiring organisation does not then have a further labour overhead when there is no work to be done;

- matrix management is an attempt by the conventional organisations to give some degree of authority to the project manager. The three different types of matrix model represent increasing levels of authority given to the project manager – namely coordination, overlay and secondment. Matrix management has been shown to have some benefits but is discounted by others due to the problems with one person having two bosses;

- the seamless enterprise exists when the functional chimneys are seen as being subordinate to key business processes. The use of tools such as four fields mapping can help to make this a reality by stimulating cross-function communication and activity;

- forming groups of individuals into teams is a complex process. There are many productivity and effectiveness benefits (synergy) to be gained from teamwork over that of a group;

- teams have a natural life-cycle which has recognisable characteristics to each part. The project manager can have a role in controlling both the emergence of the various phases and the management of negative effects when the team goes 'over-the-hill';

- Belbin, amongst others, has provided managers with a tool for identifying the personalities of individuals, which can provide a guide as to the nature of the person or mixture of people who will be required for particular tasks within a particular team;

- in order to get the most from a team, the manager can draw on the experience of others. Providing a clear and elevating goal is one of the most important points. The nature of the team can also be managed through the categorisation of the task to be carried out – creative, tactical or problem-solving;

- running meetings – as for most of project management – is a skill that can be learned;

- one of the formative ideas being applied with some success in the manufacturing sector is that of concurrent engineering. Through the action of management, time-to-market can be considerably reduced and competitiveness increased.

KEY TERMS	functional chimneys collection/entrenchment/resolution/
	cross-functional activities synergy/decline/break-up
	dotted-line responsibility personality profile
	matrix management group-think
	seamless enterprise meetings
	teamwork concurrency

REVIEW AND DISCUSSION QUESTIONS

1 Why is the functional organisation prevalent in modern business?

2 What are the disadvantages of the functional organisation?

3 Briefly list the other ways in which an organisation may be structured.

4 Why is the subject of organisational structure so important?

5 Why is the 'pure project' organisation a useful structure?

6 Why should an organisation use the matrix structure?

7 Briefly describe the three basic types of matrix organisation.

8 Why should an organisation consider very carefully before attempting to use matrix management?

9 How do the ideas of the 'seamless enterprise' differ from those of matrix management and those of functional management?

10 Why should project managers concern themselves with the way the groups they are working with interact?

11 How might a knowledge of the life-cycle of teams help the project manager?

12 Using Belbin's character profiles, indicate which of these you feel best applies to you. You may like to apply this to a group in which you are working, by then analysing each other's characteristics.

13 What actions can the project manager take to try to ensure effective teamwork?

14 Discuss the statement that, 'Project meetings regularly take up too much time and achieve very little'.

15 Show how the ideas of concurrency are along the same lines as those discussed in the 'seamless enterprise'.

REFERENCES

Ansoff, H.I. (ed.) (1969) *Business Strategy*, Penguin.

Bartlett, A. and S. Ghoshal (1990) '"Matrix Management" – Not a Structure, a Frame of Mind', *Harvard Business Review*, July-August, pp.138-145.

Belbin, M. (1993) *Team Roles at Work*, Butterworth-Heinemann, p.23.

Berne, E. (1967) *Games People Play: The Psychology of Human Relationships*, Penguin.

Davis S.M. and P.R. Lawrence (1977) *Matrix*, Addison Wesley, pp. 18-19.

Dimancescu, D. (1992) *The Seamless Enterprise: Making Cross Functional Management Work*, HarperCollins.

Donkin R. (1995) 'Shaping a Brave New World of Work: The Science of Identifying, Creating and Selecting Model Employees', *Financial Times*, 8/3/95, p. 16.

Handy, C. (1989) *The Age of Unreason*, Arrow, pp. 70–92.

Knight, K. (ed.) (1977), *Matrix Management – A Cross Functional Approach to Organisations*, Gower.

Larson C.E and F.M.J. LaFasto (1989) *Team Work*, Sage Press.

Lawler E.E. and S.A. Mohrman (1985) 'Quality Circles After the Fad', *Harvard Business Review*, January-February, pp. 65–71.

Mullins, L.J. (1993) *Management and Organisational Behaviour*, 3rd edition Pitman Publishing. p. 327.

Nichols, K., A. Pye, and C. Mynott, (1993) 'UK Product Development Survey' The Design Council.

Peters, T. (1987) *Thriving on Chaos*, Macmillan.

Peters, T. (1992) *Liberation Management*, Macmillan.

Semler, R. (1993) *Maverick! The Success Story Behind the World's Most Unusual Workplace*, Century.

FURTHER READING

Blanchard, K., D. Carew and E. Parisi-Carew (1992) *The One Minute Manager Builds High Performing Teams*, HarperCollins.

Constable, G. (1993) 'Concurrent Engineering – Its Procedures & Pitfalls', *Engineering Management Journal*, October, pp. 215–18.

Katzenbach, J.R. and D.K. Smith (1993) *The Wisdom of Teams*, Harvard Business School Press.

Kerzner, H., and D.I. Cleland (1985) *Project / Matrix Management, Policy and Strategy, Cases and Situations*, Van Nostrand Reinhold.

Leppitt, N. (1993) 'Concurrent Engineering – a Key in Business Transformation', *Engineering Management Journal*, April, pp. 71–6.

CHAPTER 6

Control of projects

It was stated in Chapter 1 that the roles of the project manager included planning, organising, directing and controlling activities. The nature of control is discussed here along with the characteristics that require controlling. Control systems theory is applied here in the same way that it is applied in the control of electro-mechanical devices. Such hard systems ideas have been shown to work well in the development of soft systems – such as those for controlling quality. Whilst certain elements assume that the system being controlled is a closed one, the principles appear to hold for open systems, which are more characteristic of project organisations.

6.1 CONTROL SYSTEMS

The most basic model of a control system is shown in Fig. 6.1. In this diagram, the output of a process is monitored by some means to determine the characteristics of the output. This data is interpreted and then fed back to the input to the

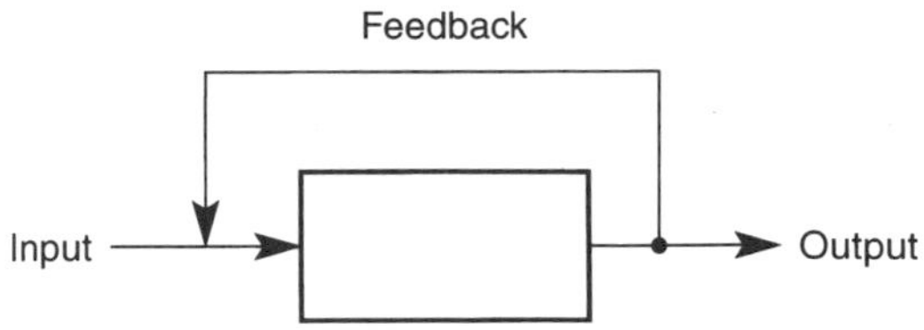

Feedback

Input ⟶ Output

Figure 6.1

process. On receipt of this information, adjustments are made to the process. By using this kind of 'feedback control system', the performance of the process can be guided by the application of corrective actions to keep it within certain limits (having defined 'acceptable deviation' from the desired performance).

The monitoring point should be set so as to take a representative measure of the characteristics in which you are interested. The nature of these will be discussed in the following sections. The action that is taken based on the feedback is the 'corrective' or 'control' action which seeks to remedy the deviation that has been noted. The intention is to keep the system stable through regular corrective action. The nature of the feedback itself is important.

Example of a control system – corrective actions and stability in a physical system

Try balancing a ball in the centre of a tray – start it moving and try to bring it to rest again ten centimetres away from the start point. Very quickly the movements of the tray get larger and the movement of the ball will generally become anything other than diminishing as the ball passes over the point without stopping. The system rapidly becomes unstable as the movement of the ball has passed out of control and soon leaves the tray completely. This is the result of instability in the system – the brain cannot make the necesssary corrective action to bring it back to rest and so the control actions get larger as the ball exhibits behaviour which is considerably different from that which is required. The movement of the ball becomes as shown in Fig. 6.2. Progamming a machine to do the same task with the application of appropriate control actions can render the system stable in a very short period of time. The pattern of motion is as shown in Fig. 6.3. This system is stable – the movement or response of the system does not go off to infinity or cause the destruction of the system (as evidenced by the ball finally running off the edge of the tray in the first test), but settles back to an equilibrium (stationary) after the initial disturbance (the move).

The application of such control systems clearly works well when there is a steady stream of output in the process, e.g. as would be characterised by the output of a production line or any operation with a standardised product. The control of projects requires the view that although there is a single event being carried out, it is the product of many interlinked smaller events (within the

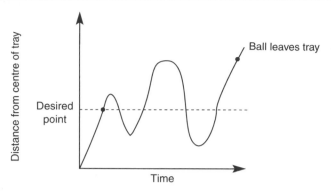

Figure 6.2 Instability

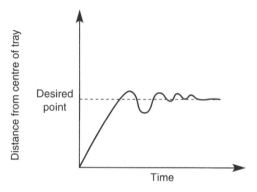

Figure 6.3 Stable system

work breakdown structure) which, like the moving of the ball on the tray, can have their progress monitored and appropriate corrective actions applied to keep them on track.

The system for overall control can be viewed as a series of smaller systems of control, which the project manager interlinks. This overall system of control will expand the larger the project becomes and, as it does so, more of the control actions will have to be devolved. The system of control systems within systems is shown in Fig. 6.4. The role of project administrators here as gatherers and processors of data is fundamental.

In Chapter 2 it was noted that there are a large number of potential constraints operating on a project. It was stated that project success depends on the achievement of the project goals within these. The major ones are likely to be cost, quality and time, though consideration of these alone will ignore others that may have just as much importance in the particular project setting, notably environmental constraints (*see* Section 6.4). The control that will be exhibited throughout this section is a mixture of feedback control and feedforward, through the setting-up of systems and implementation of management policies. The feedforward actions are those that provide a

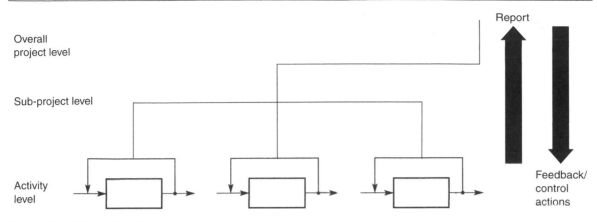

Figure 6.4 Hierarchy of control systems

degree of control or modification of the output to the process but which are carried out prior to the process.

6.2 CONTROL OF MAJOR CONSTRAINTS – QUALITY

'Quality' is defined by BS 4778 as:

> **'The totality of features and characteristics of a product or service which bear on its ability to satisfy a stated or implied need.'**

The establishment and management of an effective system to control the quality of products and services is a role of increasing importance in project management. The quality system contains a number of key elements – policies, system description and procedures. These are arranged hierarchically.

The policies for quality control are determined and set out either as part of organisational policy or as required by contractual terms set out by a client organisation. The systems are then put in place to meet the requirements of these policies and the procedures are what people at all levels of the organisation carry out on a day-to-day basis. The objective of such quality control is:

> **'To provide a formalised system within the project system which ensures that the needs of the customer or the stated objectives of the system are continually being met.'**

The system needs to be formalised and so requires much of the informality which exists within organisations to be removed. The 'customer' here is anyone who takes the output of the project activities – from an end-user of an artefact or system to a department which receives information from the project team (e.g. accounts or marketing).

There are other reasons for having a quality system in place:

- to protect the project organisation, as far as is possible, from legal liability, most notably professional negligence and product liability claims. The organisation, through its quality system, can demonstrate that it has taken 'every reasonable precaution' to ensure that the project was carried out in a way that ensures that the stated needs were met;

● it is a prerequisite for obtaining business in many markets including aerospace, defence, public procurement and the motor industry.

The emergence of the importance of quality systems has come as a natural extension of the role of specialisation. In traditional craft industries, the craftsperson would have responsibility for the quality of the output of their process – hence the use of hallmarks in silverware and other forms of labelling of the product which would allow it to be traced back to the originator. The medieval traders' guilds provided a level of quality assurance by regulating their members. As organisations have become more complex and the division of labour has been more extensive (along Tayloristic lines) the role of the quality specialist has emerged.

More recently it has become commonplace to consider not only product (or output) quality, but also the 'process' by which that output is delivered. Quality systems provide elements for assuring both of these.

Early quality systems were sets of procedures which developed with the emergence of international standards setting out how such systems should be constructed and operated. The first formalised specifications for quality systems were developed by military purchasers who attempted to provide a generic standard for systems that would ensure that the specific needs laid down in procurement contracts would be met. These relied heavily on the need for checking or inspection actions – quality was simply 'conformance to specification'. Such systems would frequently cause conflict between the people who were carrying out the tasks and the inspectors, as the implicit assumption was that it is the people at the task level who are to blame for errors. (Deming has argued for many years that it is the management system that is to blame for 85 per cent of operational errors.)

These military standards, including AQAP 1 (Allied Quality Assurance Publication), have been used for 20 years by suppliers to NATO armed forces. These and other standards (DEF-STAN 05-21, 05-24, 05-29) provided the basis for the first UK commercial standard – BS 5750 (1979). It was amended and brought into line with the ISO 9000 series of standards in 1987 and subsequently re-named, along with the equivalent German and International standards as the BS - EN - ISO 9000 series, in 1994. Most of the major automotive manufacturers have their own standards in addition to this which they require their suppliers and contractors to work under (Ford's Q1, Rover's RG2000). Recently there have been moves to integrate their requirements, thereby simplifying the task for suppliers who service more than one manufacturer.

The standards provide details of the minimum specifications for systems, based on procedural adherence to ensure the quality of the process. They should never be taken as a guarantee of the absolute quality level of the outputs of the system. They set out the way in which the systems should be operated.

The extent of the impact on the organisation depends on the particular standard chosen. BS - EN - ISO 9001 is the most extensive covering design, development, production, installation and servicing – the majority of the product life-cycle. BS - EN - ISO 9003 only covers final inspection and testing. The former will be discussed here as the commercial standards are the most widely used.

From the language used in the specifications (*see* below), it is clear that the standards were developed for application in manufacturing industry, particularly for contract manufacturers. However, the organisations that have applied the standard to date include banks, dentists, electricians, academic institutions(!), road recovery firms and distribution/logistics companies. There is clearly the need for interpretation of a generic set of rules to the specific situation. To enable this process, the BSI (British Standards Institution) has published a series of guides to accompany the standards, e.g.

BS - EN - ISO 9000 - 1 – entitled 'Quality Management and Quality Assurance Standards; Part 1: Guidelines for selection and use'.
BS - EN - ISO 9004 - 1 – entitled 'Quality Management and Quality Systems Elements; Part 1: Guidelines'.
BS 5750 Part 8: Guide to the Application of BS 5750 : Part 1 to services.
BS 5750 Part 13: Guide to the Application of BS 5750 : Part 1 to the development, supply and maintenance of software

The 20 requirements of the standard BE - EN - ISO 9001 (1994) are paraphrased below:

1 Management responsibility – there must be a defined management representative to provide a single point of contact for customers.
2 Establish and maintain a documented quality system.
3 Establish and maintain a system for reviewing customer contracts to ensure that it brings together product offered and required.
4 The design process shall have a quality control system on inputs, outputs and the process itself.
5 Document control – all documents should be controlled to ensure that the current issue is the only one in use.
6 Ensure that the purchased product conforms to specified requirements, e.g. through auditing and then supply under certificates of conformance or inspection of the incoming product.
7 Where a customer supplies a product for you to work on, it must be identified as belonging to the customer.
8 All products must be labelled during processing and must be traceable to records of component parts.
9 Processes should have the necessary degree of process control.
10 Need to keep receiving, in-process and final inspection and test records.
11 Any measurement equipment used must be labelled and calibrated as well as being suitable for the application (no mention, however, of measurement capability).
12 The product must be identified so that the inspection status (awaiting inspection, inspected and passed, failed or concessioned) is immediately obvious. This may be through the use of marked bins or appropriate tags.

13 Procedures must be identified so that when a non-conforming product is produced, there is a system for dealing with it.

14 Procedures must be identified for preventing recurrence of non-conformances through the analysis of defective data, procedural amendments, etc.

15 The product needs to be handled and stored so that there is no damage or deterioration in the product or accompanying documentation.

16 Procedures are required for the identification, filing, indexing, storage, maintenance and disposition of records.

17 'The supplier shall carry out a comprehensive system of planned and documented quality audits'.

18 Procedures need to be set up to identify needs for employee training and to ensure that records are kept accordingly.

19 Servicing must be carried out in accordance with the contract, if specified.

20 Statistical techniques must be used where appropriate.

The major requirements from the point of view of the project manager include:

- Point 2 – there is a need to provide a 'quality manual' to describe how the system works. This is a hierarchical series of documents which addresses each of the points within the standard and is structured as shown in Fig. 6.5. At the top level is the statement of policy (the policy document) which outlines the aim of the system and the structure and names of the documents below it. At the next level is the functional documentation which provides statements as to how each of the functional areas is organised. Below this are the procedural documents, which state how each piece of work is to be carried out. At the lowest level are reference documents such as technical data manuals (e.g. for materials or machine specifications).
- Point 3 – the project manager must establish regular contact points and formalised review meetings so that the assent of the customer/sponsor to progress is gained and that the original requirements are regularly reviewed.

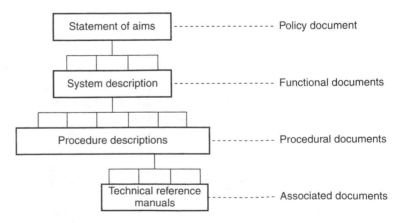

Figure 6.5 Hierarchy of quality system documentation

- Point 4 – treating one-off activities such as design as a process and requiring control of these requires much of the 'art' of such processes to be expressed as science.
- Point 17 – once the system is in place (documented and operational) the system needs to be audited in a similar way to financial auditing.
- Point 18 – people need to be appropriately trained to carry out their tasks. The project manager must be able to verify this through the production of training certificates, course records, etc. This process has been helped recently by the advent of National Vocational Qualifications (NVQs).

The process of implementing a quality system to the requirements of a recognised specification should follow the route below:

1 Establish the reason for wanting the system – is it simply to obtain business through having certification or will it provide an advantage in a competitive bidding situation? Unless this reason is established at the start of the program of implementation, it is unlikely to be effective. It is not unusual for an organisation to take two years to have fully implemented such a system, if the aim is to achieve recognition through having the quality system approved and certified.
2 Train people in working to the requirements of the system, including the preparation of documentation. This is a major task, and one that is particularly difficult for project organisations. The intention is to provide a set of procedures which describe in detail how each job will be performed. In project organisations, making these procedures generic enough to cover the variety of work that is carried out can be a real challenge. Similarly, convincing people that when they work outside the existing procedures their actions have to be documented, is often fraught. People will need to be trained in the assessment of systems to provide for step 4.
3 Create the documentation including the necessary reference manuals.
4 Carry out an internal audit (check whether procedures are being adhered to) and review (consider the efficacy of the procedures). This should be done initially by someone within your own organisation, though it is normal for it to be someone outside your immediate function. Set a plan for the implementation of any changes identified by this process.
5 Have your systems audited by an external auditor from a registered assessment body. The progression from this audit is shown in Fig. 6.6.
6 If you are granted 'registered firm' status, you may carry the BSI logo on your stationery and other publicity material. Your organisation will then be subject to periodic audits (usually annually) as well as 'flying visits' which are announced at 24 hours' notice.

The process of accreditation is not simple for an organisation going through it for the first time. Gaining accreditation can involve the use of consultants (*see* Chapter 2) to provide services ranging from training of staff to providing you with a pre-written quality manual. This latter option is not to be recommended

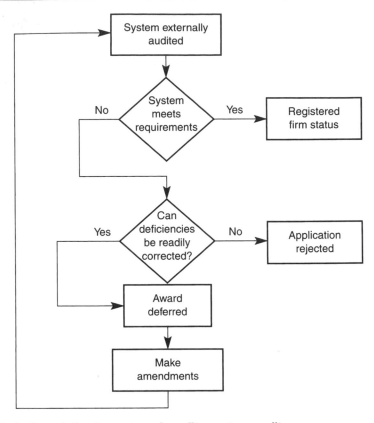

Figure 6.6 Actions following external quality system audit

as much can be gained from compiling your own, through improved under-standing of the processes and people then having ownership of that part of the quality manual.

For the project organisation, many of the structures necessary for compli-ance with such a standard will already be in place. However, where this is a requirement, the project manager should be aware that this provides an extra workload for team members – the approval process alone can absorb thou-sands of working hours. Where people are brought in on short-term contracts, the documentation services and control systems are likely to have to be pro-vided centrally. The checks and administration, which affect every part of the organisation, will require an ongoing commitment of time. This *must* be built into the schedules – expecting people to do it as an additional activity for which no time has been allowed is unreasonable and will certainly result in a system which frequently falls down.

Example – JCB reduce its supplier base

JC Bamford, the earth mover and construction equipment manufacturer, announced that it intended to cut its supplier base by up to 70 per cent over three to five years. This draconian move came as the company sought to build closer relationships with suppliers by sharing out its orders for bought-in products and services between a smaller number of companies.

The process of selecting which suppliers would be kept included the implementation of a rating system – suppliers would be graded from A to D. According to *The Engineer* (April, 1989) this would be assessed by a panel of JCB executives according to their commitment to meet the improvement objectives on a whole string of criteria. One of these was quality, and before a company could be considered to be grade B, it would have to have a quality system certified to BS 5750. Eventually all suppliers would have to be grade A rated.

The financial implications of quality performance are called quality costs. These can make an enormous difference to the return that a project generates. Quality costs are broken down into three categories – prevention, appraisal and failure. What is included in each category is shown in Table 6.1. Failure can be broken down into internal failure (that which is detected by the organisation before the customer detects it and allows rapid remedy to be made) and external failure (one which the customer detects after delivery of the product or consumption of the service). Generally, it can be stated that the failure costs are orders of magnitude higher than those of prevention and appraisal.

Table 6.1 Elements of quality cost

Category	Activities included
Prevention	Quality planning, training and auditing, supplier development, costs of maintaining a quality improvement programme or system, maintenance of all testing equipment
Appraisal	Any checking activities (and materials consumed during these), analysis and reporting of quality data, auditing suppliers' quality systems, storing records of quality results
Failure	*Internal* – any wasted activities, be they in the production of an artefact which is scrap or the generation of a document which is not read, changing or rectifying work already done because it was not right first time, downgrading goods or services, problem-solving time *External* – replacement of faulty goods, having to return to a site to re-do tasks, complaints and consequent loss of goodwill and repeat business, product and professional liability claims

Crosby (1979) researched how the performance of the quality system related to the profitability of the organisation. The findings of this work were that:

'For a well developed quality system, the costs of quality can make up as little as 2 per cent of turnover. For an organisation with a poor or neglected quality system, they can make up in excess of 20 per cent.'

A recent audit of a project organisation within the aerospace industry showed quality costs to be 36 per cent of turnover. This is a major driver and source of major cost savings if recognised and a system implemented properly. Savings are generally made through the increase of prevention and appraisal activities which in the medium term will result in reduced failure costs. The project organisation has to accept that in the short term, overall costs are likely to increase as the improvements take their time to work through the system.

Help in identifying quality cost elements is available in BS 6143 : Part 1 : 1992. Part 2 gives the prevention, appraisal and failure model and includes some sample proformas for completing quality cost reports. Both have high practical value in a project management environment. Further discussion of quality costing is contained in Dale and Plunkett (1991).

6.3 CONTROL OF MAJOR CONSTRAINTS – COST AND TIME

The detailed systems for controlling quality are novel in many industries. The systems for controlling cost and time have been in use for far longer, but still require a considerable input from the project manager in their establishment and execution. The attributes of cost and time are interlinked as previously discussed. The need is for practical tools that will identify when corrective actions are required and what they should be. The role of the project manager in cost control may be stated as:

- setting up the cost control system in conjunction with the needs and recommendations of the financial function;
- allocating responsibilities for administration and analysis of financial data;
- ensuring costs are allocated properly (usually against project codes);
- ensuring costs are incurred in the genuine pursuit of project activities;
- ensuring contractors' payments are authorised;
- checking other projects are not using your budget.

The measurement that is often taken to consider progress using cost as a measure is 'sunk costs'. That is the measure of what has been spent to a particular point in time on activities. It is notoriously unreliable as a measure of how much has been achieved, as it is perfectly possible for a project to be 80 per cent complete but to have incurred 95 per cent of the budget allocated to it. Controlling cost overruns clearly needs more than just a raw figure such as expenditure incurred. The 'earned value' concept is one attempt to make the measure more meaningful. As Archibald (1992) notes:

'The earned value of a task is the approved budget allocated to perform the task. When the task is complete, the budget has been earned.'

Many claim this to be a powerful technique provided sufficient tasks can be aggregated (added together) to give an overall picture of progress. Large tasks with long measurement periods or very small tasks cannot be analysed using this measure. The earned value can be analysed using a number of standard techniques. The budget for a project is built up of the estimates of the budgets of the elements from the work breakdown structure. The earned value on completion of each of those elements is the same as the budget it was originally assigned. This is known as the budgeted cost of work performed (BCWP). This theoretical value can be compared with the costs that were incurred – the actual cost of work performed (ACWP). The difference between these values gives the 'cost variance', i,e:

cost variance = ACWP - BCWP

This can be taken as a short-term measure of cost performance, but is often applied to give the estimates for cost to completion. If used in this way the project manager can either treat the variance to date as incidental (everything will go to budget beyond this point) or indicative (the variance experienced so far is likely to be reflected in the remainder of the activities). In the former case, the estimated cost at completion (ECAC) is given by:

ECAC = total budget + cost variance

In the latter case, the ECAC is given by:

ECAC = project budget × performance index

where the performance index = ACWP/BCWP

This technique only works once the project is well advanced and assumes that there are no particularly uncertain events in the completion stages. It is an indicator that the original estimates were less than accurate in one direction (too short or too long) and does not follow the law of probability that it will overrun on 50 per cent of occasions and under-run on others. Parkinson's and Murphy's Laws still hold. As a technique its mathematical basis is questionable, but for the beleaguered project manager it can add a degree of apparent science which often impresses project sponsors.

The BCWP shows the theoretical monetary value of the work performed up to the given point in time. This can be compared with the budgeted cost of work scheduled (BCWS) which shows the amount that should have been spent up to that point if the schedule were being adhered to. These criteria can be plotted as curves (*see* Fig. 6.7). The BCWS has an envelope within which the values can fall – this is due to the slack in the system. BCWS for critical path activities would be a single line. Whilst these ideas have an appeal, they can be misleading – if, for example, the project is overrunning on time but has been run below budget, this can show as a positive result, i.e. there is an apparent cost saving.

These measures can be summarised in the form of reports which provide the input to problem-solving processes (*see* Chapter 8). The information needs to be collated by a timing coordinator who can do so in one of the following ways:

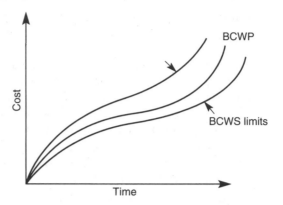

Figure 6.7 Budgeted cost of work performed (BCWP) lying within the budgeted cost of work scheduled (BCWS) envelope

- obtaining a verbal report on progress from the person or team carrying out that section of work;
- sending out and collecting a form of progress questionnaire which outlines the activities and the original targets for them which the team members complete and return to the coordinator with the current status recorded;
- detailed internal measure of progress – an assessor viewing progress as a semi-independent arbiter;
- an external assessor carrying out some form of audit on the project, with widespread powers of access to project data.

Clearly the last two are useful where independent checking of information is required, but it tends to infer a lack of trust of the people doing the work. The point is that whatever data is collected must be reliable (it is not unusual for problems to go hidden or undisclosed due to an individual's fear of retribution if poor performance is discovered). Verbal reports are fine but they can obscure important information through either of two extremes – a person who complains about 'problems' even though progress is good, and the person who will say things are OK simply because 'it is not as bad as it could be / last time we did this'. The project manager must be aware of these and look for evidence to corroborate the information, received from other sources. Thus the cost information should be matched with verbal reports of time progress from several members of the same team, in addition to the gleaning of opinion from other teams.

The climate for reporting should be set to provide a balance:

- people require feedback on how they are performing;
- people need to be clear what information to report, in what format (and what to leave out);
- the project manager needs to have a positive statement that progress is being made according to plan;

- *but* the major reports need to be the exceptions – where there is a clear deviation from acceptable performance in meeting any of the constraints imposed on an activity.

This focus on the exception is vital and must be reflected in the importance that the various reports are given. The bureaucracy of 'paying someone to read reports that you have paid someone else to write' is partially eliminated by this focus on exception.

The factor not so far discussed in relation to the reporting and feedback loop is *timeliness*. If the information or feedback is held up for any period of time, the control action will have to be more severe than if the deviation had been spotted and acted upon earlier. Take the analogy of trying to control a car – corrective actions are constantly needed to speed and direction to keep the car on the road. These come from various inputs, but predominantly from the visual feedback that the driver is getting. Imagine that a box is placed between the steering wheel and the front wheels which adds a time delay between the action of steering and the front wheels moving. Say this delay was two seconds – this probably would not cause too many problems provided the road was relatively straight. When the delay becomes 15 seconds, control becomes almost impossible. This illustrates the importance of feedback and control actions being provided in the shortest possible time – delaying the analysis of feedback can allow activities to proceed out of control for too long. On the other hand, the application of too much control in too short a time period can severely hamper progress – having to complete hourly or daily reports for an activity that is scheduled to take months is clearly inappropriate – this would result in a significant proportion of time being spent in completing reports on the work rather than the work itself. For such activities, many project managers find that reporting durations of around five days at a time works best.

As was stated in Chapter 2, the nearer to completion the project gets, the easier it becomes to forecast what the final result will be – not just in terms of cost and time, but also in terms of the technical performance of the result. Archibald (1992) uses the concept of a 'technical performance measure' to provide an objective and visible means of comparing the actual-to-predicted performance. This should be a part of the regular project review procedure as it allows other estimates based on this to be re-evaluated.

Example

A team was in the process of developing a new silicon chip for PC applications. The design specification stated that it was to run at 40 Mhz. During the development work, it became apparent that with a small modification, it would be possible for the chip to work up to speeds of 66 Mhz. The implications were passed to the next review meeting, which was able to upgrade the estimates of sales for the new chip and hence allow the manufacturers to increase scheduled production. Had the technical performance measures not been included in the ongoing review, the additional capability may not have been fully exploited.

6.4 OTHER CONTROL ELEMENTS – ENVIRONMENTAL CONSTRAINTS

This was a 'hot issue' during the early 1990s with public pressure on companies to become more environmentally responsible. Companies have responded in different ways – e.g. the electricity generators' 'dash for gas' and insurance companies which started using paperless systems. More fundamentally, legislation has changed and the impact of breaches of legislative requirements are ever more severe. The majority of project managers should be aware of this issue, as if it is not already high on the management agenda, it will soon become that way. There are, however, a number of challenges associated with environmental issues. Many authors comment that the issue of 'environmental responsibility' has been the subject of much rhetoric, but less action due to the scarcity of practical guidance. Stakeholders who will have an interest in the environmental performance of the project organisation include:

* partner organisations in joint ventures;
* clients/customers;
* team members;
* sponsors;
* insurers – obtaining the necessary insurance to protect the organisation from the effects of claims is a serious issue in many construction projects, and will often involve demonstrating to the insurers that your organisation is going to carry out the project in a responsible manner (*see* systems below);
* legislators and law enforcers (*see* EC role below).

The role of pressure groups and the media as stakeholders (in the sense that they can cause much disruption to project activities) need to be recognised. One of the effects of legislation is to make organisations' environmental performance open to scrutiny by the public and media. Publicity gained through poor performance is proving damaging to the public image of those companies and their products, directly impacting on the financial performance of the companies.

The role of the EC in providing legislation on environmental matters is considerable. The Fifth European Community Environmental Action Programme sets out the aims of the community for its environmental policy from 1993 to the year 2000. It is trying to create a worthwhile change in emphasis – to remove policies as a burden to industry and to make them self-sustaining. The requirement on industry is to become proactive rather than reactive, through the development of 'clean technologies' and the development of markets for products which are environmentally sound. This emphasis on making the process self-sustaining will occur after the enforcement of existing legislation through taxation (incentives and penalties) and legal liability.

'Eco-labelling' is well established (disposable food and household consumables containers being at the forefront of this), but the requirement for companies to treat their environmental performance as they have done their quality performance has been less successful. The parallel between the two is useful as:

- there is a requirement for policy to be made;
- documented systems are required;
- there is a standard for environmental systems – BS 7750 (*see* below);
- it will be possible in the future for such systems to be accredited and for the organisation to obtain recognition in the same way as for BS - EN - ISO 9000.

The requirements of the environmental systems standard (BS 7750) are as follows:

1 Commitment – required at the highest levels in the organisation to demonstrate that the intentions will be backed with authority.
2 Environmental policy – as for quality systems, there must be a documented policy which includes the steps that will be taken to ensure continuous improvement in this area.
3 Environmental review – carry out an initial review of the current state of environmentally relevant practices in order to provide a base for future action.
4 Organisation and personnel – ensures that all people involved in establishing and running the system have the appropriate authority.
5 Registers of environmental effects – the organisation must keep records of legislation as it affects their operation in addition to relevant permissions, e.g discharge consents, planning permissions, etc.
6 Objectives and targets – in order that continuous improvement over and above legislative requirements can be demonstrated, the organisation must provide quantitative goals for itself.
7 Environmental management programme – a documented plan of action.
8 Environmental management documentation and manual – as for quality systems, the environmental management system must be described in the form of a written manual, which must be updated with changes in practice and legislation.
9 Operational control and records – where shortcomings are identified, procedures must exist for dealing with these and preventing recurrence.
10 Environmental audits – periodic reviews must be carried out in a planned and documented way to determine the level of procedural adherence.
11 Systems reviews must be carried out in accordance with a predetermined plan to consider the efficacy of the procedures laid down in the system.

There have been problems to date with implementation of BS 7750 – the BSI has not yet appointed organisations to carry out the accreditation work. Consequently, some companies have systems in place but cannot obtain official recognition for this. Although such incidents damage the credibility of the standards, it is thought inevitable that application will be widespread by the end of the decade.

The formulation of environmental policy should be focused on four main areas:

- the organisation and its products;
- the direct environmental impact of products and processes;
- the infrastructural implications of the activities of the organisation – impact on road usage, etc.;

● external relations with the community – through education, the role of a good 'corporate citizen' (Welford and Gouldson, 1993).

6.5 PROJECT MANAGEMENT SOFTWARE AND INFORMATION SYSTEMS

Computer-based systems

Computer-based systems will not carry out the planning process for you, but in certain circumstances they will simplify the task. They should always remain a management tool. Most companies today have some form of project management software, removing the need for complex selection procedures. The first issue, however, is: 'Is a computer-based system required?' BS 6046 : Part 3 : 1992 gives some guidance in this respect:

● where there are less than 500 activities and the logic arrangements are relatively simple, the standard suggests that these can be done manually (the reality of managing 500 activities means that this is very high – 30 is more practical);
● where the activities have complex inter-relationships, a computer should be used, up to a project of 3000 activities;
● projects of 3000 activities and above should be broken down into smaller sub-projects.

Other factors in the choice of whether to plan activities manually or by computer include:

● the nature and uses of the output of the plan – does the data need to be manipulated or processed in any way, for example? If the data is only required for display, a manual system is more appropriate;
● the frequency of update of data – if the plans are going to be updated continuously or on a regular basis (daily, weekly or monthly) then the computer-based system is going to be of benefit (essential for constant-update systems).

Choice of system

Having decided on the need for a system, the choice of hardware/software combination should be based on evaluation of the following factors:

● capabilities of the system – scale (size of projects, and numbers of activities and levels in the WBS), scope (range of data that it will be required to handle, e.g. time only; time and resources; time, resources and cost) and power (ability to efficiently manipulate data as required);
● nature of the output required, e.g. charts, graphs, management summaries, and the format in which it is to be presented;
● the intended purpose of the data, e.g. resource analysis (crashing, allocation and smoothing).

Systems used to require mainframe hardware to run data through basic calculation routines such as critical path analysis and would need experts to interpret the output. The majority of modern systems are PC based and available off-the-shelf. This has many benefits for the user – the packages generally work well, are bug-free and in use on a wide scale. This has resulted in a good range of after-market guides and technical support. Some companies prefer to have tailored systems and contract themselves to one software house or consultancy company for the provision of those services. Such a contract may include a provision of the necessary hardware and ongoing support.

Modern Windows-based systems will run on 386 machines, but run better on 486 or above. These can be stand-alone (isolated from other computing resources) or networked. Networked systems provide local processing (data manipulation at the terminals) whilst being able to contribute to, and draw from, centrally held data-files. Such systems can prevent the emergence of 'islands of information' (where information is in the hands of a small proportion of the organisation). They require rules of access to the data to be defined where data integrity is important. Where projects are taking place which involve several sites or external organisations, a networked system can provide an integrating factor between them.

Discussing the nature of specific systems is inappropriate here due to their short life-cycles. Project managers will rarely have a completely free choice of off-the-shelf systems. Where a tailored system (most are customisations of standard systems) is required there are several precautions the selector should take:

- check existing sites where their systems are being used – make visits if necessary, and talk to user groups;
- check upgrade paths for the systems – can your system be upgraded when new versions of the standard software become available?
- Obtain impressions from knowledgeable users who may know 'the right questions to ask';
- evaluate carefully whether the capabilities presented are 'available now and in use' or 'in development and available shortly'. The tried and tested solutions are often more beneficial;
- capabilities should meet both existing and potential needs over the planned life-time of the system.

Computers are still not universally accepted as a working tool and many people are still resistant to the use of technology. The system becoming the domain of one or a small group of people should be avoided as this further alienates those who find systems daunting.

Modern systems produce high-quality output, and colour graphics can make quite an impact on potential customers. The output can be misleading because of the high quality of presentation. The confidence it inspires deters people from questioning the content.

The role of project management information systems (PMIS)

The control and distribution of information to the project team members and other stakeholders is a significant part of the responsibility of the project manager. It is particularly vital if the stakeholder expectations are to be managed effectively. The cycle of events that leads to the generation of reports should be as follows:

measure – record – analyse – act

If an attribute is to be measured for control purposes it should be recorded, ideally in the form in which it was collected and without any interpretation. This and other measures should be combined and analysed before action is formalised. Not proceeding with the cycle at any point wastes the previous actions. To prevent this waste, if data is not going to form part of an analysis and subsequent possible action, it should not be collected.

Computer-based PMIS are the most commonly used and allow the regular updating of schedules to provide a basis for management action. The bar charts produced by the planning system are a convenient tool for continuous monitoring and updating of plans (*see* Fig. 6.8). The work completed is shown as the top half of the bars in the chart and is indicated by dark shading. The purveyors of project management software like to help their customers believe that impressive-looking systems can be the panacea in control. This reliance on computers can lead to the following problems (Thambain, 1987):

- computer paralysis – the project manager spends all day at the computer updating the project data – this is not a value-adding or problem-solving activity;
- PMIS verification – selective treatment of data can hide problems very effectively;
- data overload – there is too much for anyone to make sense of and hence act effectively on;
- isolation – the project manager becomes a slave to the computer and becomes detached from what is really happening;
- dependence – apparently removes the role of problem analysis and decision-making from managers, leading to less effective actions and removal of proactive problem-solving;
- misdirection – the effects of problems are tackled rather than the inherent causes.

The role of the system should be to identify exceptions (as above) and provide timely control information. The decision in setting up the systems should ask 'at what point does the difference between expected and actual performance merit a control action?' This needs to take into account the fact that in any activity there will be a degree of variability. It is the role of the decision-maker to set limits (called 'control limits') at which it is determined that the deviation from desired performance is significant (i.e. would not have occurred through natural variation). The concept of applying control limits to projects is shown in Fig. 6.9.

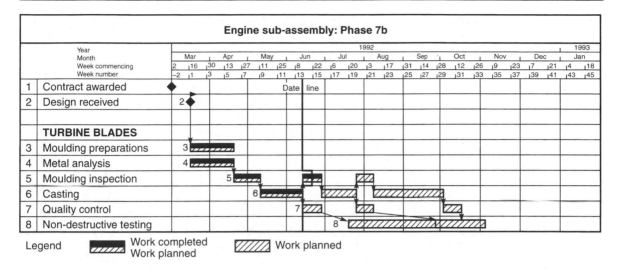

Figure 6.8 Bar chart showing work completed

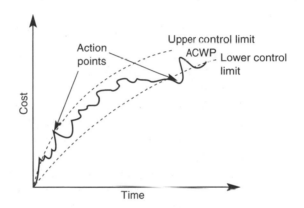

Figure 6.9 Control limits applied to progress in budget spend

6.6 STAGE-GATE APPROACH TO PROJECT CONTROL

The stage-gate system involves the decision being made actively at each milestone, whether the project should continue. The criteria for passing to the next stage must be laid down in advance – as was done using the four fields mapping planning tool where exit criteria rather than time determined when a project should pass between phases. Calling a halt to activities can save future expenditure, and must never be discounted as an option, particularly where:

- the majority of the benefits from the activities have already been achieved by the organisation;
- the initial plans and estimates have turned out to be wildly inaccurate;
- a new alternative which is more attractive has materialised;

- organisational strategy changes and the project outcome ceases to be in line with the new strategy;
- key personnel leave the organisation;
- the project requires a higher level of capability than the organisation possesses;
- to continue would endanger the organisation financially as cash flow would be considerable.

The options include the winding-up of the activities (which often causes bad feeling amongst the project team and can lead to future disenchantment) or finding ways of maximising the potential benefit whilst minimising the risk or expenditure. Many development projects have got to the point where they were about to be commercialised and the large amounts of finance required (can be hundreds of millions of pounds, particularly in industries such as pharmaceuticals) could not be provided by the originators. Taking on joint partners or licensing are possible remedies in such a case.

6.7 CHANGE CONTROL

'This business would be fine it it wasn't for our clients....'

Stakeholders change their views about their requirements of the outcome of projects. The cause cannot always be eliminated, at least not without eliminating the clients themselves. The control system has to have the capability to change the inputs to the process based on changed requirements by one or more of the stakeholders. The typical system is shown in Fig. 6.10.

The originator of the change may be any one of the downstream processes from your own project, e.g. in product development it is not unusual for products to have relatively major changes in the final stages of their development, particularly as they are about to go into production. The engineers raise change requests which are passed through a system for evaluating:

- costs and benefits;
- the priority attached to the change (whether it is cosmetic or fundamental);
- the effects of the change on other processes;
- the effects on other assumptions – particularly cost.

It is usual for this to be completed on a proforma and to be circulated until the necessary approvals have been obtained.

6.8 MANAGING AND CONTROLLING SUPPLIERS AND CONTRACTORS

For many construction projects as much as 80 per cent of the revenue generated by a project is spent with suppliers and contractors. The design and control of the purchasing function is clearly a management specialism in its own right, but is a function in which the project manager has an input. Some of the

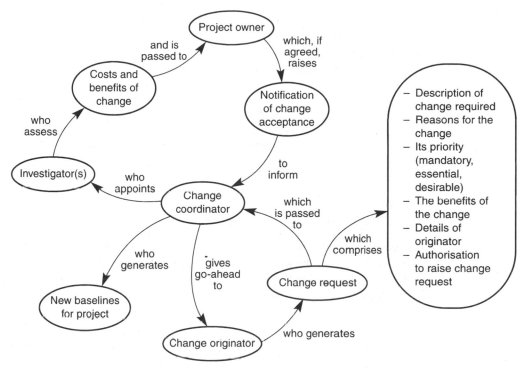

Figure 6.10 Change control system

purchasing responsibility is also typically devolved to the individual project although it is more usual for the majority to be handled centrally. There are clearly advantages to each form of purchasing as shown in Table 6.2.

Table 6.2 Centralised and localised purchasing

	Centralised purchasing	*Localised purchasing*
Advantages	• purchasing power due to aggregation of orders • better materials utilisation and stock management • economies of staffing • standardisation of purchasing procedures	• local knowledge of suppliers • low organisational inertia • local management control • enhanced supplier relationships

The trade-offs will need to be optimised on a project-by-project basis. The objectives of the purchasing system are similar – to satisfy what are termed 'the five rights'. These are inter-dependent characteristics of a supplier or contractor depending on their ability to deliver:

- the right quantity;
- the right quality;
- at the right price;
- at the right time and place, and be...
- the right supplier.

The quantity of goods or services (contractors are generally assumed to deliver a service) is determined from the schedules drawn up with the plans. Where there have been changes these are built in and the quantity calculated. The quality of goods and services may be determined through:

- trial supply of goods or services;
- prior reputation;
- certification or assessment of their quality systems.

Where contractors are hired on an individual basis, the recruiter may also seek membership of a particular professional body and possibly the contractor to provide their own legal indemnity insurance.

Achieving a purchasing decision at the right price is a difficult debate. In project organisations there is often the need for long-term relationships to be built up between buyer and supplier, though the relationship for that particular project may be fairly short. There are clearly gains to be made by applying pressure on the price to obtain the cheapest supply. In the long term, however, the supplier may go out of business or may simply economise in ways that cost you money elsewhere. Indeed Deming's fourth point is:

> 'End the practice of awarding business on the basis of a price-tag. Purchasing must be combined with design of product, manufacturing and sales to work with the chosen supplier: the aim is to minimise total cost not merely initial cost.'

The best supplier may not then be the cheapest, as there is often a trade-off in other areas.

Achieving the right time and place is the basis of much literature and the predominant complaint that industrial purchasers have about suppliers. The rating of suppliers and regular performance reviews can keep this as an issue for them. It is also one advantage that a degree of centralisation can have for the purchasing function – that of being able to track supplier performance on the basis of criteria such as late delivery. A major point to note is that it is no good blaming a supplier for late delivery if paperwork to place the order takes six weeks to be processed by the purchasing function. Giving suppliers the longest possible time in which to fulfil an order is going to be beneficial to both parties in the long term.

Being the right supplier clearly has dependence on the other four categories, but is included to start the discussion as to the way in which one selects suppliers. The choice based on price alone has been shown to provide possible short-term gains which can be more than countered in the longer term. There are several other factors which should be considered:

- are choices made on the basis of a 'free lunch' – the expansion of the corporate hospitality industry over the last ten years has been immense? This has been paralleled by efforts by many companies to be seen to be behaving ethically and state publically that their staff will not accept gifts, however small, from suppliers. There is clearly a contradiction between these two facts. The Chartered Institute of Purchasing and Supply (CIPS) has a code of conduct for their members which expressly prohibits the acceptance of gifts from suppliers;
- how are orders conveyed, with what frequency and how do the suppliers really know what your requirements are? Also, they often have expertise in both the design of their products and their application, which, as Deming suggests, should be used as a source of knowledge and improvement.

It is obviously not possible to treat the purchase of the smallest value items in the way suggested above (through partnership rather than adversarial relationships with suppliers). The use of a version of Pareto analysis (*see* Chapter 8) can identify the 20 per cent of bought-in goods and services which take 80 per cent of the project spend. It is on these that the focus of purchasing attention will rest.

The establishment of contracts between suppliers and purchasers is not an appropriate topic for a text such as this – the books on contract law are filled with horror stories of how contracts drawn up by non-experts have only worked well if they were never questioned or tested. The only advice, in a commercial environment where litigation is becoming more commonplace, is to rely on professionals in this field. In a project environment, the use of contractors is commonplace. The process by which contracts are awarded depends on the nature of the task being contracted, the relationship between the purchaser and supplier and the relative size of each. In addition, industry norms apply, e.g. in construction the allocation of contracts for trade services, whilst following basic rules, is at the discretion of the site manager. Conversely, where a contract is being placed for the supply of a major part of the project spend, the process shown in Fig 6.11 is used.

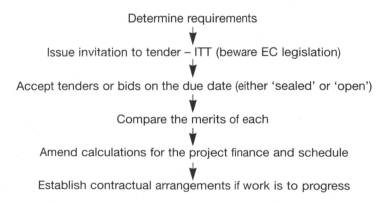

Determine requirements
↓
Issue invitation to tender – ITT (beware EC legislation)
↓
Accept tenders or bids on the due date (either 'sealed' or 'open')
↓
Compare the merits of each
↓
Amend calculations for the project finance and schedule
↓
Establish contractual arrangements if work is to progress

Figure 6.11 Establishment of contracts

The ITT must be published Europe-wide if the value of the bid is likely to exceed certain limits. Major fines have been levied by the European court against organisations who have failed to do so. The value for public contracts (central government, purchase/lease of goods or services), over and above which open European tender is required, is in the region of ECU 140 000 (c. £100 000). This is not large by the standards of much project management activity. When the bids or tenders arrive, they may be treated as either 'sealed' (not opened until a given time) or 'open' (where the information contained in the bids becomes public at the time the bids are received). The system of sealed bids is often felt to be fairer for larger contracts.

The information contained in the bids should be fed into the project's financial and time calculations and any amendments to budgets or schedules made on this basis. Contractual arrangements are usually based on standard terms and conditions, but establishing whether the supplier's terms and conditions or those of the purchaser apply is a role for legal advisors. The main objective is to ensure that the contracts can be met on both sides – breaches of contracts and the ensuing litigation rarely benefit either party greatly, but the legal industry considerably. For further discussion on the legal implications of contracts within a project environment, *see* Turner (1995).

The engineering institutions of the UK have recognised the need to provide a starting point which can eliminate some of the wrangling that goes on between suppliers and purchasers. Various bodies have compiled standard forms of contract, e.g. in the construction industry CIRIA 85 ('Target and Cost Reimbursable Construction Contracts', 1982) provides a standard form for target cost contracts and the Institute of Chemical Engineers has its 'Red Book' ('Model Form of Conditions of Contract for Process Plants: Lump Sum Contracts' 1981).

6.9 CONTROL OF THE WORK OF DEVELOPMENT PROJECTS – INTELLECTUAL PROPERTY

Intellectual property is the same as other forms of ownership in law. The role of intellectual property legislation is such that individuals or companies that develop new ideas have the opportunity to exploit them without fear of someone else copying their work. The main form of intellectual property protection is the 'patent'. If you wish to maintain control of the ownership of the product or process that you have developed (note – not software) then patenting is the major route open to you.

There is another fundamental role of the patent information for the development organisation, however, that of a 'design database'. Over 80 per cent of the records held in the patent office have expired, i.e. they are either more than twenty years old or the renewal fees have not been paid. It is estimated that as much as 30 per cent of development work duplicates that which has been done already. To avoid this, a relatively cheap search of patent office records can be the alternative to months of expensive development activity. Some major companies (including Sony and Hitachi) have representatives employed full time to scan filed applications for patents. These will often not go through the full process to become patented and so enter the public domain.

Once a development has been made, the granting of a patent depends on it fulfilling the following four criteria:

- must involve an inventive step – not be an immediately obvious derivation of an existing idea;
- not have been previously disclosed – through publication or discussion with others for example;
- be capable of commercial exploitation – the only reason that patents are granted is to enable the inventor to have the right to exploit the idea commercially;
- not be excluded – designs for new nuclear weapons for example are excluded, as it would not be desirable to have them on public display in the patent office!

Once a patent has been granted, you have the exclusive rights to:

- exploit this through commercialisation of the idea;
- licence a third party to commercialise the idea, usually for a fee;
- grant a number of parties non-exclusive licenses to the technology.

PROJECT
MANAGEMENT
IN PRACTICE:
**THE LIFTER
PROJECT**

In 1990 the Lifter Company saw that the market potential existed for a new model in its range. They needed new management control systems as this was the first development project to use the ideas of concurrent or simultaneous engineering. The project manager summed up his role in controlling the project in Fig. 6.12.

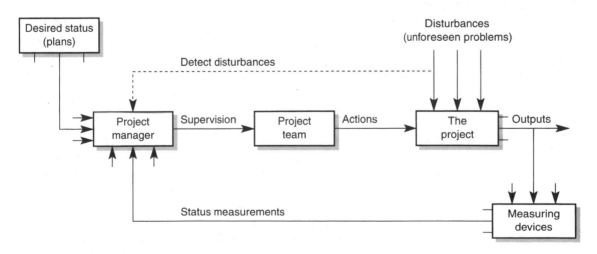

Figure 6.12 Management control loop for the Lifter project

The company was not completely used to this way of working and found the new methods harder to adapt than was originally envisaged. Consequently, when reports were compiled at the end of August 1992, the original launch date of March 1993 started to look very unlikely. The plans were re-drafted, as shown in Fig. 6.13, and further resources re-allocated to the project. The schedule at this point seemed to be under control. However, analysis of the costs incurred was produced for the next quarterly review, in October. There was considerable over-run – partly due to the extra resources being brought in to address the overrun in time (*see* Fig. 6.14, p. 166). The project manager at this stage felt that the total project costs (the 'baseline') would be more in line with original estimates, as more engineering activity had been carried out as the project progressed. He did not envisage that much activity would be required after the launch date.

Case discussion

1 Discuss the differences in profile of costs incurred due to working towards concurrent engineering.
2 From the plans of Fig. 6.13 and the history of the project to date, is it realistic to think that the project will be completed with only a small amount of slippage?
3 What data, other than costs incurred and estimated times, might help the project manager to form a better overall picture of progress?

PROJECT MANAGEMENT IN PRACTICE: **PREPARING QUALITY MANUALS USING FLOWCHARTS**	One of the major challenges of attempting to gain certification to a recognised standard such as BS-EN-ISO 9001, is the volume of paperwork that has to be generated. For the project organisation particularly, the timescale in which this has to be completed will be short, and so it is often viewed as a burden. The BSI now recognises certain flowcharting methods as being valid replacements for large quantities of text. These have the added benefit of providing a method by which people can be helped to understand processes, which can in turn form the basis of improvement activities. Figure 6.15 (p. 167) is a form of four fields map, which shows the means for meeting the criteria set out in section 5 of the standard (Document Control).
SUMMARY OF KEY POINTS	● a feedback control system provides monitoring of the output of a project at the activity level, processes the information and then instigates corrective action to the process itself; ● the nature of the feedback determines whether or not the system is stable; ● all constraints must be the subject of control; ● quality control systems will need to be established and can be recognised through achieving certification to BS -EN - ISO 9000 series of standards; ● costs can be monitored through the application of the 'earned value' concept; ● timeliness is essential to the provision of feedback; ● technical performance monitoring provides an ongoing input to future forecasts of the outcome of the project activities; ● environmental control systems can be established alongside quality control systems where there is a need to do so;

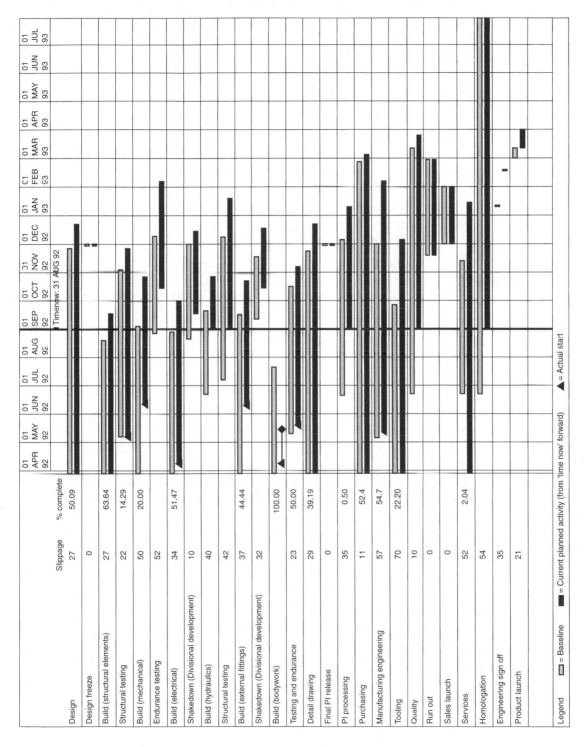

Figure 6.13 A summary of the project against the baseline set on 22/06/92

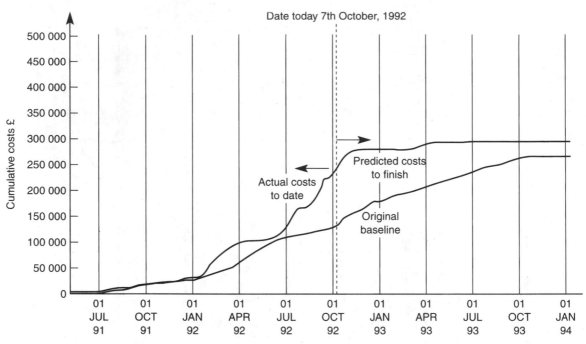

Figure 6.14 Cost control curves for Lifter project

- project management information systems (PMIS) provide the means for achieving the measure–record–analyse–act system for ensuring the minimisation of waste in the control system;
- the stage-gate approach to projects requires that certain hurdles are set for the project activities to proceed between stages;
- change control is needed to ensure that the effects are considered before they are implemented;
- purchasing can be arranged centrally or locally and can spend as much as 80 per cent of the project revenue. It is well worth controlling in order that the best is obtained from suppliers of goods or services, using a framework for items which take large parts of the spend which considers quantity, quality, price, time and place, and the supplier;
- selection of suppliers often takes place on the basis of tendering or bidding;
- contracts should be professionally prepared.
- In the development of new products or processes, patent records are a source of design data, and patenting provides legal protection for the results of the design process.

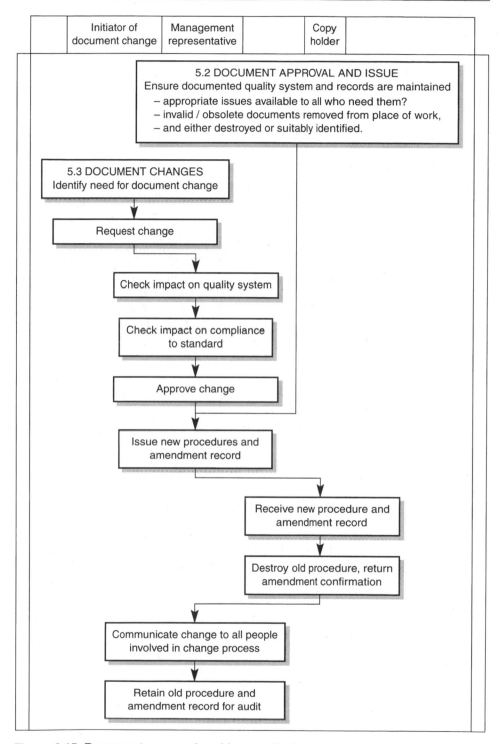

	Initiator of document change	Management representative		Copy holder	

5.2 DOCUMENT APPROVAL AND ISSUE
Ensure documented quality system and records are maintained
– appropriate issues available to all who need them?
– invalid / obsolete documents removed from place of work,
– and either destroyed or suitably identified.

5.3 DOCUMENT CHANGES
Identify need for document change

Request change

Check impact on quality system

Check impact on compliance to standard

Approve change

Issue new procedures and amendment record

Receive new procedure and amendment record

Destroy old procedure, return amendment confirmation

Communicate change to all people involved in change process

Retain old procedure and amendment record for audit

Figure 6.15 Document approval and issue criteria
Source: Excelsis consultants

KEY TERMS	feedback control systems	estimated cost at completion (ECAC)
	corrective/control action	budgeted cost of work scheduled (BCWS)
	BS - EN - ISO 9000	technical performance measure (TPM)
	quality manual	BS 7750
	audit and review	stage-gate
	earned value	5-rights
	actual cost of work performed (ACWP)	tendering / bidding cycle
	budgeted cost of work performed (BCWP)	intellectual property
	variance	patents

REFERENCES

Archibald R.D. (1992) *Managing High Technology Progams and Projects*, 2nd edition, Wiley.

Baily, P., D. Farmer, D. Jessop and D. Jones (1994) *Purchasing Principles and Management*, 7th edition, Pitman Publishing.

Crosby, P. (1979) *Quality is Free* McGraw-Hill

Dale, B.G. and J.J. Plunkett (1991) *Quality Costing*, Chapman & Hall.

Thambain, H.J. (1987) 'The New Project Management Software and Its Impact on Management Style', *Project Management Journal*, August.

Turner, J.R. (1995) *The Commercial Project Manager*, McGraw-Hill.

Welford, R. and A. Gouldson (1993) *Environmental Management and Business Strategy*, Pitman Publishing.

Further information

Copies of the British Standards contained in this chapter can be obtained from:
Sales Department
British Standards Institute
Linford Wood
Milton Keynes
MK14 6LE

More information on intellectual property can be obtained from:
The Patent Office
Cardiff Road
Newport
GWENT
NP9 1RH

FURTHER READING

Goldratt, E.M. (1990) *The Haystack Syndrome: Sifting Information Out of the Data Ocean*, North River Press.

Hines, P. (1994) *Creating World Class Suppliers: Unlocking Mutual Competitive Advantage*, Financial Times/Pitman Publishing.

Hutchins, G. (1994) *Taking Care of Business: How to Become More Efficient and Effective Using ISO 9000*, Omneo/Oliver Wight Publications.

Lamming, R. (1993) *Beyond Partnership*, Strategies for Innovation and Lean Supply, Prentice Hall.

McGoldrick, G. (1994) *The Complete Quality Manual: A Blueprint for Producing Your Own Quality Manual*, Financial Times/Pitman Publishing.

CHAPTER 7

Management and leadership in project environments

The literature on the subject of management and leadership is vast. A search of a single university library yielded in excess of 6000 references – the system simply did not bother to count beyond this. The subject is well studied in many disciplines and so provides for an overlap with the organisational behaviour and the human resources management specialisms. There is also a substantial literature which is practitioner based which has much to offer the practising manager and student alike.

This chapter considers the basics of management and leadership and cites some of the key historical developments in this area. A structure is provided for the literature and the role of new management theories or 'paradigms' is considered. The need for the manager to show leadership and treat time as a valuable resource is highlighted through the consideration of time management.

CONTENTS

7.1 THE ROLE OF LEADERSHIP AND MANAGEMENT IN PROJECTS

The structure employed for these discussions is shown in Fig. 7.1. The assumption is made that management has a positive role to play in the achievement of project goals. The figure shows the major contributory factors in this. At the highest level, the generic ideas concerning project management are deconstructed into three major components which all have an input into the individual project manager/leader's role:

- management – the technical discipline of applying and administering authority over others which is given through the formalised structural arrangement of the organisation
- leadership – the quality of obtaining results from others through personal influence
- individual skills and attitudes which the project manager possesses

Figure 7.1 shows the components of the individual project manager's role in planning, organising, directing, controlling and motivating the people concerned with the achievement of the task. Apart from the three characteristics already mentioned, the nature of the task being undertaken, the motivations of the individuals in the team, the organisational structure and the elusive notion of 'culture' are all inputs to determining the role that the project manager should play. This in turn determines the style that will be adopted which leads to the concept of each project or task being a 'test of management effectiveness'. Should the factors that the project manager uses prove to have been used effectively then there will be a positive influence on the outcome. This is not to simplistically say that the outcome itself will be positive, as there are many external factors that can have a more significant effect. Therefore, the discussion of the role of management in this chapter is limited to the factors that are internal to the organisation or the project team itself.

Managing is a term that implies capability to direct and administer the work of others. It does not imply technical specialism, though this is often required, but the term 'manager' should imply a knowledge of the issues involved in 'managing'. The definition of management has been stated to include a measure of power or authority given by the organisational structure. Managing is therefore considered to be task-related.

As Drucker, a most respected author on the subject of management, commented:

'The manager is the dynamic, life-giving element in every business. Without his leadership, the resources of production remain resources and never become production. In a competitive economy above all, the quality and performance of the managers determine the success of the business, indeed they determine its survival. For the quality and performance of its managers is the only effective advantage an enterprise in a competitive economy can have.' (Drucker, 1955)

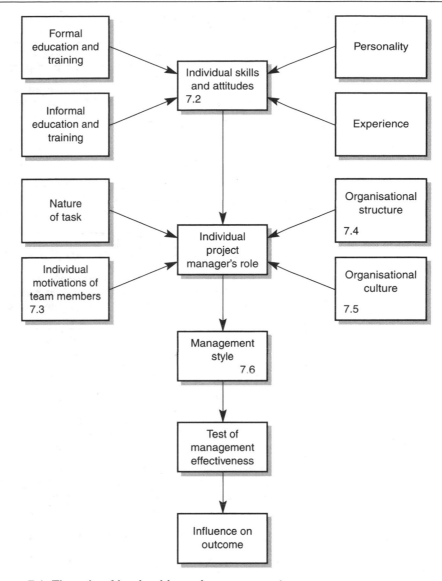

Figure 7.1 The role of leadership and management

Leadership

Leadership involves the influencing of others through the personality or actions of the individual. The definition is therefore people-related. A framework for the study of managerial leadership is given in Fig. 7.2.

The earliest approaches to leadership were the 'traits' approach. The context was militaristic, aligned to the notion that born leaders are the type of people who could lead a group out of the trenches and into attack. The idea that 'lead-

---

```
┌─────────────────────────────────────────────────────────────┐
│              ┌──────────────────────────────┐                │
│              │  QUALITIES OR TRAITS APPROACH │                │
│              └──────────────────────────────┘                │
│                                                               │
│         Assumes leaders are born and not made. Leadership     │
│         consists of certain inherited characteristics or      │
│         personality traits. Focuses attention on the person   │
│         in the job and not on the job itself.                 │
│                                                               │
│            ┌──────────────────────────────────┐              │
│            │  THE FUNCTIONAL OR GROUP APPROACH │              │
│            └──────────────────────────────────┘              │
│                                                               │
│    Attention is focused on the functions and responsibilities │
│    of leadership, what the leader actually does and the       │
│    nature of the group. Assumes leadership skills can be      │
│    learned and developed.                                     │
│                                                               │
│          ┌──────────────────────────────────────┐            │
│          │  LEADERSHIP AS A BEHAVIOURAL CATEGORY │            │
│          └──────────────────────────────────────┘            │
│                                                               │
│    The kinds of behaviour of people in leadership positions   │
│    and the influence on group performance. Draws attention    │
│    to a range of possible managerial behaviour and the        │
│    importance of leadership style.                            │
│                                                               │
│               ┌───────────────────────┐                      │
│               │  STYLES OF LEADERSHIP  │                      │
│               └───────────────────────┘                      │
│                                                               │
│    The way in which the functions of leadership are carried   │
│    out and the behaviour adopted by managers towards          │
│    subordinate staff. Concerned with the effects of           │
│    leadership on those being led.                             │
│                                                               │
│   ┌──────────────────────────────────────────────────────┐   │
│   │  THE SITUATIONAL APPROACH AND CONTINGENCY MODELS      │   │
│   └──────────────────────────────────────────────────────┘   │
│                                                               │
│    The importance of the situation. Interactions between the  │
│    variables involved in the leadership situation and         │
│    patterns of behaviour. Belief that there is no single      │
│    style of leadership appropriate to all situations.         │
└─────────────────────────────────────────────────────────────┘
```

Figure 7.2 A framework for the study of managerial leadership
Source: Mullins, 1993. Reproduced with permission

ers are born and not made' is contentious and highly dubious (as illustrated in Fig. 7.3). Great leaders in all spheres of human endeavour have developed their skills and attributes (as discussed in Section 2.6) to the point needed for the task they are undertaking. Both of these are teachable – provided the individual wishes to learn. Intelligence is one of the few characteristics that cannot be taught, though this has rarely been a constraint to success. Much of the research into establishing the precise characteristics of a leader has been inconclusive or contradictory. The more recent approaches (functional or group approach, leadership as a behavioural category, style) have to some extent followed the same pattern. The emergence of the 'contingency' models recognises what might have been expected, that there is no single 'recipe for leadership' which, if followed, will make you instantly successful.

Figure 7.3 Trait approach to leadership
Reproduced with the kind permission of King Features Syndicate Inc.

Zaleznik (1977) questions whether it is possible for an individual to be both a manager and a leader in the same context. He considers the conflict between the two:

'What is the best way to develop leadership? Every society provides its own answer to this question, and each, groping for answers, defines its deepest concerns about the purposes, distributions and uses of power. Business has contributed its answer to the leadership question by evolving a new breed called the manager. Simultaneously, business has established a new power ethic that favours collective over individual leadership, the cult of the group over that of personality. While ensuring the competence, control and the balance of power relations among groups with the potential for rivalry, managerial leadership unfortunately does not necessarily ensure imagination, creativity, or ethical behaviour in guiding the destinies of corporate enterprise.'

Whilst there is clearly a role for both project managers and leaders, the term management will be used from here on to denote both the management of the task and the leadership of the people involved.

7.2 INDIVIDUAL SKILLS AND ATTITUDES

The model of Fig. 7.1 shows the inputs of personality (discussed in Chapter 5), experience (from previous activities within and outside the work environment) and (in)formal methods of training and education (*see* below).

In Section 2.6 the various skills and attitudes that could be required of a project manager were discussed. Many of these are learnable, in particular personal management (the management of yourself, as opposed to personnel management which is the management of people) and the ability to motivate a team. Personal management will be discussed here and motivation in the following Section (7.3).

The basis of the study of personal skills management is the application of Deming's fifth point:

'Improve Constantly and Forever Every Aspect of Product and Service Provision.'

The best place to start with any management change is yourself. Most managers would like to have extra time, and no matter what project you are involved in, time is one resource that is not replenishable. The successful project manager has learned to apply some form of structured method to the allocation of that resource. Whilst there are many excellent proprietary time management systems, the discussion here will be of the general principles rather than the characteristics of any one particular example.

DeWoot (quoted in Godefroy and Clark, 1989) shows that for American managers who had not had any time management training:

49% of their time is spent on tasks that could be done by their secretaries;
5% is spent on tasks that could be delegated to subordinates;
43% is spent on tasks that could be delegated to colleagues;
3% is spent on tasks which justify the input of their talents and abilities.

Many project managers work long hours with their own work always being subject to delays and fitting the description 'running to stand still'. This leads to poor decision-making as time is not properly allocated to the analysis and consideration of the issues involved. Their work takes on a pattern where they have no basis for making the decision as to whether to take on or reject further tasks and so take on more than they can realistically handle. For many people, this is a way of remaining useful as they are seen to be busy, but in reality they are rarely effective.

Time allocation fits three broad categories:

- proactive – working on plans that are beyond the timeframe of 'that which needs to be done immediately' with the emphasis on 'problem prevention'. If one considers management to be a process and have a 'management product', the quality of that product will be determined by the effect that it has on both the short- and long-term performance of the project they are managing;.
- reactive – there is a problem, work to solve it. This is also known as 'fire-fighting' or 'busy work' and is a style of management which can be very rewarding in that the constant attention of that manager is required (Zeus culture) but stress is high and progress on innovative matters haphazard;
- inactive – resting between the bouts of proactive and reactive work. Does not include thinking time, but does include time spent outside work.

The basis of any time management system is that it provides a logical base to work from in deciding how to prioritise time between the three categories. The effects of good or bad time management are shown in Fig. 7.4.

One of the major effects of poor performance in management is stress. This is pressure which, through the natural reactions of the human body, generates symptoms ranging from anxiety to death in the individual. The body generates adrenalin (for 'fight or flight') which is not worked off by the body – particularly in sedentary occupations. Whilst a certain amount of pressure is beneficial and leads to enhanced performance as an individual rises to a challenge, the negative side is 'stress.' (*see* Markham, 1989). By far the most helpful guide to the individual managing stress has come in the form of the 'four Ps' (unknown, 1995):

Figure 7.4 Effects of time management on the behaviour of individuals

- plan your way out of the situation that is causing you the stress;
- pace yourself – don't try to do everything at once;
- pamper yourself – reward yourself for goals accomplished or plans completed;
- piss yourself laughing – the healing power of laughter is enormous.

The approach to improving time management involves taking a little of that commodity to plan and involves the classical business strategy development cycle:

- analyse the current situation – the best way of doing this is to chart the amount of time that you spend during a period of several weeks on certain tasks – record them in a table such as Table 7.1. This is generally a fairly depressing exercise, especially when you refer to the next section. The priority column should rank the importance of the item being considered from one (will contribute to long-term objectives) to five (totally irrelevant diversion).

Table 7.1 Time usage analysis

Start time	Activity	Time taken	Priority	Comments

- set goals and targets for short-, medium- and long-term (broken down into professional, financial, personal and any other) objectives, which must be SMART:

  S – specific and written down – this is a fundamental starting point for both personal and project management, defining, specifically where it is that you want to be (discussion of the need to set objectives often uses the metaphor of a journey – you would not start out unless you knew where it was you were going);

  M – measurable – there should be a definable point at which it can be objectively determined that the goal has been achieved;

A – achievable – the objective must be physically possible;

R – realistic – for yourself to achieve this, without being too conservative (goal should be uplifting - *see* Chapter 5);

T – Time-framed – having a limit on the date by which it will be achieved.

Where there is a discrepancy between the objectives you have set for yourself and the way in which time is allocated, the plan to achieve those objectives must be changed as follows:

1 Set the plan in place as to how to achieve those goals – there is a certain amount of time that we have to allocate to each of the above areas of activity. This amount of time should reflect the priority that each takes, e.g. the time outside contracted working hours – is that to be spent doing extra work, time with family, in front of the television or on social or sporting activities? Most people can put these in a ranking. The achievement of a certain goal should be associated with the allocation of a certain amount of time to it.

2 Use specific techniques to keep to the above (*see* Table 7.2).

Table 7.2 Techniques to keep to a plan

Use a diary or other form of time-planner ('the shortest pencil is better than the longest memory') – record activities rather than trying to remember them – this only takes up valuable space in your mind.

Say 'no' to non-goal achieving tasks – do not add to your current task list.

Handle each piece of paper once only – this rule avoids the little time-bombs (memos that required action by a date which is approaching rapidly) that sit in an office because you have not got round to tackling them.

Use checklists and to-do lists to save you having to remember events and to enable you to rationally sequence them. Do not avoid difficult or unpleasant tasks. Get them done and out of the way so that your time may then be more positively employed.

Make telephone calls with a fixed duration – e.g. by calling five minutes before a meeting you limit the time of the conversation to five minutes.

When you talk to someone have your agenda written down and record the results of the discussion. Don't handle information twice.

Allow people to make and implement decisions for themselves – they do not need to bring all basic issues to you – the rules for making the decisions should be established.

Do not allow interruptions to disturb meetings or periods when you need to be engaged in proactive work.

Do not be constrained by the normal work practices of time and place (if allowable).

3 Constantly review your performance – the use of a diary along with the repetition of the time evaluation form from time to time can show the magnitude of improvement. Some of the most successful people keep a 'Journal'. This is a record of their performance, both good and bad, written at regular intervals (daily/weekly). This form of honest self-analysis is excellent for charting progress, particularly over a period of years and providing support to the idea that taking charge of your time can yield enormous benefits. As one very successful project manager put it, 'What better way of showing that you are ready for the responsibility of managing other people than by taking effective control of your own time? How on earth can you hope to be an effective manager of other people, if you are incapable of managing yourself?'

One thing at a time – the idea of focus that has been applied to such effect in the development of manufacturing strategy (the operation that focuses on meeting a narrow range of needs will be more successful than that which tries to meet a wider range) is also applicable to personal time management. Focusing in on the goals to be achieved and eliminating distractions can clear the way of unwanted activities.

The last two Ps are vital if you are to be successful as a project manager. The former takes on the ideas of balance in your life as a whole through sport or other recreation, whilst having fun is a major spur to better performance as well as a great stress reliever. Peters (1992) quotes a Californian marketing company as having a number of strategies to encourage the 'fun' back into work including regular water-pistol fights in the accounts department.

Having cited these methods for improving your time management, these kinds of skills are only the basis of a longer period of sustained self-improvement. Formal post-experience education for managers is a major industry and most forward looking organisations promote individuals taking time to study through providing study leave or flexible working arrangements. Some organisations have gone as far as creating their own study centres (e.g. Unipart University). Informal methods of learning are just as valuable through reading new books and journals in addition to sharing knowledge and ideas with colleagues and people from other organisations (often referred to as 'networking').

7.3 INDIVIDUAL MOTIVATION

The modern project manager has a responsibility both to the organisation and to the team members to ensure that they are provided with a high level of motivation. People work better and faster when they have pride in their work. The individual will need to gain satisfaction from the tasks they are assigned, as work generally occupies a significant part of their lives (call this a 'social duty'). By providing for the needs of an individual, their performance can be made less uncertain and, to a degree, managed for benefit to both the individual and the organisation. The major theories of work motivation are shown in Fig. 7.5.

Scientific management

Figure 7.5 includes the work of Frederick Taylor in the development of the principles of scientific management. This is included as its importance is largely historic, but it had an unprecedented effect on management thinking. Despite the principles being nearly a century old, there is still much evidence of their application.

The principles of scientific management or 'Taylorism' are most applicable to repetitive work. They are:

1 Work should be studied scientifically to determine in quantitative terms how it should be divided and how each segment should be done. The aim is to maximise efficiency of the activity and is achieved through measurement, recording and subsequent analysis.
2 The worker should be matched scientifically to the job, e.g. where a task has a physical input to it, the physique of the individual should match the requirements of that task by, for example, using a well-built person to move heavy loads.
3 The person carrying out a task should be trained to do it as per the results of the analysis – it must be carried out exactly as designed and closely supervised.
4 The person carrying out the task should be rewarded for following the prescribed method exactly by a substantial monetary bonus.

(Taylor, 1911)

The result of Taylorism is the separation of the work task from any thinking process by the individual. Any attempt at motivation is purely financially based. Support activities are carried out by trained individuals. The advantage of the system for working is that the task is made very simple, which means that an individual can get very proficient at it and can be replaced with relative ease. The downsides are considerable, however, with the person being alienated from the task they are doing and having no real input to the conversion process. This alienation can be passive in the form of losing of interest in the process ('don't care' attitude) ranging to destructive (pilfering, sabotage, deliberate waste, bomb threats, militant union action).

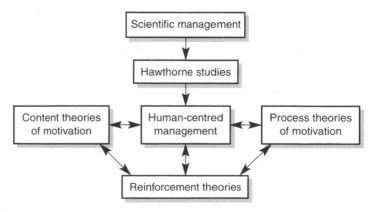

Figure 7.5 Main theories of work motivation

The Hawthorne studies

The Hawthorne studies were carried out to assess the impact of working conditions (temperature, light, noise) on the motivation and hence the productivity of individuals (Roethlisberger and Dickson, 1939). They focused on a group of production workers and showed that initially, when the lighting level was increased, the level of productivity of the people also increased. The link was made – improving the lighting – improves the motivation – improves productivity. The lighting was increased on subsequent occasions with the same result. The lighting level was now returned to its original level and the productivity still increased. This caused the initial hypothesis to be rejected – there was a much more important factor at work. There is a fundamental rule of measurement – check that the measurement process does not affect the performance of what you are trying to measure. Whilst the measurement process was relatively unobtrusive, what was causing the change was the attention being paid to this group of workers. This finding was far more significant than the finding about physical conditions. There is a clear implication for practical application here – paying attention to groups improves the likelihood of good performance.

Figure 7.5 shows three paradigms of modern motivation theory/management behaviour:

- content theories – focuses on what motivates an individual at work. Key theories include the 'hierarchy of needs' and 'motivation-hygiene';
- process theories – focuses on how particular behaviour is initiated, or the process of motivation. Key theories include 'expectancy';
- reinforcement – focuses on how desirable patterns of behaviour can be reinforced.

Content theories

Maslow published his theory on the 'hierarchy of needs' in 1943 (*see* Maslow, 1970). These are shown in Fig. 7.6. This analysis of needs is based on the notion

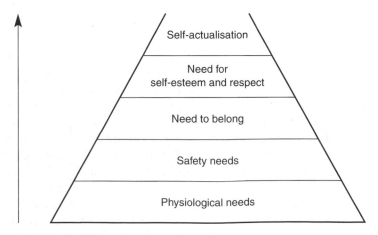

Figure 7.6 Maslow's hierarchy of needs

that individuals will have basic requirements to be content at one level. Once these are met on an ongoing basis, their needs move to the next level, and so on. As he stated, 'Man is a wanting animal and rarely reaches a state of complete satisfaction except for a short time. As one desire is satisfied, another pops up to take its place'. This theory has intrinsic appeal as it enables the person designing a working environment to meet the needs of an individual at an appropriate level – providing the elusive motivation through an individual pursuing as yet un-met needs.

The first set of needs are physiological – food, shelter, etc. Maslow argues that until the basics are met, someone will not be looking for higher order needs, such as recognition. Safety needs are the next level up the hierarchy where the provision of the basic needs is seen to be enduring rather than transitory. Above this is the need to belong, which represents 'man the social animal'. This may be to a social group or to a recognisable team, something which will give them an identity. The need for self-esteem and respect comes next with the thoughts of others about an individual counting in their own self-image. The need for self-actualisation – or to be the best person you can be – is the highest level of needs. Maslow did recognise that this order was not universal and that individuals would have their own hierarchies.

Herzberg's work to produce his 'motivation-hygiene' theory focused on the provision of rewards to the individual. He categorised needs from the task as either 'hygiene' factors or 'motivational'. Hygiene factors are those needs that, unless satisfied, will have a negative effect on motivation. Once a level of satisfaction is reached, increasing the level still further will not increase motivation. Pay is considered to be one such factor for many people. Motivators are those factors which, the better they are met, the higher the motivation that results from them. Recognition is one such factor.

Process theories

Vroom (1964) first developed one of the main theories in this category – that of 'expectancy'. The theory considers that people have a choice of the amount of effort they expend (termed the 'motivational force') in a certain situation. This will depend on their perception of the likelihood of them receiving a desired outcome from this. The first-level outcomes are performance-related (the results from the task directly – the satisfaction of doing a good job, for example). The second level is the extrinsic benefits that are achieved, such as praise from a colleague or superior, promotion or payrise. The theory was further developed by Porter et al. who considered the element of motivational force being translated into effective work, through the skills and abilities of the individual.

Further revisions of this work have taken place, all building in more or different factors to try to provide a theory which is universally applicable. Human behavioural processes are far more complex than the models can allow, particularly where science dictates that a single exception disproves a rule. Such theories in practical application may help in explanatory roles, but rarely are effective in a predictive mode.

Reinforcement

Reinforcement as a means of influencing behaviour is often, somewhat cynically, related closely to the manipulation of people. It forms a significant part of popular 'how to manage' books (including Blanchard and Johnson, 1982) and is summarised by the way in which good behaviour can be positively reinforced. The five rules for providing this are given by Skinner (1973) as:

1 Be specific – praise should refer to specific achievements and be backed up with current information.
2 Be immediate – do the praising as soon as the good performance becomes obvious. This will enable the individual to make the link between the good action and the praising.
3 Make targets achievable – help individuals to break down tasks so that they consist of a series of achievable and recognisable milestones (or even 'inchstones'), and praise on the completion of each.
4 Remember the intangible – praise may be more of a motivator to future performance than pay or status.
5 Make it unpredictable – the passing comment of praise can be far more rewarding than the expected 'pat on the back'.

There is, however, an underlying assumption of rationality in the above theories – that an individual's environment can be logically designed and their needs met on an individual basis. Whilst this is clearly desirable, not only the environment but the system of reward (usually based on promotion and the pay system) has to be designed. Doing so in a large organisation will obviously be an immensely time-consuming activity if the principle that 'the system of reward should be designed to meet the motivation system of the individual,' is adhered to. Practically stated, if the individual is motivated by purely financial considerations (which is only a few per cent of the population), then their reward system should be financially based. If they are seeking recognition through status or title, then this should be provided (or offered as a potential reward).

Other factors that affect the motivation of the individual include:

- location – there are differences between the motivation systems and expectations of traditional rural communities and those from urban backgrounds;
- length of service of the individual – one with long service (beyond two to five years) is going to have different needs from someone new in a job. If a project is being run with a new team, the focus for early management action should be to provide guidance and early feedback so that expectations of the individual are defined. Working with uncertain assessment criteria is very unsettling as you have nothing to rate yourself against. As Goldratt (1990) said:

'Tell me how you measure me and I will tell you how I will behave. If you measure me in an illogical way, do not complain about illogical behaviour.'

- previous work environment – people react and mould to the constraints placed on them – man is a surprisingly versatile animal. Change in attitude and role does not always come with changing jobs or joining a new project team. For this reason many new manufacturing companies have placed age restrictions on new employees who are going to work in line environments. The objective is that they required people who had not been sullied by the intense management–union fighting at the end of the 1970s or whose spirit had not been broken by too many years in a Tayloristic environment.

The literature is probably most fragmented in the area of motivation. Vroom (1964) cites over 500 different studies on the impacts of various factors on motivation. What the figure for 1995 would be....

7.4 STRUCTURAL IMPLICATIONS FOR PROJECT MANAGERS

The role of organisational structure has already been discussed in Chapter 5. The following section considers some of the cultural implications of the applications of various organisational structures. The application of Taylorism required a highly developed organisational functional hierarchy. The evolution of the more modern management paradigms has changed this considerably. There are implications of structure for motivation of the individual. The issue has already been raised of the system of promotion for project managers and how this is often not as clear as for line personnel.

Taiichi Ohno is widely accredited as the designer behind the Toyota production system. His role in project engineering, as Womack *et al.* (1990) showed, is significant. They compare the way in which Western auto producers organise their product design teams with those of the lean producers. The Western approach is to organise people by functional group, e.g. engine designers would have graduated from being component designers and, if successful, may hope to progress to power-train design. This provides a clear progression path for individuals, but a designer simply progresses as a designer with no increasing appreciation of the implications of their work on the manufacturing process. As the authors comment:

> 'Ohno and Toyoda, by contrast, decided early on that product engineering inherently encompassed both process and industrial engineering. Thus they formed teams with strong leaders that contained all the relevant expertise. Career paths were structured so that rewards went to strong team players rather than to those displaying genius in a single area of product, process, or industrial engineering, but without regard to their function as a team.'

The subject of promotion is treated by Peter and Hull (1970):

> 'In a hierarchy, anyone will be promoted to their level of incompetence.'

This is known as 'The Peter principle' and was used by the authors to explain why, in their experience, so many managers appeared to be lacking in the basic qualities needed for the task of managing. Their theory relates to the above very closely – they noted that competence in a line task would generally be rewarded by further promotion up the line of authority. The further they were promoted, the further they moved from the specialism for which they had first been promoted for being competent in.

7.5 CULTURAL IMPLICATIONS FOR PROJECT MANAGERS

Culture itself is almost impossible to define. This is because of the number of different cultures that exist within any one organisation and the fact that even the most detailed deconstruction would provide an inaccurate picture of the totality. At the simplest level, the culture of a group or team can be described as relating to one or more of the Greek gods – Apollo, Zeus, Athena and Dionysus. These ideas were developed by Handy (1985) and show how the nature of the group will need to influence the style of management that is practised, if the two are not to clash. The styles, their characteristics and the advantages and disadvantages of each are shown in Table 7.3.

Table 7.3 Culture of organisations

Name	Description of culture	Characteristics	Advantages	Disadvantages
Apollo	Role	Formalised, rule-based, focused on individual specialisms	Stable, predictable, visible	Stable, predictable
Zeus	Club	Entrepreneurial, focused on single leader, autocratic style	Little structure to prevent dynamism	Little logic to what is done, total dependence on one person
Athena	Task	Group gathered with common purpose	Creative, dynamic	Expensive to maintain, needs constant stream of new tasks and highly qualified people
Dionysus	Existential	Organisation that share resources but is not dependent on each other	Allows each to be self-determining, little structure,	Relies on individual responsibilities and risks, needs high level of personal development

Table 7.3 is of interest in providing the kind of managerial overview that is often more useful than an academic description of the same issues. When the 'so-what' test is applied, some further amplification of the effect of culture in attaining management success is required. The fundamental principles are that the culture should reflect the team membership and the task, and the management style should be in line with that culture.

In a project environment, it is almost inevitable that the role of the project manager will have much in common with that of a line or operations manager for periods of time, e.g. in the execution phase of a project to develop a new material, there was much testing and retesting of samples to be undertaken. Similarly at all levels in all projects there will be routine tasks that have to be performed, documentation being a good example. In this situation, the Apollo culture prevails. Using a group which is best described as having an Athena culture (a motivated, highly trained taskforce) to carry out such tasks will cause disinterest due to the lack of scope in the task for creativity.

In the Zeus organisation, an autocratic boss rules by their word alone. Many businesses are run in this way – usually small businesses (though Mirror Group Newspapers had this form when it was owned by Robert Maxwell). This kind of boss makes the decisions for their people and will control absolutely, jealously guarding their knowledge of how the business operates. Projects run in this way may get the task achieved, but often at the expense of the project team and other stakeholders. Where the task is anything other than the simplest, attempting to get one person to consider all the issues involved is impossible. There are times though, for example when a project is running behind and desperate measures are called for, when short-term gains may be made by taking this approach. This kind of leadership (along with others) is discussed in DeBono's *Six Action Shoes* (1993).

The Apollo organisation is highly structured – relying on the idea that breaking the task down into small units creates pockets of specialism. Many organisations have this kind of culture – government departments, large companies. The roles of departments and individuals have already been discussed under the topics of line management. As previously stated, one of the major drawbacks is the lack of creativity that this engenders, in addition to a degree of bureaucracy. Bureaucracy is often typified by a kind of behaviour that obstructs progress. A storekeeper at a major company refused to allow a project manager to have the equipment he needed for a crucial part of his project as he claimed that the item was not logged on the computer system. When the manager pointed it out to him on the shelves in the store, the storekeeper would still not release the equipment as without the necessary listing on the computer system, the correct paperwork could not be generated. Following an investigation of the business processes, the storekeepers were abolished and the stores run on a take-as-needed basis, with key suppliers filling the shelves directly.

The Dionysus and Athena cultures rely more heavily on the role of the individual than the other two. The Dionysian culture is represented in some ways by the university culture in the UK. They are seen as groups with very loose ties that are bonded to the organisational nucleus by the need for the services that they provide – such as administration, buildings and maintenance, technology provision and, mostly, funding for both individual activities and collective projects. Other professions have a similar culture – the medical profession (particularly hospitals) where the sharing is of central facilities.

Consequently it should be no surprise that certain problems have arisen:

- medical practitioners resenting the change in the organisation of hospitals in the National Health Service – the number of managers in NHS hospitals has risen from 1000 to over 20 000 in the past five years. As one doctor put it, 'They are great if you want to get a new carpet laid, but no use for helping us to actually improve the service we provide to patients'. The conflict has been that there is an increase in imposed authority on the clinical staff from the managers and a considerable increase in the amount of bureaucracy that needs to keep such managers fed with tasks to achieve (*see* Parkinson's Law of 1000 below);
- quality systems have been shown to be less applied in organisations that have Athena, Dionysus or Zeus cultures. Quality systems invariably lead to a degree of preceduralisation that would fit well with an Apollo culture, but again it is an example of the characteristics of one being superimposed onto another;
- matrix management often fails to yield the results planned – the Apollo culture of the functional organisation being overlaid with an Athena culture which is task centred.

The effect of the early work on the planning of projects should be taken into account. The ideas of work breakdown structure are likely to lead to a functional arrangement and the kindling of an Apollo culture. The project may be far more dynamic than this and require more of an Athenean approach.

Parkinson's Law of 1000 – once you have a corporate staff of 1000 people, they can become totally self-sustaining in work generated within the company, without any need for external interaction. That is, they can generate enough work to keep themselves busy (generally by paying people to read reports that you have paid others to generate), without adding one penny of value.

7.6 MANAGEMENT STYLE

Cooperation – coercion scale

Cooperation is based on educating the individual as to the reasons why it is in their interests to participate in your venture as an active contributor. This is the focus of the humanistic movement and works well in ventures which require active participation rather than grudging acceptance. The style of management that is required is accommodating – ensuring that the needs of the individual are met through the activities and the group support.

Coercion is based on using whatever functional devices and authority exist to force the individual to carry out a particular task – the basis of Taylorism.

This works well in the short term where there is a specific task to be carried out. The style of management is confrontational as there is no commonality of purpose between the individual and their superior.

7.7 THE DEVELOPMENT OF MANAGEMENT THINKING

There are two distinct approaches to management thinking. They can be broadly categorised as either academic or populist. There was a time when academic thinking was based on the work of a few key individuals whose theories had been proved through limited trials. As is often the case, some of the most advantageous work was done first. The application of psychology and other sciences to management actions, have resulted in the wide literature that was referred to in the introduction.

All the above discussions on the academic literature can be summarised in a move from Taylorism at the start of this century to a new humanism at the end (*see* Table 7.4). The emergence of humanism is the result of society demanding a new management agenda, the reversal of fortunes of Taylorism (the industrial strife at the end of the 1970s showed that whilst the Tayloristic systems had provided the Western world with an unprecedented standard of living, it had gone past the point where it was going to continue to be beneficial) and the study of world-class performers in all sectors. Those companies that were showing world-class traits invariably were those that had the greatest ability to harness the creativity of all the individuals within their organisa-

Table 7.4 The Tayloristic versus the humanistic agenda

	Tayloristic agenda	Humanistic agenda
Level of needs met	Most basic level – physiological and possibly safety	Higher level – need to belong up to self-actualisation
Role of individual	Automaton carrying out specialised task under stated rules	Individual with freedom and autonomy
Advantages for system	Predictability of outcomes	Intrinsically motivated individuals, providing caring creativity
Advantages for individual	Unchallenging, safe, ordered existence	Challenging role with chance for self-determination
Role of management	Designer and controller of work tasks	Provider of scenarios and facilitator
Responsibility for outcomes	Lay with project manager	Shared between all members of the team

tion. In addition, modern expectations, as gleaned in schools, mean that people are far less likely to agree to work under such conditions. The new management is not universal nor is it without critics or opponents. The move to what has been termed 'anthropocentric management' is also not easy. Letting go of hard-won control sits uneasily with people used to working in Zeus or Apollo cultures. It is almost certain that future organisations will move away from these structures.

The popularists are characterised by books and articles based on either personal management experience (such as Harvey-Jones, 1988) or that of a collective of organisations (including *In Search of Excellence*, and others by Tom Peters). The basics are the sharing of what the authors consider to be elements of good practice that have wider application. These are often distilled into principles that one is tempted to treat like laws of physics – fundamental and immovable, which all guarantee a management revolution. However, if there is one lesson to be learned from these texts, it is that the ability to remain flexible and customer-focused are the only constants. *In Search of Excellence* was notable in that many of the companies that were studied and considered to be excellent, soon ran into financial trouble. These popularist texts have an important role to play in the ongoing development of managers and maintaining an interest in how the virtues of customer (or stakeholder) focus and flexiblity can be best applied.

7.8 THE DEVELOPMENT OF NEW MANAGEMENT PARADIGMS

The modern manager who reads widely would be forgiven for being confused by the range of management paradigms or theories which all appear have to universal application. The temptation is either to go ahead and try the ideas, or just get on with what you are doing and hope that, like many fads, it will pass. Total quality management, the lean paradigm and business process reengineering are amongst the most significant and influential to emerge over the last ten years. What is clear from the literature examining the success of such changes in management thinking is that success is far more likely to come from adaption of a particular idea, rather than its wholesale adoption. The role of the successful project manager will be to keep up to date with changes in management thinking, but take an intelligent approach as to which changes will add value. As Nohria and Berkley (1994) commented, 'Wary of fads, the pragmatic manager considers context, focuses on outcomes and makes do'.

Furthermore:

'Management ideas should be:

- adopted only after careful consideration;
- purged of unnecessary buzzwords and clichés;
- judged by their practical consequences;

- tied to the here and now;
- rooted in genuine problems;
- adapted to suit particular people and circumstances;
- adaptable to changing and unforeseen circumstances;
- tested and refined through active experimentation;
- discarded when they are no longer useful.'

This concept of 'making do' or constantly making small changes and observing the results on a continuous treadmill of improvement is possibly the most significant. The project manager is especially well positioned to adopt this approach, as their role is central to achieving predetermined outcomes.

As Harvey-Jones (1988) commented,

'Increasingly companies will only survive if they meet the needs of the individuals who serve in them; not just the question of payment, important as this may be, but people's true inner needs, which they may even be reluctant to express to themselves. People want jobs which have continual interest and enable them to grow personally. It goes without saying that they want adequate rewards, but in my experience people are less greedy, and far less motivated by reward, than capitalist theory would suggest. It is certain that every individual not only expects, but should be entitled to a reward which recognises his contribution. The needs of one's people are also wider than just the paypacket. They wish to feel that they are doing a worthwhile job which makes some contribution to society.'

PROJECT MANAGEMENT IN PRACTICE: DOESN'T TIME FLY?

It was 7.30 on a Tuesday morning, when John Edwards, general manager of the Jenkins Company's main factory, turned onto the M3 to drive to his office in Basingstoke. The journey took about twenty minutes and gave John an opportunity to reflect on the problems of the plant without interruptions.

The Jenkins Company ran three printing plants and had nationwide clients for their high quality colour work. There were about 350 employees almost half of whom were based at Basingtstoke. The head office was also at Basingstoke.

John had started with Jenkins as a fresh graduate ten years previously. He was promoted rapidly and after five years became assistant manager of the smaller plant in Birmingham. Almost two years ago he had been transferred to Basingstoke as assistant manager and when the manager retired he was promoted to this position.

John was in good form this morning. He felt that today was going to be a productive day. He began prioritising work in his mind. Which project was the most important? He decided that unit-scheduling was probably the most important – certainly the most urgent. He had been meaning to give it his attention for the past three months but something else always seemed to crop up.

He began to plan this project in his mind, breaking down the objectives, procedures and installation steps – it gave him a feeling of satisfaction as he calculated the cost savings that would occur once this project was implemented. He assured himself that it was time this project was started and mused that it should have been completed a long time ago. This idea had been conceived two years ago and been given the go-ahead but had been temporarily shelved when John had moved to Basingstoke.

John's thoughts returned to other projects that he was determined to implement: he began to think of a procedure to simplify the transport of materials from the Birmingham plant; he thought of the notes on his desk; the inventory analysis he needed to identify and eliminate some of the slow moving stock items; the packing controls which needed revision and the need for a new order form to be designed. There were a few other projects he remembered needed looking into, and he was sure he would find some time in the day to attend to them. John really felt he was going to have a productive day.

As he entered the plant, John was met by the stock controller who had a problem with a new member of staff not turning up. John sympathised with him and suggested that he got personnel to call the absentee. The stock controller accepted that action but told John that he needed to find him a person for today. John made a mental note of the problem and headed for his office. His office manager, Mrs James, asked him whether she should send off some samples, or would they need to be inspected? Without waiting for an answer, Mrs James then asked if he could suggest a replacement for the sealing-machine operator, as the normal operator was ill, and told him that Pete, the manufacturing engineer, was waiting to hear from him.

John told Mrs James to send the samples. He noted the need for a sealer-operator and then called Pete, agreeing to meet in his office before lunch.

John started on his routine morning tour of the plant. He asked each supervisor the volumes and types of orders that were being processed that morning, how things were going, and which orders would be run next. He helped one worker find storage space for a container-load of product which was awaiting dispatch, discussed quality control with an employee who had been producing poor work, arranged to transfer people temporarily to four different departments and talked to the dispatch supervisor regarding pick-ups and special orders which were to be processed that day.

Returning to his office, John reviewed the production reports against his projected targets and found that the plant was running slightly behind schedule. He called in the production foreman and together they went through the machine schedules, making several changes. During this discussion, John was asked by someone else to agree several labelling changes to their products and received a telephone call for the approval of a revised printing schedule.

John next began to put delivery dates on important orders received from customers and the sales force (Mrs James handled the routine ones). Whilst doing this, he had two phone calls, one from a salesperson asking for a better delivery date and one from the personnel manager asking him to book time for an initial induction meeting with a new employee. John then headed for his morning conference at the executive offices. He had to answer the chairman's questions on new orders, complaints and potential new business. The production director also had questions on production and personnel problems. He then had to see the purchasing manager to enquire about the delivery of some cartons, and also to place an order for some new paper. On the way back to his office, John was talking to the chief engineer about two current engineering projects. When he reached his desk, he lit a cigarette and looked at his watch – it was ten minutes before lunch.

'Doesn't time fly', he commented as Mrs James entered his office to put some papers on his desk. 'No,' she replied, 'Time stays, we go.' Wondering about the meaning of this, he headed for the canteen.

After lunch he started again. He began by checking the previous day's production reports and the afternoon followed the pattern of the morning. Another busy day, but how much had he accomplished? All the routine tasks had been managed, but without any creative or special project work being done. He was the last to leave the plant that night.

As he drove home he pondered the role that he was paid to fulfil, and wondered where the time to carry out any innovative thinking had gone today. He was sure that he had planned intelligently and delegated his authority. He acknowledged the need for a personal assistant, but saw that as a long-term project as the chairman was having a blitz on the overhead created by non-direct staff.

Case discussion

1 Identify the tasks which John should have done himself, and which he should have delegated.
2 Discuss how he uses his time – what are the main problems?
3 How effective do you feel John's 'management by walking about' is?
4 How could he improve his time planning?
5 Would employing a personal assistant for John really 'add value' or just be another overhead cost on the company?

SUMMARY OF KEY POINTS	• the skills and attitudes of the project manager will be determined by personality, experience, and both formal and informal education and training;
	• the role that an individual project manager will play depends on many factors including the nature of the task, the individual motivations of team members, the structure of the organisation and the culture in addition to the project manager's own skills and attitudes;
	• the concept of a 'test of management effectiveness' is introduced to show the effect that the role of the project manager can have on the achievement of outcomes for all stakeholders;
	• leadership is categorised by the influence of the individual on people whereas management is centred on people being treated as one of a number of resources;
	• time is a non-replenishable resource and must be managed accordingly;
	• stress is caused by your body stifling its natural urge to 'fight or flight', i.e. aggressively confront the source of the stress or run away from it;
	• craft-based industries were replaced during the last century by organisations with tasks designed according to the principles of scientific management. These relied on financial reward as the prime motivator;
	• financial reward is only one means that management can provide as a motivator. Meeting certain other needs through the work task can be more beneficial (Maslow) as well as treating people as individuals rather than automatons;

- scientific management is being replaced in developed countries by jobs designed to meet the higher needs of the individual (the humanist movement);
- cultures may be broadly described as either role (Apollo), club (Zeus), task (Athena) or existential (Dionysus). Each has different roles for management and situations where it is applicable;
- management can be based on either coercion or encouraging cooperation;
- new management paradigms should be screened very carefully before being adopted by the manager. The hype should be eliminated and a realistic evaluation of their ability to add value to the 'management product' carried out.

KEY TERMS

management and leadership   humanism
stress   culture
time management   cooperation
motivation   coercion
scientific management (Taylorism)   management paradigms
hierarchy of needs

REVIEW AND DISCUSSION QUESTIONS

1 Differentiate between the task of leading and managing a project.
2 Show the influences that an individual project manager will bring to the role.
3 What are the influences from within an organisation on the role that a project manager takes?
4 Why might the study of time management be fundamental to a project manager?
5 Using Table 7.3, examine your own time-management performance over the period of one or two days. How does this relate to the goals that you have set yourself?
6 From your analysis in question 5, show what strategies you are going to use to keep yourself on track to the targets you have set for yourself.
7 Compare the work of the major thinkers on motivation. What influence has each had on modern management?
8 Why is it reasonable to think that as managers, our action can have an effect on a project outcome?
9 Why do people need to have a clear promotion path in their jobs? What other motivators would you provide for people?
10 Distinguish between the four basic types of organisational culture as outlined by Handy (1985). Give examples of each and show how they each meet the needs or constraints imposed on the organisation in which they operate.
11 Why is it necessary to ensure that the style of management meets the culture of the organisation?
12 Show how the emergence of humanism changes the way in which people are treated within organisations.

13 Compare one major popularist text (e.g. *In Search of Excellence*) with an academic journal article of your choice. What are the purposes, potential audiences, and likely effects of each of these? In your view, what is their role in forming management thinking?

14 How might a project manager differentiate between management paradigms that may prove beneficial and those which are going to be of no benefit?

REFERENCES

Blanchard, K. and S. Johnson (1982) *The One Minute Manager*, Fontana.

DeBono, E. (1993) *Six Action Shoes*, Fontana.

Drucker, P. (1955) *Management* Butterworth-Heinemann (first published in 1955 – many later editions are available and still as relevant to the discussion of the role of management).

Godefroy, C.H. and J. Clark (1989) *The Complete Time Management System*, Piatkus.

Goldratt, E.M. (1990), *The Haystack Syndrome*, North River Press.

Handy, C. (1985) *Gods of Management*, Pan Books, revised edition.

Harvey-Jones, J. (1988) *Making It Happen: Reflections on Leadership*, Collins pp. 249–50.

Herzberg. F., 'Work and the Nature of Man', Granada Publishing, 1974.

Markham, U. (1989) *The Practical Guide to Using Stress Positively*, Element Books.

Maslow, A.H. (1970) *Motivation and Personality*, Harper & Row, 2nd edition.

Mullins, L.J. (1993), *Management and Organisational Behaviour*, 3rd edition, Pitman Publishing.

Nohria, N. and J.D. Berkley (1994) 'Whatever Happened to the Take-Charge Manager', *Harvard Business Review*, January-February, pp. 128-37.

Peter, L. and R. Hull (1970) *The Peter Principle* Pan Books.

Peters, T. J. and R.N. Waterman (1982) *In Search of Excellence – Lessons from America's Best-run Companies*. Harper and Row.

Peters, T. (1992) *Liberation Management*, Macmillan, p. 602.

Porter, L.W., Lawler, E.E., and Emmet, E., (1968) *Managerial Attitudes and Performance*, Irwin.

Roethlisberger, F. J. and W.J. Dickson (1939) *Management and the Worker*, Harvard University Press.

Skinner, B.F. (1971), *Beyond Freedom and Dignity*, Knopf.

Taylor, F.W. (1911) *The Principles of Scientific Management*, Harper.

Womack, J., D. Jones and J. Roos (1990) *The Machine That Changed The World*, Rawson Associates.

Vroom, V.H. (1964) *Work and Motivation*, Kreiger Publishing.

Zaleznik, A. (1977) 'Managers and Leaders: Are They Different?' *Harvard Business Review*, May–June, pp. 67–78.

FURTHER READING

Adair, J. (1988) *The Action-Centred Leader* and *Effective Leadership: A Modern Guide to Developing Leadership Skills*, revised edition Industrial Society.

Alexander, R. (1992) *Commonsense Time Management*, Amacom.

Forsyth, P. (1994) *First Things First, How to Manage Your Time for Maximum Performance*, Institute of Management / Pitman Publishing.

Handy, C. (1985) *Understanding Organisations*, Pelican, 3rd edition.

Jay, A. (1987) *Management and Machiavelli*, Business Books, revised edition.

Tack, A. (1984) *Motivational Leadership*, Gower.

CHAPTER 8

Problem-solving and decision-making

During the execution phase of a project particularly, the project manager will be faced with the need to solve a whole range of problems rapidly and effectively. As it will not be possible to pre-plan all eventualities, the objective of this chapter is to show how such situations can be handled. Most of the techniques meet the criteria of being simple enough to be used by anyone, though some of the mathematics can be considerably more involved. Decision-making is considered as part of a generic problem-solving process.

Price (1984) describes one of the conflicts that exists in management:

'Business is a risky undertaking. According to those who have devoted their lives to the proper study of mankind, Man is a risk-evasive animal. From what I have seen, risk addicted seems closer to the norm. There is excitement in taking risky decisions and it is possible to get hooked on it; it makes you feel good.

Risk, unnecessary risks are taken by the thousand every day. Often they are unnecessary simply because they are made in the light of inadequate knowledge, but it boosts somebody's self-esteem to make them with an air of omniscience, which is one of the resons why we are on the whole, such poor quality performers.'

There is another view, namely that the modern project manager is overloaded with data rather than information; the information revolution has provided the means to access large quantities of numbers quickly, often without the means to assimilate them. Handling such volume complexity without succumbing to 'data paralysis' is a significant task and one of the value-adding roles that management can play.

The project manager should have the option either to try to provide a structure for making 'rational' decisions, or rely on gut-feel and experience and hope that this is appropriate.

CONTENTS

8.1 THE PROBLEM FRAMEWORK

One of the key roles of a manager is to handle problems that challenge them in their own role, as well as being a resource for members of the project team to turn to for help. Problem-solving is a core management skill, but, like leadership, one that too often is assumed to be an inbred attribute rather than an acquired skill.

For the purposes of this discussion, a problem is defined as:

'The gap between an actual situation or the perception of it and the required or expected situation.'

The two properties, expectation and perception, are subjective and based on the viewpoint of the individual (*see* worldview in Chapter 2). Many issues presented to managers fail this definition; people perceive that there is a problem without identifying the gap. Clarifying the reality of the situation with objective measures is a precursor to the problem-solving process. Part of the role of the project manager in this process is the gathering of the possible worldviews. This requires the skill of being both involved, yet objective.

The nature of the problem determines the point of departure for the manager. This can be categorised as:

- requiring an immediate reaction – the timescale of a decision requires a 'conditioned reflex' rather than a 'considered response'. Such a situation would include the threatening of the well-being of an individual;
- response to a crisis – the problem can be considered within a relatively short-time period, i.e. an undesirable state of affairs has occurred – you need to do something about it soon;
- emerging problem – some undesirable state of affairs appears likely to happen – what are you going to do to resolve it?
- response to an opportunity (*see* Reebok below) – speculative problem-solving or avoidance in advance of an undesirable situation (missed opportunity);
- strategy formulation – the plotting of a course to a desired situation over a period of years.

The time period of the first kind of problem means that the response or intended solution must be either instinctive (such as to run away) or ingrained through training (to remove the source of potential danger). There is scope in the latter for a major component of any discussion on problem-solving – that of proceduralisation. This is not restricted to emergency situations, but a major component of any work situation today. This proceduralisation or systematisation can be defined as:

'the enaction of a predetermined reponse to a given set of conditions'.

The systematisation of problem resolution depends on identifying the situation. The programmed response is then initiated, as shown in Fig. 8.1.

The pre-programming of actions has a number of advantages:

- once a method has been defined for resolving a situation, it can be refined and improved;
- by removing thought processes from the actions, they are, to a great extent, independent of the individual carrying them out;
- if a predetermined procedure is followed, actions are traceable back to the people who carried them out;
- the actions are then the responsibility of the organisation rather than the individual;
- should the procedure fail, the identification of the fail-point is considerably helped, as the steps can be re-traced.

The alternative is that the problem-solving cycle is invoked. As for the planning process, the cycle is iterative (involves repetition of steps if the output does not meet recognised or emerging conditions). The remainder of this chapter will consider the possible approaches to problems with a degree of novelty – those that are being solved for the first time and those that are being considered for proceduralisation. There is a downside, not least of which is the removal of the individualism in the performance of that part of the task. No one has yet achieved an effective procedural description for carrying out the job 'as if you cared personally about the outcome'.

The problem-solving model (Fig. 8.1) shows the process moving from determination if a standard procedure exists to choosing a definition for the problem. Classical problem-solving focuses very heavily on providing a definition for the problem – indeed it is often stated that 'if you can define the problem you are working with, you are half way to a solution'. The definition must include the statement of the gap between the two states: actual/perceived situation and desired/expected situation. Without these two, the problem is said to be 'unbounded'. Once the problem has been defined in this way, the process can move on to the next stage – the construction of various alternatives. At this point the process leaves the analysis of the problem, at least temporarily and moves to the synthesis phase. This transition involves the first major piece of decision-making. The logic of the process is fairly simple at this point – there

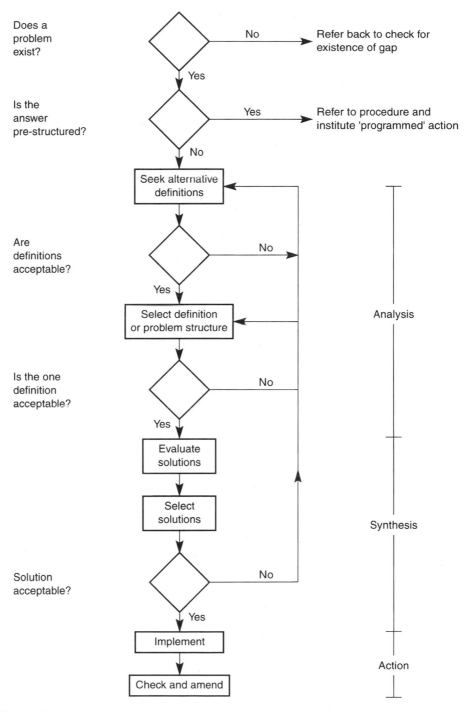

Figure 8.1 Systematic problem-solving model

only needs to be a decision made if there is a choice of definitions or solutions. Where only one exists the implications need to be considered, but without wasting time on non-decisions.

In the previous chapter the extremes of management style were identifed as 'coercive' and 'cooperative'. The natures of the decision-making processes are different. For the former, the project manager would be the key decision-maker. In the latter, many of the decisions would be devolved, either to the individual with the most knowledge or responsibility for this part of the project, or to the group as a whole. This devolution removes a large part of the decision-making role of the manager. Part of the process of devolution involves seeking ideas from others. This ensures that the set of possible solutions can bridge the problem gap – and includes 'brainstorming'.

Brainstorming

Taking a group out of their normal work situation to ponder a problem can be immensely beneficial – both to the organisation and the group. The dynamics of the brainstorming process are aided by adherence to a few rules:

- provide a basic structure to the task of decision-making – groups are generally very bad at looking for structure or logic in decisions;
- the benefit is from the extraction and combination of ideas from a variety of people – the object of the exercise is therefore to facilitate this;
- give people the opportunity to do some pre-thinking on the problem – the subconscious mind has an enormous capacity and can provide solutions without the input of conscious effort;
- at the start of the meeting an ice-breaking exercise will help people to relax and provide a 'safe environment' for the generation of ideas;
- all ideas must be written down – use whiteboards and 3M's post-it notes, for example;
- express ideas as the participants state them – paraphrasing removes the original meaning and adds a slant of your own. If in doubt as to the veracity of the point being made, seek clarification;
- do not allow any criticism of ideas put forward – this will destroy the credibility of that person and you will be unlikely to gain much more from them;
- do not permit one or a small group of individuals to dominate the proceedings – this will exclude potentially valuable input from others;
- summarise and record the outcome of the brainstorming session and then circulate it to all those concerned – the after-meeting feedback is a further source of solutions and ideas, as people think of all the things that they would like to have contributed during the session.

Decision-making as a process is the period involving the seeking of alternatives through to the end of the comparative evaluation stage. The inputs to this process are:

- strategic – in order for an organisation to retain coherence the decisions made in the projects that it undertakes need to fit with the overall strategy outlined for the organisation;
- fundamental/political – each person brings their own viewpoint to the decision-making process. This will range in form from bias (often undeclared) to forthright statement of personal beliefs;
- quantitative modelling;
- subconscious elements – obtaining peoples' legitimate reservations about a decision can be a preventor of 'group-think' provided the atmosphere can be created in which people feel free to try to elucidate such thoughts.

The nature of the decision-making process depends on the system that the decision concerns. In Chapter 2 a basic overview of systems was given which showed the application of the input/output/constraints and mechanisms model to a project system. Further examination of this is needed to determine whether it is:

- an open system – having interaction with systems outside through the flows of material or information;
- a closed system – being self-sustaining in informational and material terms – operating in isolation.

It is tempting when considering systems to look for the closed-system model. If this is possible, the modelling process involves defining variables from within the system and then optimising these. As Wu (1994) comments:

'Many of the traditional concepts in organisation and management theory consider an organisation such as a production system as a self-contained, closed system.'

This leads to inappropriate models of behaviour being constructed, as they do not show the dynamic nature of the interchange between the systems and their external environments, i.e. they were open systems.

The use of open-system models is not as attractive, however, as by definition they require the variables from external factors to be continuously introduced and the nature of the environment to be dynamic and inherently unstable. This instability is reflected in a tendency for the behaviour of the system to be unpredictable.

8.2 MODELLING SYSTEMS FOR DECISION-MAKING

Drucker (1956) states the reasons for poor decision-making as being:

- data not properly ordered or structured;
- too much time spent developing answers to problems rather than the statement of the problem;
- an inability on the part of the decision-makers to consider all the variables/ factors involved;
- an inability to evaluate the impact of extraneous factors.

The growth of the use of personal computers, and the availability of a great range of highly capable software, mean that there exists relatively cheap means of processing large quantities of data. There is little excuse now for the data not to be properly ordered or structured. The ease of preparation of graphs and other graphical techniques should have removed this as a cause. The same argument could also be applied to the third of Drucker's points, as the ability to build more data into decision-making models has been greatly enhanced. The second and fourth of the factors are procedurally linked to the decision-making process and are only removed by:

- increased awareness of the potential of both of these to affect the process;
- focus on the removal of the damaging effects of poor decisions, i.e. make the decisions more robust.

There has been a considerable growth in the use of sophisticated models in decision-making. The application of scientific models to the solving of management problems has developed into a specialist branch of management known as 'management science' or 'operational research'. The temptation is to view the output of management science analysis as having a high degree of truth, because the mathematical models that are used are very difficult for a lay person to dispute. In reality management science is one of the tools that can be employed in decision-making, rather than being the totality of the process.

The model of the system may take on one of many forms, including:

- a descriptive model – using words or graphical means to describe the action or performance of a system, e.g. systemigrams (Chapter 2);
- a geometric model – expressing an object in a mathematical form (as used in computer-aided-design systems);
- a mechanistic model – determining the inputs to and outputs from a system;
- static predictive – taking a limited picture of the state of a system at a particular point in time and using various mathematical techniques to predict the future performance;
- a dynamic predictive model – a 'real-time system' which takes a constant review of the inputs to a system, providing the most up-to-date forecast of future performance.

Taking a generic view of the modelling process, a model of a system is defined as:

A system which is constructed under controlled conditions, whose behaviour mimics that of another system where it would not be possible for those conditions to be controlled (economically or physically).

Jennings and Wattam (1994) describe the benefits of using modelling as:

- time contraction – it is often possible to speed up events to show the effects of time on a system and use it in the prediction as to what will happen after a period of time, without necessarily waiting that long;

- what-if – the decision-makers have the option to manipulate a model and determine a range of scenarios based on their own individual predictions of the conditions as to what the external environment for the system will be;
- error avoidance/detection – there are many systems that can shadow the decisions made by others and act as a course filter for marginal decisions or ones where there has been an error. Such systems are often used both in mechanical design and stock-market trading.

In addition:

- it is possible to examine the fundamental assumptions on which a model was based;
- parameters can be optimised without the need for potentially expensive trial and error with reality;
- the sensitivity to external effects can be measured.

Modelling involves a cycle of activities which are akin to Deming's PDCA (*see* Chapter 1) – the model is designed, built, tested and then amended based on the comparison of the performance of the real system and the model. The model is then updated based on this performance. The process itself involves:

- making assumptions about the behaviour of systems;
- simplification of the system parameters;
- estimation of the likely values of unrelated variables.

8.3 HANDLING UNCERTAINTY IN DECISION-MAKING

There are two basic paradigms associated with handling uncertainty – the mathematical and the managerial. The research literature on improving mathematical models for handling uncertainty is vast. Most requires the input of an expert statistician to be used effectively. This approach tries to impose a degree of certainty onto the system, through treating the causes of the uncertainty. The alternative (managerial perspective) is to provide a basis for handling the effects.

As an example, a company are about to launch a new product onto a market in which they have previously operated. They feel that there is a considerable degree of uncertainty as to whether the new product will be a success. They have a number of possible routes open to them:

- firstly, analyse, using the best data available, the possible sales patterns for this product;
- secondly, do rough predictions and spend the rest of the time looking for options as to what will happen given various scenarios — both good and bad.

In the former case, the managers are unlikely to have much input to the process by which forecasts are generated, nor faith in the results. In the latter case, the process is visible and the options given market conditions can be evaluated.

This also involves setting up frameworks which can be improved on for future product launches – they can review what they decided would happen given a certain set of conditions, then how their reaction to this would work. The first looks at handling the cause of a problem, the uncertainty inherent with product volume forecasting, and tries to remove it. The second accepts that variability exists but focuses on the task of pre-evaluating various management strategies given various sets of conditions.

8.4 MATHEMATICAL MODELLING TECHNIQUES

The use of mathematical models in decision-making is widespread, ranging from basic spreadsheet calculations to the most advanced statistical techniques. Table 8.1 indicates the most used techniques, a description of their usage and survey results indicating the degree to which they are employed with either frequent or moderate usage in industry (from Forgionne, 1983).

Table 8.1 The use and level of application of a variety of mathematical modelling techniques in decision-making

Technique	Description	Utilisation (see note below) (%)
Simulation	Computer modelling of a scenario	87.1
Linear programming	Optimal allocation of restricted resources to maximise or minimise a variable (such as price or cost)	74.2
Network analysis through CPM or PERT	Obtaining the logic of both precedence relationships and time requirements in a project environment through graphical means (*see* Chapters 3 and 4)	74.2
Queueing theory	Shows how a system reacts when faced with a random (stochastic) customer who demands the services of that system	59.7
Decision trees	Graphical method for describing the flow of decisions depending on the possibilities available at each juncture. May be pursued as a statement of possibilities or with statistical analysis	(not included in this survey) 60 (estimated)
Markow processes	To determine, in a sequential manner, the probability of the occurrence of certain events	(not included in this survey) 30 (estimated)

Note: Forgionne (1983) shows the percentage of respondents to their survey who indicated frequent or moderate usage of the techniques

Each of these techniques required differing levels of mathematical skill to use effectively and would justify a chapter on each. For a detailed discussion of linear and integer programming, queueing theory and Markow processes, *see*, for example, Anderson *et al.* (1991), and Dennis and Dennis (1991). The role of simulation, network analysis and decision trees are discussed below.

8.5 PROBLEM-SOLVING TOOLS

The basic problem-solving tools of the project manager include Pareto analysis and Ishikawa/fishbone diagrams.

Pareto analysis

Pareto was an 18th century economist, who found that 80 per cent of the wealth of Milan was held by 20 per cent of the people. This 80/20 'rule' often recurs – many companies find that 80 per cent of their profits are generated by 20 per cent of their products or services (*see* Fig. 8.2), or that 20 per cent of their clients provide 80 per cent of their business. The Pareto principle applied to problem-solving means that part of the initial analysis is to discover which 20 per cent of causes are causing 80 per cent of the problems. The effort of the problem-solvers can then be focused on establishing solutions to the major factors. Over time, the 80 per cent of problems have been removed, but the principle is still valid, stated simply – apply effort where it is going to yield the greatest result.

Ishikawa/fishbone diagrams

The fishbone diagram is a simple graphical technique which can help structure a problem and guide a team into seeking further information about the nature

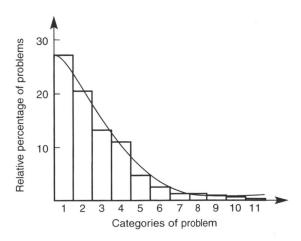

Figure 8.2 Pareto analysis

of the system under consideration. The effect is shown on the right-hand end of the diagram. The causes are then broken down into categories and these are then further deconstructed to show what contributes to that problem from those categories.

The problem of late delivery of software to clients is considered in the example shown in Fig. 8.3. As can be seen, the problem is broken down into four main subject areas – management of the team, specification of the software, the people in the development team, and the hardware on which they are working. Each of these is then broken down. The predominant cause is shown by highlighting the particular area – in this case it is the changing of the specification during development.

Further problem-solving tools (also called tools of quality control) may be found in Bicheno (1991), Ozeki and Asaka (1990) and Mizuno (1988).

8.6 CAUSE-EFFECT-CAUSE ANALYSIS

Several challenges frequently emerge during the problem-solving process:

- the problem is complex and difficult to structure;
- people enter the discussions with solutions in mind rather than the analysis of the problem itself.

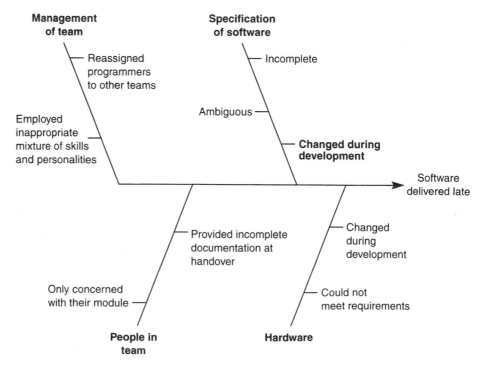

Figure 8.3 Ishikawa/fishbone diagram applied to late delivery problem

This leads either to stagnation in the process due to the inability to handle the complexity or inappropriate solutions being given lengthy discussion time. Neither of these is likely to promote good decision-making. Amongst the problem-solving techniques that have sought to overcome these challenges is cause-effect-cause analysis. This is appropriate where:

- a trained, literate and skilful facilitator is available;
- the group are open to consideration of new problem-solving methods.

The objective is to analyse what the group states to be the undesirable effects of the problem (the gap) to find the root cause or causes. These can then be systematically addressed, rather than attention being focused on the effects. This is an excellent way to bound a problem and come up with a detailed description of its nature. The technique is not novel, but has recently been popularised by Goldratt in his treatment of it as part of his 'theory of constraints'. It has also been used by others including Obeng (1994). Used as above it can be very powerful. It has been found from experience to be less useful for solving tactical problems than for strategic ones as the skills and rigour of checking the logic of the system are not always available at the lower levels of companies.

The Japanese use the technique of asking why a problem occurs five times (the five whys) – this gets to the root of the problem as they see it, though it is likely to suggest a single root cause rather than, as often happens, several. The process is similar for constructing cause-effect-cause analysis – the logic has to be preserved in both the reality of the effects listed (do they exist?) and for the linking of causes to effects, for the tool to work.

The task order should be completed as follows. It looks odd to start with, but, like the construction of network diagrams, will become clear once you have practised using it:

- list the effects of the problem you are tackling – development projects are always delivered late, for example. These must all be real entities, i.e. it must be agreed that these do exist as statements in their own right;
- start with this as one bubble in the middle of a page (*see* Fig. 8.4);
- select another of the effects and show how this relates to the first – either as a cause or an effect. Show the result as in Fig. 8.5. This should then be read as: IF A THEN B, e.g. IF [it rains tomorrow] THEN [we will not be able to complete the site testing];
- select other effects and build these round the first two. Many will be inter-linked, though at first sight they appeared unrelated. Go as far as you can, again each time checking the links you have made to ensure that the logic is followed;

Figure 8.4

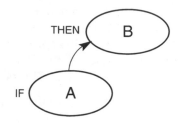

Figure 8.5

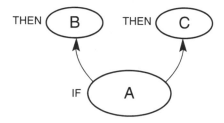

Figure 8.6

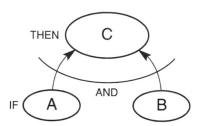

Figure 8.7

- where one cause has a number of effects, this should be drawn as in Fig. 8.6;
- where there is more than one cause linked to an effect, this should be as Fig. 8.7, if there is dependency on both of them, i.e. IF [A] AND [B] THEN [C]. If the dependency is on either [A] OR [B] for [C] to exist, this is drawn without the 'banana' linking the two.

It is often necessary during the course of constructing the diagrams both to amend the entities and add others, e.g. in the example that follows, the link between [doesn't allocate time well] and [permanently tired] is not entirely logical. The additional entity [goes to bed late] was added to keep the logic flow. It was obviously necessary to check, as before, that this entity was real. The example shows how a problem concerning the poor performance of a person was analysed. The limited set of effects were listed as:

[Bill's performance at work is poor]
[He works slower]
[He has a bad attitude]
[He is often late]
[He is permanently tired at work]
[He appears more interested in fishing]
[He does not allocate his time well]

These are then formed into the diagram shown in Fig. 8.8. The additional entities and logic links are a matter of opinion to some degree. A further example of how this technique can be used to structure problems is included at the end of this chapter. For further developments of this technique, see Goldratt (1993).

8.7 DECISION TREES

A similar technnique in format to the cause-effect-cause analysis, decision trees can be treated at a simple qualitative level or by detailed consideration through

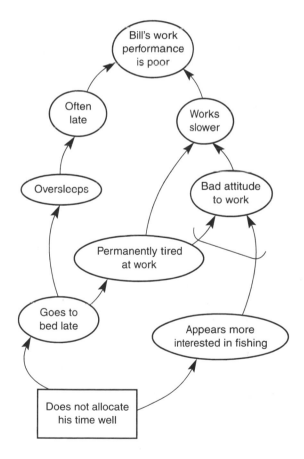

Figure 8.8

the addition of probabilities/distributions to each of the events. Greenwood (1969) shows a basic format for constructing decision trees in Fig 8.9.

The decision points are shown as squares whilst possible outcomes are shown as circles. The possibilities and implications of decisions are therefore clearly identified provided all the decision points are shown. The qualitative treatment of the structure has merit in its simplicity and speed of construction. Further analysis of the probabilities of the chance events occurring can be made, providing a means for assessing the likelihood of needing contingency plans. The use of 'expected value' measurements can be both derived from and applied to this tool. The likelihood of the outcome of an event is assessed, and the cost/benefit in monetary terms calculated based on this outcome. The expected value of the branches can then be calculated from the sum of the subsequent expected values.

Example

A decision has to be made on whether to fund project X or project Y. Each has two possible outcomes. For X, it has a 75 per cent chance of yielding £100 000 but a 25 per cent chance of yielding only £20 000. For Y, it has a 50 per cent chance of yielding £200 000 and a 50 per cent chance that there will be no yield. The decision tree in Fig. 8.10 illustrates the problem.

The financial decision is based on the sum of the expected values of the yields of each branch of the decision tree:

For project X – expected value = $(0.75 \times 100\ 000) + (0.25 \times 20\ 000) = 80\ 000$
For project Y – expected value = $(0.5 \times 200\ 000) + (0.5 \times 0) = 100\ 000$.

The assumption is that we wish to maximise the yield, therefore project Y should be pursued.

This method is attractive in that relatively complex models can be constructed and evaluated quickly. The figures for probabilities and values of

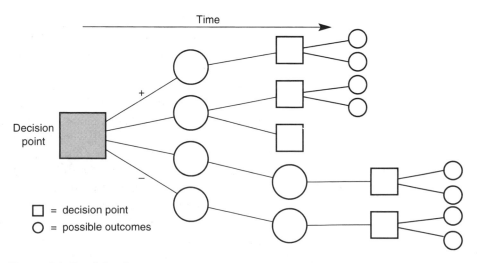

Figure 8.9 Decision trees
Source: Greenwood (1969)

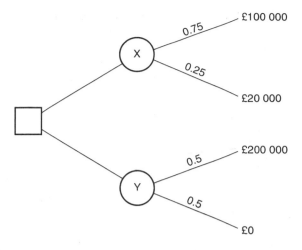

Figure 8.10

return are both a matter of prediction, so the outcome will be determined by the quality of the data the model is provided with.

8.8 SIMPLE DECISION FRAMEWORKS

Many complex decisions are best made if they can be broken down into the desirable elements of the outcome of that decision. Techniques for aiding in this process include the use of attribute analysis and force-field analysis.

Attribute analysis involves breaking down the decision into a set of desirable outcomes. These are then placed alongside the choices in the decision process and rated accordingly. For example, a company wishes to choose a supplier for a project. There are five alternative suppliers (A to E) which are arranged across the top of the table as shown in Table 8.2. The desirable outcomes are arranged down the table (knowledge and experience, reputation, etc.). The manager of the team can then rate the individual suppliers on their perception of how they will perform on each of those outcomes/attributes. The rating is given out of ten, and then totalled for each supplier.

This form of attribute analysis assumes that each of the attributes is of equal importance. Where one is considerably more important than another (e.g. reliability of delivery times may be vital if this is a critical path activity), it can be given an increased weighting – making the score out of 30, say, for that attribute. The totals are viewed in the same way as before. This is clearly a fairly arbitrary means of arriving at the decision, however it is simple to construct and allows a degree of traceability back to how a decision was made. It also enables people to have a discussion on each of the attributes and come up with some relatively objective measure.

Table 8.2 Supplier selection using unweighted attributes

Attribute	A	B	C	D	E
Knowledge and experience	6	7	7	9	8
Reputation	6	6	7	9	10
Prone to strikes/bankruptcy	4	6	9	9	9
Significance of their support	4	8	7	9	9
Design appreciation and conformance	7	7	8	8	9
QA system	5	6	8	9	9
Defects and warranty claims to date	7	6	8	9	10
Reliability of delivery times	6	6	6	9	10
Cost control	7	6	7	6	6
Service level	8	7	8	8	10
Total	60	65	75	85	90

where 1 = very bad
       10 = excellent

Force-field analysis examines the strengths of different influences on a decision. This is best illustrated through the following example (*see* Fig. 8.11). The decision to stand for election to a representative body (student's union council, parish or town council, club committee, etc.) has a number of implications. Firstly, the time input to get elected may be substantial and the fear of losing the election significant. There is an opportunity cost – other work has to be put off until after the project is complete (which generally proves to be a poor career

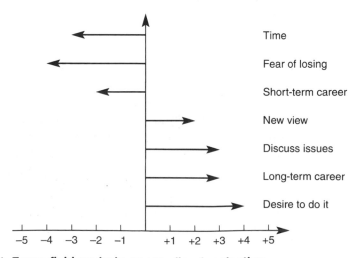

Figure 8.11 Force-field analysis on standing for election

move, at least in the short term). There are benefits, such as the requirement to take a new view on a subject and to discuss issues that affect your life. It may improve your CV and career prospects. A major consideration is also whether you want to be elected. These influences can then be rated on a 0-5 scale as being positive (stand for election) or negative (find something better to do). The influences with some numbers assigned are shown in Fig. 8.11. As can be seen, by summing the positive (+12) and negative influences (-9) and subtracting the negative from the positive, the decision was positive.

8.9 DECISION-SUPPORT SYSTEMS

The principle which decision-support systems embrace is that there is sufficient knowledge existing for the subject to be considered complex, and therefore can be better interpreted through the abilities of computers to deal with large amounts of information. The knowledge must exist within the system, and this is provided through the contribution of experts in the relevant subjects.

The most basic form of decision-support system is a database. The data is structured in 'fields' which the database system can manipulate and structure as required. One example is the database of poisons held at Llandough Hospital in Cardiff – the effects of the poison, and its antidote or appropriate treatment are held on a central computer which other hospitals can access by telephone. The decision on the appropriate form of treatment is taken without the need for guesswork by the treating doctor. Another use of the information on that database is to track back from the symptoms to the nature of the poison.

A further development of the database is the expert system – otherwise known as artificial intelligence. The expert system takes the expert knowledge, usually gained from an individual or a number of individuals over a period of time. Curtis (1995) states:

'An expert system typically:
- incorporates expert knowledge in a particular subject area, usually by storing and representing this as rules or other representative forms (knowledge base);
- separates the general knowledge from the details of a particular case under consideration to which the knowledge base is applied (particular context);
- clearly distinguishes the knowledge from the mechanism of reasoning (inference engine);
- possesses an interactive user interface for providing explanations, justifications and questions to the user;
- provides, as its output, advice or decisions in the area of expertise.'

The logic IF [A] THEN [B] is simple for computers to handle. Decision-taking far more often involves the logic IF to a certain extent [A] THEN to a certain extent [B]. This is known as 'fuzzy logic' and needs further examination before it is amenable to computer analysis.

This system of rules can be modelled directly as a system, although for people who do not have this level of programming skills, the use of an expert system 'shell' is likely to be the most beneficial.

8.10 THE IMPLICATIONS FOR DECISION-MAKERS OF CHAOS THEORY

Projects represent goal-oriented systems. The conventional models of planning (through network analysis and discounted cash flow, for example) treat projects as closed systems, hence the rapid redundancy of the project plans (as discussed in Chapter 6). As shown in Chapter 6, systems can be represented as exhibiting either stable, predictable characteristics, or instability, where the reponse of the system is unpredictable. The successful project organisation will have systems that operate on the boundaries of stability, a state away from that of equilibrium. As Stacey (1993) explains:

> 'The theory of chaos explains the nature of the border area between stability and instability: it is a state in which a system combines both stability and instability to generate patterns of behaviour that are irregular and inherently unpredictable, but yet have a structure.'

There is an apparent contradiction in this statement: irregularity and unpredictability imply random behaviour, but the patterns generated have an implicit order. The conflict is resolved by stating the timeframe over which the system performs has a degree of predictability – it is considerably shorter than conventional wisdom would have us believe. Furthermore, the nature of the predictability is not at the same level of precision – figures should be considered to the nearest order of magnitude rather than the nth decimal point.

Chaos theory is the result of investigations into the behaviour of non-linear feedback systems (Gleick, 1988). The work has been carried out by analysing the behaviour of mathematical models at the boundaries between the point where they are stable and hence predictable, and when they go unstable (the output becomes infinite).

The implications of this work include the realisation of the importance of the system's starting point. Stacey further notes:

> 'In "bounded instability" or "chaos", the system operates to amplify tiny changes in starting conditions into major alterations of consequent behaviour. This is called "sensitive dependence on initial conditions".'

Changes that are so small that they could not feasibly be detected are shown to have a totally disproportionate effect on the behaviour of the system, and in particular the dimension that project management is most concerned with – namely the output. This kind of sensitive dependence gave rise to what is known as the 'Butterfly effect' – the notion that a butterfly flapping its wings on one side of the world, causes a storm to break on the other (the weather is a good example of a chaotic system).

The attainment of success is not then focused on the mechanistic determination through mathematical models of decision paths. This would be to ignore the inherent assumptions in those models, namely that they are closed-loop stable systems. This is a very contentious view, though one that is borne out regularly in practice. This questions the role of the techniques discussed in Chapters 3 and 4 and shown in Table 8.1. The implication for management decision-makers is that the need is for ongoing vigilance to see trends emerging and to look for the occurrence of short-term patterns (the systems overall may be considered to be chaotic, but within limited timeframes there may be a degree of order). These short-term patterns are called 'fractals' in mathematical terms and can be demonstrated graphically (*see* Stacey, 1993 and Penrose, 1989). Fractals have the property that no matter what magnification they are viewed under, the shapes are roughly the same. They provide little hope, however, of the ability to predict the performance of systems – the differences between starting conditions being too small to measure, and hence are of little use in predictive work.

In such systems long-term planning is unworkable as the state of future patterns cannot be determined, particularly in strategic decision-making. An examination of the effectiveness of technology strategy was carried out by Schnaars (1989). He reports that forecasts were generated based on searches of past data for trends, projections forward from limited initial data, dubious patterns and historical precedent. The result was an overall success rate of less than 20 per cent in the forecasts he surveyed. In the majority of cases the tendency was for the forecasters to become emotionally involved in the technology that they were forecasting and hence wildly over-estimate the markets and rates of progress of technology. This bias to the forecasts was highly significant and showed that there were considerably more predictions for growth markets than could possibly exist in reality. The notable exception was the explosion in the world market for personal computers, which was understated by several orders of magnitude. The Schnaars survey is not necessarily a representative sample of all forecasts made, but it should be stated that it is rare for prior forecasts to be held up for inspection to see how well they represented the future they were predicting. The truly clear crystal ball is still in development....

Commenting on the management science literature, Schnaars further states:

'The technical books worship calculation in a chaotic world that negates the very premise of the techniques they champion. The models they propose are of especially limited value on the softer applications, such as new product and technological forecasting, where numbers are scarce and irregularities occur regularly.'

The practical implications for project managers trying to assemble or assess forecasts which act as a basis for financial justification are:

- avoid emotional involvement with technology – it may be technically very exciting, but this will not necessarily mean successful commercialisation;
- check the fundamental market conditions, in particular are the support systems and the culture present to adopt the development?
- stress the cost:benefit from the perspective of your stakeholders or customers.

There is a further implication for management. There have been many management paradigms which have emerged over the last ten years, all promising the possibility of great rewards. The results (Maylor, 1995) have been very mixed. The only management initiatives which have been proven are those that focus on attaining strategic flexibility – the ability to move from one mode of competitive advantage to another. This is in line with chaos theory – the inability of any single management paradigm to provide long-standing competitive advantage is now undoubted.

8.11 THE IMPORTANCE OF THE FOLLOW-UP ACTIONS

Many poor decisions have been 'rescued' by the work which followed. This process will be aided the more people have 'bought in' to that decision. Gaining that kind of commitment will only work if the style of management is participative – confrontational management will focus the decision back on to the decision-maker. This can be of benefit if the manager wishes to insulate the team from external elements.

Example – Reebok launches 'the pump'

Reebok launched their 'pump' range of sports shoes at a show where they had not planned to do so and despite their marketing plan being incomplete. The pump offered the wearer new levels of comfort due to part of the shoe being inflatable – it would then mould exactly to the contours of the wearer's foot. The case is an excellent example of opportunism – their chief executive officer was attending a European trade show and saw that there was little by way of innovative new products being presented. He made the decision to launch the product at that show, without waiting for the normal cycle of development to be completed. This was a bold move which gained the company a great deal of positive publicity – the follow-up action, however, made the decision a good one. The company was then mobilised to carry through the implications of this decision and appears to have managed to do so well. Had the company itself not been so capable, the decision, in retrospect, would have been a very poor one.

PROJECT MANAGEMENT IN PRACTICE: **THE USE OF CAUSE-EFFECT-CAUSE ANALYSIS**

A board meeting was held at the Mighty Sealing Company. There was growing concern about the competitive environment in which the company was operating. Board members were asked to state what they felt the major problems were. They highlighted eight issues. These were:

1 Existing market is in decline.
2 Sales people do not sell effectively.
3 We have insufficient sales support material.
4 We have an inadequate entry barrier (to the markets in which we operate).
5 We are confused as to which products we should sell.

6 We are unable to exploit new markets.

7 We do not really understand our market environment.

8 There is increasing competition.

These problems or 'un-desirable effects' (UDEs) provided the basis for constructing the logic diagram (the 'current reality tree'). Other entities (or logic elements) were introduced to the tree to clarify the logic (*see* Fig. 8.12, p. 216). The current reality tree shows that there are many effects (including the most significant – the decline in sales volume), but that there is one major cause, over which the company have some control – UDE no. 7 – [we do not really understand our market environment]. This finding provided the basis for the next steps.

Understanding the competitive environment would rely heavily on the company: customer interface – the sales force. In order to understand the role and conflicts that the sales people have, a series of 'selling effectiveness clouds' were constructed (*see* Fig. 8.13, p. 217). Issues included the conflict of 'time on the job' where the sales force are with prospects and clients and 'time off the job' where they are undertaking training. These two tasks clearly rely on one another, but are in conflict.

In order to start to resolve these conflicts, the same form of logic diagramming was used. The result: the 'future reality tree' where the root causes are put in place to result in a particular desired effect (in this case sales volume grows). This is shown in Fig. 8.14 (p. 218).

The method shown allowed a complex problem to be addressed in a systematic way, and initiatives put in place to help better understand the processes that were taking place. How these would then contribute to the desired objective could then be mapped.

Case discussion

1 What is the benefit of constructing a 'current reality tree'?

2 Why is it necessary to insert additional elements into the tree?

3 Why would focusing on 'selling effectiveness' lead to the better understanding of the market?

4 Explain the reason for the cloud which considers the conflict between 'salesmen perceive selling is an art', and 'selling is a science'.

5 Evaluate the 'future reality tree' – does it resolve the UDEs listed at the start of the exercise?

SUMMARY OF KEY POINTS

- a problem is the gap between perceptions of an actual situation and that of the expected or required situation;
- problems may be categorised according to the required reaction time and the nature of the response required;
- problem responses may be programmed through procedures or reasoned through the problem-solving cycle;
- a model may be constructed either qualitatively (through descriptive modelling) or quantitatively (through mathematical modelling) to provide a representation of reality which can be tested under controlled conditions;

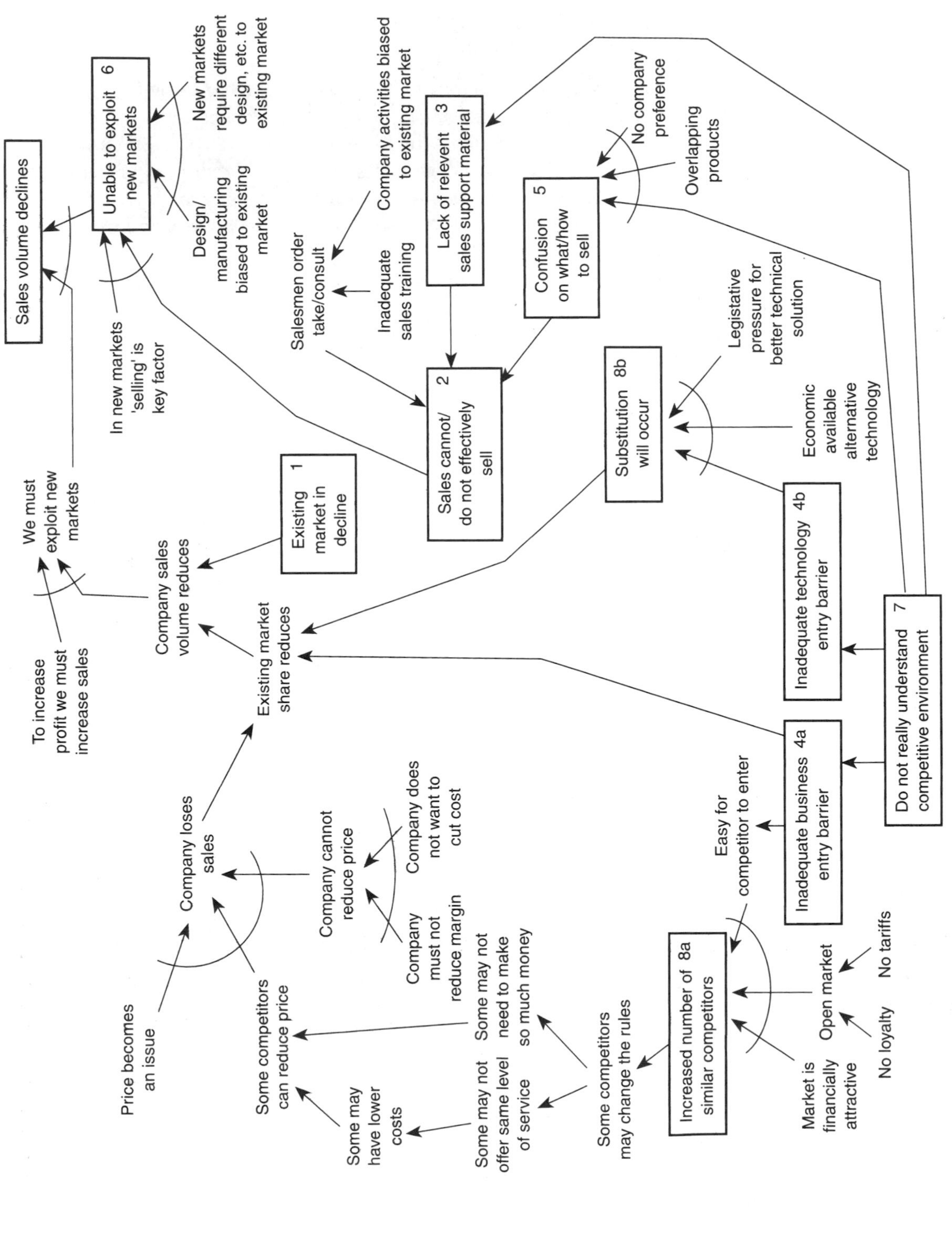

Figure 8.12 Current reality tree

Figure 8.13 Selling effectiveness clouds

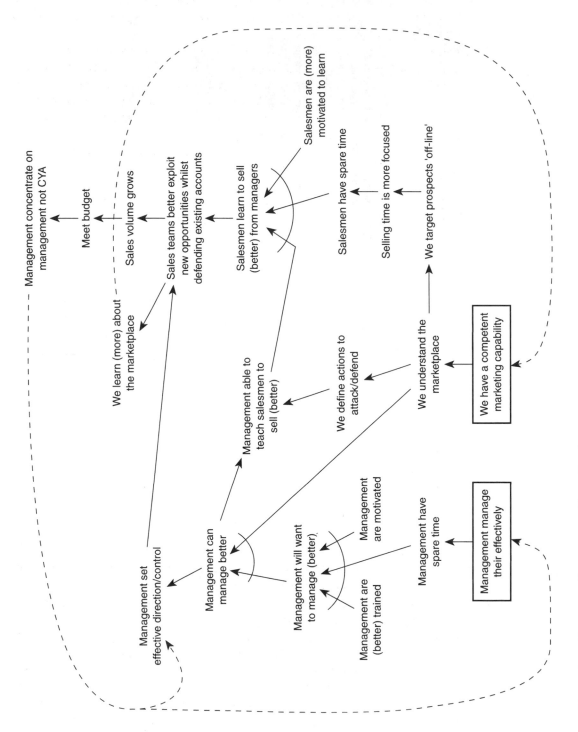

Figure 8.14 Future reality tree – selling effectiveness

- uncertainty can be handled either through statistical means, calculating the most likely set of events, or through managerial action to make the system more robust to the effects of uncertainty;
- various mathematical tools can be employed to take away the need for subjective decision-making in some areas, whilst providing decision support in others;
- Ishikawa/fishbone diagrams provide a graphical method for structuring problems; Pareto analysis provides a guide as to which problems to tackle first;
- cause-effect-cause analysis provides a graphical technique for finding the 'root' of a problem through structuring the logic of the situation;
- other problem-solving tools include decision trees where the route that actions take can be graphically evaluated and probabilities then assigned to each route if required;
- decision-support systems are normally computer-based and allow expert knowledge to be expressed as a series of rules which are then interpreted by the system;
- gut-feel and experience have a vital role to play in decision-making, and this can be structured through techniques such as 'breakthrough thinking';
- chaos theory renders many of the assumptions about long-term planning invalid, and shows the need for organisations to develop their strategic flexibility in order to respond to the effects of this chaos rather than try and adhere to plans or forecasts that try to ignore it.

KEY TERMS	problem-solving cycle	cause-effect-cause analysis
	programmed actions	decision frameworks
	bounding a problem	decision trees
	brainstorming	attribute analysis
	management science/operational	force-field analysis
	research	decision-support systems
	what-if analysis	expert systems/artificial intelligence
	Pareto analysis	breakthrough thinking
	Ishikawa/fishbone diagrams	chaos

REVIEW AND DISCUSSION QUESTIONS

1 Discuss the statement made by Price in the introduction to this chapter – that '..Man is a risk-addicted animal'.

2 How might the tools outlined in this chapter reduce the risk in decision-making?

3 Show the advantages of having pre-programmed actions
   (a) as part of a health and safety policy – for example in the event of a fire
   (b) in the handling of client enquiries
   (c) for the installation of new work procedures.

4 Show the effect of time on problem-solving and give practical examples of each of the different timescales.

5 What is the role of 'brainstorming' and how might it be used to greatest effect?

6 What are the major inputs to the decision-making process and how might these be best harnessed to ensure that the decision-making process is effective?

7 What are the basic forms of systems model? Give an example of each and their role in a project environment.

8 As a project manager in a development activity for a new range of computer software, discuss how uncertainty may be handled.

9 You are the coordinator of a moderately complex project. The following problems have arisen during the execution phase of previous projects with the resulting delays as shown. Use an appropriate technique to show which of the problems you would focus your attention on and show the results of your analysis graphically.

Problem	Delay (days)
A Late delivery from suppliers	36
B Last minute re-design of assembly due to customer change of specification	7
C Suppliers fail to meet the quality levels required in goods supplied	41
D Schedule did not leave enough time for testing	5
E Components did not fit together when assembled	6
F Customer rejected initial trial system	12
G Engineer left team during the project	16
H Office move was scheduled for during the completion phase	5
J Hauliers firm sacked by customer due to dispute over delivery times	3

10 Select a problem with which you have been involved, and use the Ishikawa/fishbone diagram to structure the causes of the problem. Indicate what you feel to be the biggest causal factor.

11 State the same problem using cause-effect-cause analysis, showing the relationship between the various facets of the problem. Does the root cause you indicated above still hold?

12 Use a decision-tree model to show the effect on your finances of various decisions regarding the choice of a holiday this summer.

13 Discuss the role that decision-support systems such as expert systems will play in the decision-making of the modern project manager.

14 Discuss the benefits of ensuring that all 'hard' and soft information is included in the decision-making process.

15 Why has chaos theory changed the way we regard systems?

16 Forecast what the home of ten years' time will contain in the way of labour-saving gadgets and entertainment. If there are 30 million homes in the UK by this time, consider how many of these will have taken up this technology. Filter these ideas by considering:
(a) the cost:benefit to the purchaser.
(b) whether your view is affected by your enthusiasm for the technology.
(c) whether there would be hard statistical evidence which could be drawn upon to prove your estimates of the likely take-up of the new technology.

REFERENCES

Anderson, D.R., D.J. Sweeney and T.A. Williams *An Introduction to Management Science* (1991), 6th edition, West.

Bicheno, J. (1991) *34 for Quality*, Picsie Books.

Curtis, G. (1995) *Business Information Systems*, 2nd edition, Addison Wesley, pp. 536–7.

Drucker (1956), *Nation's Business*, The Chamber of Commerce of the US, April.

Dennis, T.L. and L.B. Dennis (1991) *Management Science*, West Publishing.

Forgionne, G. (1983) 'Corporate Management Science Activities: An Update', *Interfaces*, vol. 13, no. 3, June.

Goldratt, E. (1993) *Theory of Constraints*, North River Press.

Gleick, J. (1988) *Chaos: The Making of a New Science*, Heinemann.

Greenwood, W.T. (1969), *Decision Theory and Information Systems*, South Western, pp. 83–104.

Jennings, D. and S. Wattam (1994) *Decision-Making: An Integrated Approach*, Pitman Publishing.

Maylor (1995) *Beyond Competitive Advantage: A Competitive Relevance Approach to Manufacturing Strategy*, Matador Conference, April.

Mizuno, S. (ed.) (1988) *Management for Quality Improvement: The 7 New QC Tools*, Productivity Press.

Nonaka (1988) 'Creating Organisational Order Out of Chaos: Self Renewal in Japanese Firms', *California Management Review*, Spring, pp. 57–73.

Obeng, E. (1994) *All Change: The Project Leader's Secret Handbook*, Financial Times/ Pitman Publishing.

Ozeki, K. and T. Asaka (1990) *Handbook of Quality Tools – The Japanese Approach*, Productivity Press.

Penrose, R. (1989) *The Emperor's New Mind: Concerning Computers, Minds and the Laws of Physics*, Oxford University Press.

Peters, T. (1987) *Thriving on Chaos*, Macmillan.

Price, F. (1984) *Right First Time*, Wildwood House, p. 66.

Schnaars, S. P. (1989) *Megamistakes: Forecasting & The Myth of Rapid Technological Change*, Free Press.

Stacey, R.D. (1991) *The Chaos Frontier: Creative Strategic Control for Business*, Butterworth–Heinemann.

Stacey, R.D. (1993) *Strategic Management and Organisational Dynamics*, Pitman Publishing, pp. 208–46.

Wu, B. (1994) *Manufacturing Systems Design and Analysis*, 2nd edition, Chapman & Hall.

FURTHER READING

Cooke, S. and N. Slack (1991) *Making Management Decisions*, 2nd edition, Prentice Hall International.

Goldratt, E. (1995) *It's Not Luck*, North River Press, 1995.

Littlechild, S.C. and M.F. Shutler (eds) (1991) *Operations Research In Management*, Prentice Hall.

Rivett, P. (1994) *The Craft of Decision Modelling*, Wiley.

CHAPTER 9

Project review

Once the main part of the work is completed, it is very tempting to move on rather than ensure that the work is completed and the maximum benefit yielded from it. How the last phases of 'check and act on the results of the checks' are managed will determine to a large extent the views of stakeholders on the outcomes as well as set the chances for future project success.

These final processes carry a number of paradoxes which the project manager will have to address:

- *trying to make the review process objective whilst taking into account a rich picture of the events surrounding project performance;*
- *relating procedural conformance to project performance;*
- *the establishment of long-term programmes of improvement whilst being assessed on short-term measures which are predominantly financial;*
- *meeting the needs of the organisation as well as the stakeholders.*

Such conflict is not easily resolved, particularly where weak guidance is provided from senior management. These same people may be demanding ever greater performance, without providing the means to improve. Increasing the level of investment in the business or technology is not going to provide a basis for a competitive position which cannot be copied. Improving the processes carried out through management action is the only way for this to become a sustainable process.

Considering the role of world-class performers through benchmarking and adapting their principles is just one tool in the improvement process. The role of the project manager will become increasingly important provided they can find ways to adapt to the changes required.

9.1 PROJECT COMPLETION AND HANDOVER

The major elements that will require the attention of the project manager during this phase are:

- ensuring there is an incentive for the project to be finished and that activities are completed;
- ensuring documentation is provided;
- closing down the project systems; particularly the accounting systems;
- constructing the immediate review of activities – providing a starting point for all improvement activities;
- disposal of assets that arc surplus to requirements;
- providing the best basis for future projects;
- ensuring that all stakeholders are satisfied;
- providing the basis for future reviews of activities.

The situation the project manager needs to avoid is where a project spends 90 per cent of its life 90 per cent complete. Finishing the activities so that resources can be released for other work and minimising the costs incurred during the close-down phase are vital. There is a trade-off to be considered here – how much time and resource should be put into the closing of activities? At one extreme, there is a temptation to abandon the activities in a great rush to move onto other tasks. Such action risks undue haste and removes the possibilities for maximising the benefit of the review, for example. At the other, a close-down process can become drawn out, nothing is really finished, and the overhead costs of the activities remaining keep escalating. Which approach is taken often depends on the success or otherwise of the project – it is clearly much more desirable to spend time closing a project which is an apparent success, whereas a disaster is more likely to be rapidly abandoned. As already discussed, the review process is equally important in either case, as are the other activities listed above.

In the kind of organisation where people are brought in on contract, for the duration of that project alone, and are paid a time rate (according to the amount of time they spend working on it), there is little incentive for the work to be finished on time. Indeed, it is within their interests to ensure that things go mildly wrong and result in the plan of work being extended. The provision of some form of bonus for early completion should be considered where personnel have an active input to the result. Contractors and subcontractors should be treated as suppliers in this respect and be eligible for development effort.

Documentation

The purpose of providing documentation is:

- to give the customer of the output of the project guidance on the operation and maintenance of the item provided;

- to provide evidence that the project has been completed in a proper manner;
- to provide the basis for one form of the assessment activity;
- to allow any future work on the same system to be based on good information rather than assumptions.

In addition it should be noted:

1 If it is left to the end to write documentation, much information can be lost, as staff are already re-assigned to other activities and the task gets left to certain individuals to complete. This can be a soul-destroying task and one that most people dread. The reluctance to carry out this kind of task can be explained by the application of Handy's cultural model of the four gods – documentation of a system requires a formal culture, whereas the project activities required task or existential working. Including this activity as part of the work breakdown structure is vital, rather than hoping that it will be carried out as an un-accounted extra. Where time is short, this activity should not be regarded as the one that can be 'squeezed' to provide slack for other hard-pressed activities.

2 The nature of the documentation includes the formal items presented throughout the course of the work and the communication documents and notes of individuals. Individuals need to keep their own logbooks of events, discussions and agreements. The professional institutes require these to be kept during training as the basis for assessment of training programmes. Their long-term use is becoming more important as the issue of professional liability becomes more pertinent. Such a document might provide valuable material should an individual be implicated in an enquiry involving professional negligence.

3 Formal documentation includes contract, permissions, letters and memoranda. All documentation with legal ramifications must be kept, but many memoranda and generally circulated documents are kept when they are never likely to be ever needed again. The number of filing cabinets that an individual has does not indicate their importance. Indeed, developments in file management technology have enabled most filing cabinets to be eliminated, by using a document storage system that incorporates a scanner which digitises the original image of the document and stores it on a magnetic disk. A policy should be established for documents generated by wordprocessors, as to whether these need to be stored in hard-copy form (i.e. on paper) or whether the inclusion of floppy disks in records is acceptable. Such magnetic media is not a guarantee of security as they can be corrupted by heat or magnetism and systems change, resulting in incompatibility of formats.

4 BS-EN-ISO 9001 states the requirement for record storage: that the organisation should provide a filing system for the information, in which there is a guide as to the disposition of any item of information and that these records are kept for a suitable period of time. The larger the project, the longer it is likely that records will have to be kept, though seven years is typical.

5 Much effort is spent on data security – organisations jealously guard what they consider to be commercial information and many have a ban on disclosure to outsiders. Many companies have their own versions of 'The Official Secrets Act' which employees or contractors, particularly in new product development, are required to sign prior to commencing work. However, there is in general too much effort spent on keeping information from customers and competitors.

   Clearly in defence and other sectors that have national security matters at stake, this is a real issue, but the majority of companies jealously guard material that would not benefit competitors or other adversaries and is generally historical. Even cost data is highly transient and so unlikely to be beneficial to outside parties.

The close-down activities should form part of the detailed planning – and the derivation of checklists can provide an objective means of ensuring that the finishing tasks are carried out. Such a checklist is:

- an *aide-mémoire* in addition to formal work allocation;
- evidence that the close-down tasks were planned;
- evidence, when completed, that the tasks were carried out, by whom and when.

Closing down the project systems

The activity curve shown in Chapter 2 shows that, in general, the level of activity falls off as the project nears completion. This is accompanied by a slow-down in the spending rate – both on labour and materials. As people leave the project team it must be remembered that the systems, in particular the accounting and quality systems, are still operational. For the accounting systems, it is likely that people will know the codes against which items could be charged. Rather than deplete new budgets, there is always the temptation to try to get expenditure set against other budgets. In order to ensure that costs are not run up against project codes, the project manager must ensure that further unauthorised expenditure is curtailed. There will, however, be late invoices being received from suppliers and possibly overhanging administration activities which will need to continue being charged. These must be paid and are one of the reasons why the financial position at the end of major work does not always provide a good indicator of the financial performance of the project overall.

   Formal notice of closures are issued in many industries to inform other staff and support systems that there are no further activities to be carried out or charges to be made.

   In contract project activities, the legal termination of activities occurs at the time when the customer 'signs off' the project. It is often tempting for work to continue after this has occurred and for the team to provide the customer with 'free' consultancy. Many service projects have this element, in particular in information technology. However, no organisation can afford to:

- cut the customer off completely at this point and ruin the possibilities for future business;
- continue to provide services for which they do not charge.

In reality, if this 'consultancy' is required on an ongoing basis, it is likely to indicate that other aspects of the project execution were less well managed. This could be in particular the handover process or the failure of documentation to identify solutions to problems. Where the completion criteria for projects are left open, you are more likely to end up providing further benefits with possibly no hope of obtaining payment for them. The provision of further services outside the remit of the plan but required by the customer should be included as a quality cost (*see* Chapter 6).

Conducting project reviews

The review system contains key elements, providing further control or corrective actions and closing the loop of plan-do-check-act:

- immediate 'post-mortem' on the activities;
- immediate remedial and improvement action;
- long-term audit and review;
- strategic and procedural changes.

The formal long-term review may prescribe major procedural or strategic changes. The one that is carried out as a completion phase activity is intended to provide rapid feedback on the performance of individuals and systems that the dispersing team members can take away with them. It is the basis for identifying short-term needs, such as procedural changes or changes in skills required by individuals. People need rapid feedback on their own performance – the organisation should provide this in order that:

- they know what aspects of their performance should be repeated;
- managers can identify training or educational requirements;
- the organisation can assess the utility of individuals to future teams.

A further role of the post-mortem is to provide a case-history of the project which is then a guide as to the documentation that will be required, over and above that already compiled, for the long-term audit.

The assessor or reviewer in this case should be someone who has been associated with the project and knows the challenges – physical, political, environmental, financial and personal that were faced during all phases. The likely reviewers are the sponsor and the manager, though many feel that the manager could not be expected to be sufficiently objective about the process.

One of the tools which is of considerable benefit to short-term improvement is an audit of the management by the team (assumes that the team is managed by an individual rather than being autonomous). Such characteristics as attitude, skills, approachability, openness, ability to delegate authority yet share responsibility, ability to represent the project team to others, and willingness to embrace change, may be assessed. This kind of management questionnaire can demonstrate very clearly that the manager is serious about improving the 'management product' through continuous self-improvement, rather than just preaching the message to others.

The feedback gained by individuals (both managers and team members) provides reinforcement for good skills and behaviours and a path for change where improvement is required. This data is a vital input to the work of the human resources function, in identifying satisfaction levels associated with different ways of working and levels of motivation.

Disposal of assets

Assets left at the end of activities include:

- project hardware;
- surplus stocks;
- administration facilities.

The surplus stocks represent waste – they were not needed and should not have been supplied. It is considered inevitable that this will happen, but is not desirable (*see* 'Seven Wastes', Section 9.5 page 237). Other project hardware that is not absorbed by the controlling organisation needs to be disposed of. This is often carried out with the view that as the job is finished, the sooner they are eliminated from the accounts, the site or just from view, the better. Valuable material is put in skips, left to rot or any number of other options that any entrepreneur would balk at. Trying to encourage people to think of beneficial means of disposal of assets is unnatural for many – they have the attitude that the organisation can afford it and often that 'the paperwork would cost more to raise than would be raised in revenue from its proper sale'. This is, however, more symptomatic of galloping bureaucracy than detachment of the individual from financial results. Theft of assets is also a major consideration which the project manager needs to take into account to minimise – losses through this can be significant and conventional security measures are not always as effective as may be required.

Ensuring that all stakeholders are satisfied

Marketing influences much of our consumer behaviour, consciously or otherwise, from the clothes that we wear to the brands of groceries we buy. Selling success is an unpopular concept on this side of the Atlantic, but one that should be considered in enhancing the customers' image of the project organisation. The data for such promotion should come from the review process (for total disasters, the potential and opportunities for improvement come from the same source). The concept of the 'product surround' should be utilised – actual performance accounts for 20 per cent of people's perceptions (and hence impact) but costs 80 per cent of the budget to achieve. The 80 per cent of the impact of the work carried out comes from 20 per cent of the spend. Put simply, '... an ounce of image is worth a pound of performance'. Achieving good publicity can have internal benefits as it is seen that items of good performance are being both looked for and recognised – organisations are often regarded as only after 'catching you out for doing something wrong'.

9.2 LONG-TERM PROJECT AUDIT AND REVIEW

The process of auditing and reviewing activities at a slight time distance from their execution is a part of normal life in many project organisations. This is due to the timeframe over which the results of the actions and the way in which they were carried out become evident. The return-on-development activities may take even longer to yield the benefits that were attributed to them during the planning process. This should form part of the normal project processes, just as planning does. The process itself requires:

- a reason to exist;
- time;
- information;
- resources;
- credibility.

The reason for reviews is often described as 'praise of the unworthy followed by punishment of the innocent'. The reason must go beyond this and be set out clearly in the terms of reference. The main goal is to ensure that continuous improvement activities are in place and are followed through. It also provides a point at which the responsibility of the project manager can be objectively assessed.

Time must be allocated from other activities and an appropriate auditor/reviewer arranged. The project manager should be involved in the process. Information should be provided along with the necessary access and authority to obtain further information. It should be resourced, either from central overhead allocation or an amount set aside from the project funds to carry it out. As for the manager, the process must be given credibility. The research should be carried out in a manner which is rigorous but fair, and there should be no hidden agendas (praise or punishment).

The auditing process involves:

- establishing the procedures – the formal statement of intent as to how activities should be carried out, whether financial, quality or environmental;
- checking documentation and other records of practice to show that they have been followed;
- presenting a report detailing the areas where there are deficiencies or irregularities.

An audit is often viewed as a negative process, i.e. it is trying to catch people out. However, it is responsible for identifying inconsistencies, double-checking information as well as seeking alternative viewpoints on the proceedings. There will regularly be conflict into which the players may try to draw the audit team.

The review process involves:

- studying overall performance relative to constraints;
- identifying areas where the procedures failed or have otherwise been shown to be inadequate;
- reporting on the areas and suggesting improvements.

It is a real skill and art to carry out a worthwhile review process. Getting the truth, or many versions of it, and attempting to make sense of the conflicts (as for audits, but with a more open mandate) are common tests. It is always going to be a subjective exercise – this factor is worth remembering. Two different teams, given the same project, are likely to produce totally different reports. This will depend on the skills and biases of the individuals. The review should differ from the audit in one further dimension – that of the focus. Audits look internally, whilst reviews should take into account the impact of the project on the environment as a whole. The changes that were impressed by the environment should also be considered.

The nature of the feedback will differ from the post-mortem type of review. Changes are rarely made to procedure-level events at this stage – the procedures may have already been changed considerably and the context is unlikely to be completely the same again. Where the greatest impact will be felt is in strategic issues – the role of the project manager, of suppliers and the imposition or relinquishing of controls on activities can be examined. Above all, it is likely that a full picture of performance indicators will be available by this time and provide a more complete picture of the accuracy of forecasts and the veracity of other planning assumptions.

In the execution of a formal audit or review, the criteria under consideration will to some extent determine who should be the auditor or reviewer. Expecting someone without accountancy skills, experience or qualification to carry out a financial audit, is unlikely to produce usable or credible results. The criteria for the assessor also require a degree of independence. There is often the tendency in formal organisations which run projects in matrix form for one department or function to assess another's projects and vice versa. This arrangement, whilst being convenient and usually very cost-effective, can be counter-productive as there is the equal chance of complicity or hidden agendas as the departments have old scores to settle. This 'culture of distrust' is perpetuated by such arrangements and simply adds another degree of paying someone to check the work that you have paid someone else to do in the first place. Whilst it can expose incompetence, the audit/review procedure has to be seen as a value-adding activity, rather than simply an opportunity to be negative about the work of others.

The implication of the above is that there can be a worthwhile role for the project audit and review process. An assessor works with the project sponsor and manager to look for areas for improvement. In reality, if you want to find the major areas for improvements, the people who are in the best position to provide this information are those that were directly involved with the activities – the project team themselves. This knowledge is collated with the assessor taking a collaborative role rather than an adversarial one, and utilising their experience to be fair and openly objective, rather than having to indulge in political games-playing. The view should be holistic – no one aspect of the project performance should be considered in isolation and data should be corroborated wherever possible. Substantiating the claims of suppliers (both internal and external) by verification with their customers is always a good check of data. Maintaining a focus which looks externally as well as at the internal data sources ensures that the fundamental objective of 'meeting customer requirements at lowest cost' remains on the management agenda.

Table 9.1 shows the nature of both procedural audits and performance reviews that can be used to assess a project. It shows a variety of criteria and

Table 9.1 - The use of project review and audit

Criteria	Procedural	Performance
Financial	Audit on accounting systems	Assess return on investment, assess cost variances with plans
Time	Conformance to plan	Customer satisfaction with the timeliness of completion and the costs required to provide this
Quality	Conformance to quality manual	Performance level of project output, perceptions of quality by customers and stakeholders
Human resources	Treatment in accordance with contract / legal conditions of employment, or organisation policy	Team spirit, motivation, attitude survey
Environmental	Conformance to policy set out in environmental management manual	Absolute level of environmental impact of project activities
Project planning	Conformance to plan	Cost of the planning process assessed and appropriateness of techniques
Project control	Were measures in place and did corrective action take place?	Did the control activities provide the basis for significant improvement actions?

their methods of assessment. As stated during the work on control, if you only measure financial performance measures, do not be surprised if the focus of the project team rests on short-term performance gains. Carrying out such assessment shows the team how seriously the organisation regards the criteria set out. If policy statements at senior management level are not backed up by the allocation of assessment effort *and* resources for improvement as a result of these assessments, the policies will become discredited.

9.3 CONTINUOUS IMPROVEMENT

'Management-speak' – the language of the (so-called) management expert, now includes many Japanese words. One of the more common of these is 'kaizen' – meaning 'continuous improvement'. Deming's fifth point concerning continuous improvement of products and processes was stated in the section of work on time management. Improving the management process and product clearly forms part of this development.

Many Japanese companies have had representatives interviewed to try to find the secret of their success, particularly in the automotive, electronics, white goods and other repetitive manufacturing sectors. Their steel and other process industries have continued to improve their performance and are often the standard by which their competitors are judged. The continuous seeking of improvement of all activities is the basis of this competitive and performance advantage.

A culture known as the 'learning organisation' is encouraged where the importance of the contribution of individuals is acknowledged. In the current environment, this route to gaining competitiveness is the one which others are going to find difficult to emulate. Competitiveness gained through technology can be overcome or equalled with the purchase of that technology. Similarly for systems and procedures, these too can be fairly quickly copied. The one resource that is very difficult to duplicate is people. Training and education is the basis for people improving themselves and this takes time to achieve. Whilst your competitors may try to poach good staff through better salary offers, giving them a path for improvement can be the way not only to make them more valuable, but of retaining this one non-duplicatable asset.

One of the challenges facing management is how to enthuse people about improvement activities, particularly when improvements in efficiency could result in them becoming 'surplus to requirements' or victims of 'down-' or 'right-sizing'. This kind of industrial 'treachery' is one of the key union oppositions to modern working practices. It is clear that despite the protests of many managers, the people who are left in today's paired-to-the-bone organisations are having to work harder. With this backdrop, persuading people to take a longer-term view can only come from:

- example set by senior management;
- methods of assessment;
- pay systems.

The first point is fairly self-evident and the second was discussed above. The third was alluded to in Chapter 5 in the discussion of motivation. The movement to multi-skilling and requiring people to be more flexible has resulted in the emergence of 'pay by skills acquired'. Staff with a high degree of proficiency in a number of tasks reduces the dependence on individual characters and increases the flexibility of the organisation as a whole.

9.4 BENCHMARKING OF PERFORMANCE AND PROCESS

This is another example of current management jargon which has spawned a large amount of business for the consultancy industry. Organisations are being told, 'how can you be certain that you are as good as you say you are, unless you compare your performace with that of others?' This is a very persuasive logic, but before engaging in any benchmarking activities, a deeper understanding of the possibilities and protocols should be explored.

A benchmark is a reference point – some standard by which other phenomena are judged. It is a temporarily fixed point, with the location or magnitude decided by relevant metrics or measures. The original use of benchmarks was claimed by the early map-makers who needed certain reference points by which to judge others – in this case in spatial distance along three dimensions from the reference point. The distances having been assessed, the new point could also be considered to be a reference point, though the accuracy would be diluted the further one went from the original data.

The large-scale commercialisation of benchmarking activities was begun by Rank Xerox in 1979. Managers from their American operations were encouraged to go to view how their Japanese operations were being managed and compare their performance. Where there were performance differences the methods used were noted to explore the possibilities for adapting the methods to their own plants. Initially fairly informal, the methodology has become more formalised and is viewed as one of the best ways for obtaining ideas for improving both performance and processes. During the compilation of this text, the response from project managers to questions regarding the relevance of benchmarking was on the whole favourable. The most widespread adoption of the use of benchmarking was in manufacturing industry. A CBI/Coopers & Lybrand survey of the top 1000 companies in the UK found that of the 105 respondents to their questionnaire, two-thirds were engaged in benchmarking with 82 per cent regarding it as a success.

The initial approach to benchmarking involved consideration of very basic data, usually financial ratios which provided a means of comparison of the overall effectiveness of management. Other areas of management activity, including maintenance management, have followed this focus on key ratios, though the approach is often limited by the interpretation of the data. Figures without explanation of their means of collection and the meanings of each with clear bounds established as to what they include, are misleading. This understanding of what lay behind the numbers caused problems at a large UK specialist manufacturer when their German holding company carried out a benchmarking study to compare ratios of direct to non-direct staff. The UK operation appeared to be significantly over-staffed with non-directs compared to other companies in the group. On analysis, however, the comparison was not valid as the definitions of direct and non-direct employees were very different – the German company, for example, counted transport operatives as direct employees, whilst the UK operation counted them as support (non-direct) staff. The comparison was between unlike sets of statistics.

The generation of benchmarking data does have clear benefits. The nature of the comparison can be with:

- functional – those conducted within the same functional part of the organisation;
- internal projects – others conducted by the same organisation;
- generic – process-related studies comparing projects with similar processes;
- competitor benchmarking – comparison with competitors.

The objective is to find how the best performers are doing and how these results are achieved. Thus a functional benchmarking exercise is clearly limited to the level of improvement, but it provides a good starting point and is likely to be highly cost-effective. The use of internal studies again develops benchmarking experience among staff and can be considered to be 'safe' as the information is developed and kept in-house. Generic processes are where the most benefit can often be gained, but where the comparisons are likely to be the most difficult. Consider the project activities associated with publishing a book. If the publisher wished to decrease the time to market, they might consider benchmarking themselves against one of the newspapers, who regularly have to take copy from writers and turn it into printed material within a few hours. For most text books, the development process takes months. The methods or processes are similar, the end-product is considered to be very different.

Competitive benchmarking is possibly the most difficult to execute effectively, due to the defensive attitudes of organisations towards their performance. This most certainly should involve a 'code of conduct' including retaining confidentiality of data. The activities do not necessarily involve site visits as much of the information can be collected and exchanged by telephone. Other data is often in the public domain and, whilst it is almost always out of date as soon as it is printed, provides useful indicators, particularly where a project organisation is at the start of their improvement activities.

Any of the criteria set out in Table 9.1 where data is gathered as part of the review (check) process, can be used to provide benchmarks. The minimum criteria are that an organisation consistently improves on its own benchmark data, and targets for improvement form an intrinsic part of organisational strategy.

One key measure that is often cited in large benchmarking studies (such as the Worldwide Manufacturing Competitiveness Study, Andersen Consulting 1995) is that of productivity. Most simply stated, this is the output achieved per unit of input resources. In operations management, this may be associated with units per hour of output of production lines. In project management, whilst the measure can be applied to some of the execution phase of the project where repetitive tasks exist, applying it to one-off activities is unlikely to be useful. It was stated in Chapter 6 that it is difficult to control activities where there is a non-tangible output, such as in design. As the output and the output rate are very difficult to define (designs produced per month does not consider the quality of the design and can focus attention on the wrong priorities – speed over quality or completeness) productivity at this level is also likely to be meaningless. Overall productivity measures (such as engineering hours per major design activity) are more useful but again focus on speed rather than quality. The achievement of 'right first time' is a worthwhile goal, and so measures of numbers of engineering change requests or manufacturing problems which are accredited to design are more relevant.

In a discussion of this vital aspect of performance assessment, Kaplan and Norton (1992) show how providing a kind of scorecard which contains both process and performance measures can be beneficial. For each of the following categories, both goals and measures are constructed:

- financial perspectives (how do we look to shareholders?);
- customer perspectives (how do customers see us?);
- internal business perspectives (what must we excel at?);
- innovation and learning perspectives (can we continue to improve and create value?).

This kind of balance to measures can now provide the basis for benchmarking activities as the organisation seeks to improve its scores. The focus on results and scores is echoed by Schaffer and Thomson (1992) who contrast the performance of results-oriented initiatives with those of activity-centred programmes. A measure of activity-centred progress would be the number of improvement programmes being carried out within an organisation or the number of staff who have been through the quality improvement training programme. Measures of performance include the percentage improvement in customer satisfaction as a result of improvement activities and reductions in quality costs for example.

9.5 TOWARDS WORLD-CLASS PROJECT MANAGEMENT

The output of a benchmarking activity can be the data that establishes which organisation is either 'best-in-class' or even 'world-class'. These two terms are widely used and not always consistently! Best-in-class (BIC) implies that in one or other aspects of performance measure, the organisation is rated as being the best within a limited class of organisations, such as a competitive group. This is often confused with being truly world-class, where the performance of that attribute would rank alongside the best in the world *in that mea-*

sure. A world-class company is one that is considered to be world-class in a number of measures. In the recent benchmarking exercise cited above, world-class companies were those which had achieved considerably better performance in measures of quality and productivity than their counterparts. These may be considered now to be benchmarks for other manufacturing industries. This discrepancy between what constitutes world-class performance and managers' perceptions of it was highlighted recently when a survey showed that 78 per cent of companies questioned said that they were world-class. On further investigation, only 2 per cent of these were achieving world-class levels of quality or productivity.

From the above discussion, it can be seen that the definition of world-class performance is open to debate and that this is not always totally objective. More than one company can be world-class at any one time in any one sphere of activity, though the gap between the world-class performers and the others can be considerable. In general, the Japanese automotive assemblers are considered to be the epitomy of such companies, though little research has been carried out in the project management environment. The way in which their operations have been improved has been summarised and can be adapted to the project environment.

Suzaki (1987) shows that the fundamental characteristics for being progressive can be compared to conventional organisations as follows:

- structures (organisational) are flexible rather than rigid to accommodate changes in customer requirements;
- the organisation focuses on optimisation of the entire flow of work through it, rather than through a single area or department (*see* below);
- open communications from flat organisational structures as opposed to tall hierarchies leading to long chains of command (where messages get interpreted and changed at each link in the chain);
- agreements between parties (including suppliers) are trust-based rather than contractual;
- skills base of the teams is wide to allow flexibility rather than narrow and specialist;
- suppliers are much fewer in number and have long-term agreements;
- education and training are significant parts of work activity rather than inconvenient distractions from the work in-hand.

Whilst improving performance by providing a single recipe for success has been the output of many consultants' reports, the role of adaptation of principles has already been stressed in Chapter 5. The concept of the 'lean organisation' was first developed by Womack *et al* (1990) and provides a series of principles for eliminating non-value-adding activities. This continues the ideas of Henry Ford who is quoted as saying: 'if it doesn't add value, its waste'.

These principles may be applied to the project environment as shown in Table 9.2. The first of these points concerns the flow of information through a

Table 9.3 Lean principles applied to project management

Line management	Project management
Integrated single-piece workflow produced just in time	Information treated as inventory and processed immediately rather than spending long periods of time waiting
Absolute elimination of waste	See section below on Seven Wastes
Focus on global rather than local optima	Focus on achieving the goals of the organisation through this and other project activities and considering the project in this light rather than as a totally independent item (develops idea of the role of the stakeholders)
Defect prevention	Defect prevention
Multi-skilling in team-based operations	Multi-skilling in team-based projects
Few indirect staff	Few indirect staff

project organisation as a manufacturing engineer would plan the routing of a product through a process. The focus is on the simplification of flows so that it becomes visible where problems and hold-ups are occurring. In order to not be seen to be idle, people tend to build up inventories of tasks to be completed, regardless of the consequences of this hold-up in the flow of information being progressed. Consequently problems get hidden. The role of simplification is to move the type of information flow from that shown in Fig. 9.1 to that shown in Fig. 9.2. In the latter case, there are no inventories. This means that periodically a person may complete their tasks with no further work to be done. In this case, rather than them creating inventory for downstream activities, they may engage in other work through being multi-skilled.

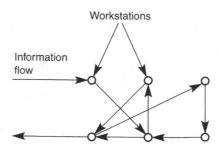

Figure 9.1 Complex information flow around system

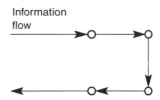

Figure 9.2 Simplified information flow through system

Apart from becoming faster at processing information, the above leads to improved responsiveness – customer requests and the inevitable changes can be implemented more quickly. This subject of waste can be expanded using the framework provided by Suzaki (1987) of the Seven Wastes:

- do not carry out activities above and beyond what is required by the customer either in terms of quality or quantity;
- eliminate waiting time either for people or project information;
- the movement of information, people or materials is generally a non-value-adding process;
- eliminate the need for processes which generate the need for further processing;
- eliminate the wastes associated with the building up of inventory (as above);
- avoid the waste of motion – not having materials or information on-hand when needed and having to go and find them;
- continuously strive to reduce the waste caused by defects or mistakes, as discussed in Chapter 6.

Wherever possible tasks should:

- simplified – procedures are often needlessly complicated and open to too much interpretation;
- combined – putting together tasks through multi-skilling can eliminate the transfer time and reduces the need for hand-over information;
- eliminate non-value-adding tasks, such as bureaucracy, constricting accounting systems and computer-planning systems, which absorb large proportions of managers' time, etc.

The above represents some very basic disciplines which can be applied throughout the project organisation. Whilst it is often tempting to seek technological solutions, 90 per cent of all improvement comes from the application of what is termed 'common sense'.

Further improvement activities need to be focused on the entire value-chain or value-network. It is not unusual for 60 per cent or more of a project spend to be with external suppliers and unless these are also engaged in improvement activities, the scope for performance improvement of your own organisation is distinctly limited. The concept of removing local optima is applicable here, e.g. where a supplier provides you with materials that are required for the execution phase of a project and will be used at a steady rate during this phase, there is little point in them delivering the entire order at the start of work, even though their machines may be geared to produce in such quantities. This would provide a local optimum, namely at the suppliers. The purchaser now has a stock or inventory which will require storing, checking and possibly guarding – all activities that involve costs. The optimum can be redistributed to benefit all parties, with staged deliveries, for example. Helping suppliers to become more responsive is part of many initiatives currently being promoted. Better utilisation of their expertise is provided through the Toyota production system, where suppliers are given a rough specification for the needs of a product and required to carry out design activities themselves. They can in this way achieve better designs as their manufacturing processes can be accommodated in the component design.

9.6 THE ROLE OF THE PROJECT LEADER IN WORLD-CLASS PROJECTS

Having identified several disciplines as being at the heart of seeking improvement, Womack *et al.* (1990) and Jones (1992) highlight the differences in roles between conventional Western project managers, and their Japanese counterparts, the 'shusas'. Originally developed as part of the Toyota production system, the shusa is responsible for cross-function activity, particularly in new product development. The project reflects far more than in Western companies the importance given to what is termed this new 'supercraftsperson'. The key differences with the Western system (as typified by coordination matrix management structures) are in:

- the level of authority that the shusas have – they have real power in the organisation, compared to the matrix manager who has to act as a coordinator;
- they have the opportunity to make a real impact of their own personality and skills into the project, with less interference from senior management;
- the progression from these projects is to senior management rather than it being seen as a step which will do little to further a functionally-based career;
- the shusas have power over the career-path of individuals, including the assignment to future projects;
- the shusa provides a guide to force the team's attention onto difficult trade-off issues in design.

The development of project leadership as a career, with its own promotional path, is an emerging feature of progressive organisations. Consequently, the project manager will be at the forefront of management activity and will have a role that is recognised, as it is in Japan. Only those that can develop the skills discussed here will be eligible for what are some of the most fundamentally challenging careers, those of the project managers of the 1990s and beyond.

PROJECT
MANAGEMENT
IN PRACTICE:
**NEW PRODUCT
DEVELOPMENT
AT TOYOTA
FORKLIFT
TRUCK – THE
X300 PROJECT**

The whole design cycle is described by the system shown in Fig. 9.3. As can be seen, each step of the process is identified and quality assurance procedures assigned.

Terminology used in Fig. 9.3:

PPC – Process plan chart – flowchart showing the steps involved

FMEA – failure mode effect analysis – product or process review method, which assesses the likelihood of failure, the effect or severity of that failure and the probability of it being detected

QCP – quality control plans

QA – quality assurance

Assigning the procedures in this way at the outset, enables quality to be 'built in' to the product. Processes are designed so that the right people have the right information at the right time and designs should be 'right first time'. The review of designs is an ongoing activity, rather than one that takes place at the end of the process. This ensures that checks are made very close to the time each part of the process is carried out, and amendments are incorporated before further cost is added.

Quality assurance starts with the information that the design process is being fed. The market research (note the departments involved from Fig. 9.3) provides an explicit statement of customer needs using a 'Quality Deployment Table', the output of a process known as 'Quality Function Deployment'. This method reduces the risk inherent in converting customer attributes into the language that the product developers understand, namely engineering characteristics. Further data on actual customer usage of products is obtained in this way, in this case from visits to dealers as well as customer and market research carried out by outside companies. Tools such as FMEA (*see* above) are applied to (a) designs at an early stage to ensure robustness and (b) the process by which the final products are to be made.

The review systems for product planning, product design and product preparation are shown in Figs 9.4 and 9.5. A very high degree of systematisation exists, though the driver is not bureaucracy but customer satisfaction. Information flows are studied, and where work is becoming held up (engineering 'bottlenecks') additional resources are provided to identify and solve the causes, preventing delay.

The transfer to production was completed with a high degree of control. The product specifications were identified and transferred to the requirements of the machines on which the products were to be made (process capability). An objective of design was to work within the capability of the available production technology. Similarly, rather than wait for the product to arrive in production for workers to be trained on its manufacture, training was scheduled as the transfer process was ongoing.

1 Design review 1 (DR1) is the process for ensuring that the unique selling points of a product are going to be achieved by the outline design. These should not have been removed or compromised by trade-offs in the process. At the same time, competitor analysis will reveal how long these features will provide competitive advantage, based on a knowledge of their products and design capability.

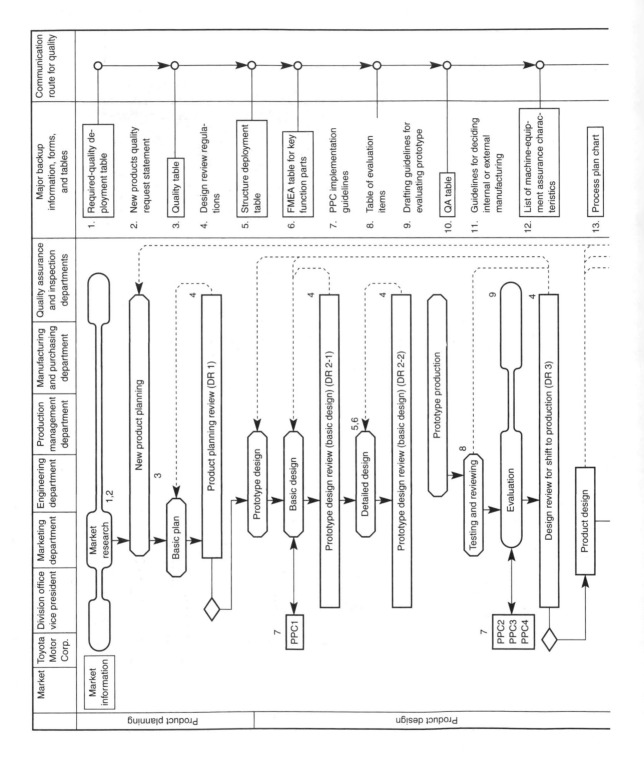

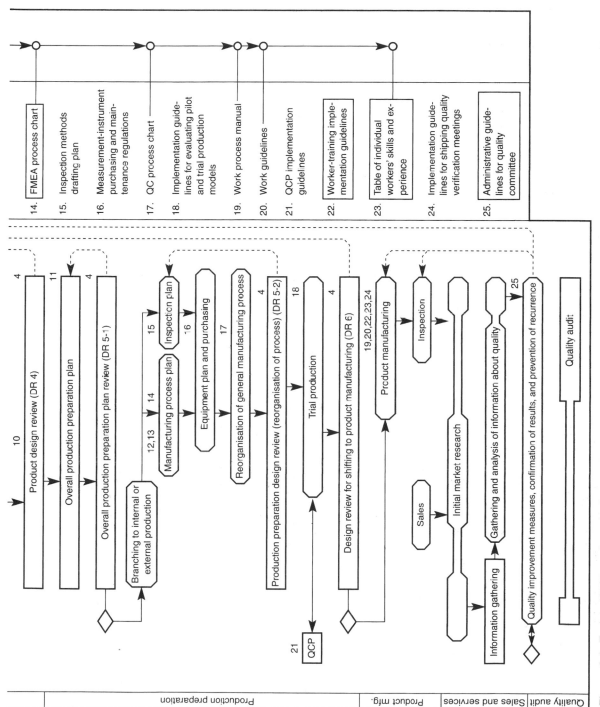

Figure 9.3 Toyota X300 project design cycle

Source: Kurogane (1993). Reproduced with permission.

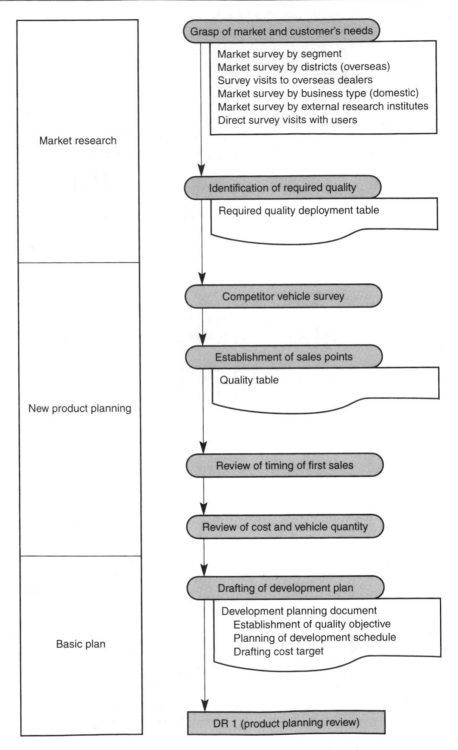

Figure 9.4 Product planning system

Source: Kurogane (1993). Reproduced with permission.

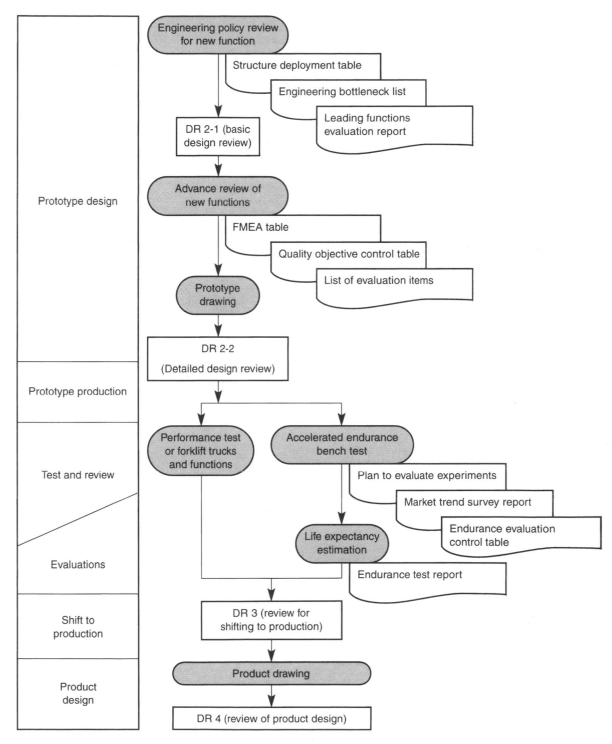

Figure 9.5 Product design system

Source: Kurogane (1993). Reproduced with permission.

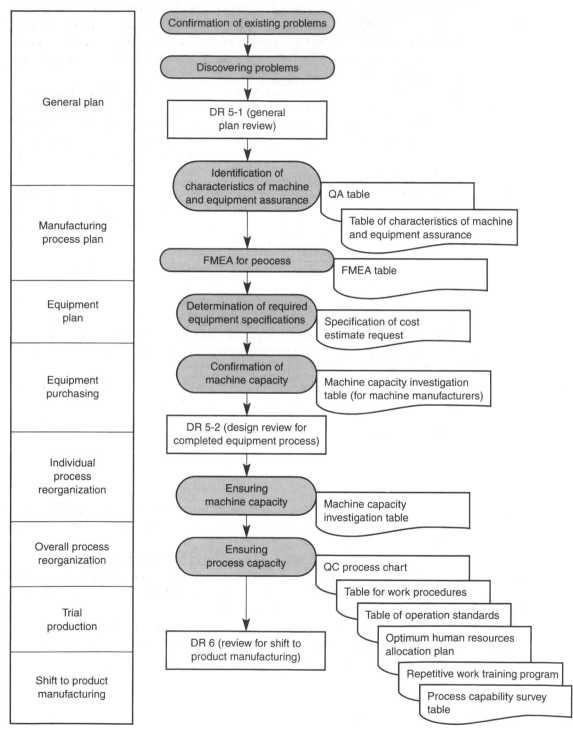

Figure 9.6 Production preparation system
Source: Kurogane (1993). Reproduced with permission.

2 Design reviews 2,3 and 4 (prototype design review, review for shifting to production, and product design review) assure that the quality objectives are being met. This process used to be carried out by a user group, who would be asked to evaluate prototypes prior to production, but was abandoned due to cost and unreliability.

3 DR5 (production preparation review) provided a checkpoint on the production preparation plan, particularly on elements of product quality, availability and cost. This is a feasibility check and does involve a corporate evaluation point. As production engineering had been involved from an early stage, however, the production preparation plan was very rapidly prepared, with minimal alterations or amendments to the product design.

4 DR6 (review for shifting to product manufacturing) was the 'engineering sign-off' point, during which not only product quality was again reviewed, but also the checks on process capability, staff training and the readiness of the manufacturing area to accept the new product.

All these processes ensured that the product was not 'thrown over the wall' between departments, and that there were no surprises when the plans landed in one department for further processing. All the time, the likely outcome was being reviewed against objectives and the theme of it being a superior product reiterated. The involvement of all departments in the development process ensured a very rapid development time and policy deployment through the participation of high-level staff assured consistency with corporate objectives.

The above was a highly successful project with a highly competitive product being available on time, and within the development budget. Further improvements in the process are planned, based on the results of the review processes. Each provides a basis for future lessons to be learned and for refinement of the process and its control system.

Case discusssion

1 Identify why the various design reviews should take place. How might they represent an improvement over and above a single design review process at the end of the product design stage?

2 Why is the 'voice of the customer' so important in this process?

3 Discuss the nature of the changes that can occur in passing information about customer requirements from a marketing department, to the engineering department to the manufacturing department.

4 Show how relating the customer attributes, in their own words, to 'engineering characteristics' may help the provision of a product that is more in line with their needs.

SUMMARY OF KEY POINTS

- the project activities must be wound-up so that all activities are completed and systems closed-down;
- documentation needs to be provided to form the basis of reviews and guidance for the users of the project outputs;
- checklists are vital to ensuring that completion activities are formalised;
- project reviews can be carried out as a form of post-mortem by the project manager on completion of activities;
- formalised audit and review usually take place some considerable time after completion;
- one of the close-down activities is the promotion of the results to stakeholders – part of managing their perceptions of events;
- audits check conformance whilst reviews look at overall performance – both can be general or focus on a number of areas including finance, quality, time, planning and environment;
- continuous improvement is at the heart of the progressive or 'learning' organisation;
- benchmarking involves establishing a reference performance (a benchmark) against which your organisation compares itself;
- benchmark data can provide the basis for establishing a 'scorecard' of performance;
- world-class organisations are those that can show that they are the best performers in a number of separate performance measures;
- lean management, whilst developed in a manufacturing context, has much potential for application in project environments through the pursuit of the absolute elimination of waste;
- the role of project managers in future will be seen as having a career path of their own in highly challenging activities, rather than being secondees from line management roles.

KEY TERMS

professional log books	scorecard
document storage systems	results-oriented
close-down checklists	activity-centred
customer sign-off	world-class
project post-mortem	best-in-class
audit and review	lean management
kaisen/continuous improvement	elimination of waste
benchmarking	shusa
productivity	

REVIEW AND DISCUSSION QUESTIONS

1 Discuss why a project may spend '90 per cent of its time 90 per cent complete'.
2 Show the activities that must be completed during the final phases of a project, categorising them as either 'check' or 'act' functions.
3 Why might compiling project documentation be considered such a burden to the team, yet be so essential?

4 What issues must be considered when deciding how far post-delivery service should extend (such as providing free consultancy with new IT systems)?

5 Why should the immediate post-project review be seen as being so beneficial to the project team, yet less so to the organisation?

6 Construct an audit questionnaire of management performance which could be given to members of a project team. Test this on someone who has managed you. What areas would you suggest for improvement?

7 Consider each of the possible stakeholders and decide which aspects of project performance they are most likely to want to hear about.

8 Distinguish between audits and reviews.

9 What are the criteria which should be taken into consideration when selecting an auditor/reviewer?

10 Considering the very varied nature of the different audits and reviews that can be carried out, is it likely that these can be done at one time by one person?

11 Discuss how the process of continuous improvement is vital if organisations are to continue to exist.

12 Discuss how benchmarking may be used in a project environment.

13 Explain the differences between world-class and best-in-class standards.

14 The concept of lean organisations has been developed from manufacturing management studies. Discuss the similarities and differences between automotive manufacturing and a project environment with which you are familiar and evaluate whether the lean principles have application in that environment.

15 Why is it important for the project leader to have real authority, as is the case in world-class automotive design acitivities? How might the skills of project management help in cultivating such people?

REFERENCES

Andersen Consulting (1995) 'Worldwide Manufacturing Competitiveness Study'.

Jones, D.T. (1992) 'Beyond the Toyota Production System: The Era of Lean Production' *Manufacturing Strategy*, Chapman and Hall.

Kaplan, R.S. and D.P. Norton (1992) 'The Balanced Scorecard – Measures That Drive Performance,' *Harvard Business Review*, January–February.

Kurogane, K. (ed.) (1993) *Cross-Functional Management: Principles and Practical Applications*, Asian Productivity Organisation.

Lean Enterprise Benchmarking Report (1992) Andersen Consulting/Cardiff Business School/Cambridge University (second report published 1994).

Schaffer, R. H. and H.A. Thomson (1992) 'Successful Change Programs Begin With Results', *Harvard Business Review*, January–February.

Suzaki, K. (1987) *The New Manufacturing Challenge: Techniques for Continuous Improvement*, Free Press.

Womack, J. P., D.T. Jones and D. Roos (1990) *The Machine That Changed The World*, Rawson Associates.

FURTHER READING

Akao, Y. (1990) *Quality Function Deployment: Integrating Customer Requirements into Product Design*, Productivity Press.

Akao, Y. (1991) *Hoshin Kanri: Policy Deployment for Successful TQM*, Productivity Press.

Hines, P. (1993) *Mutual Competitive Advantage*, Financial Times/Pitman Publishing.

Schonberger, R.J. (1992) *World-Class Manufacturing*, Free Press.

INDEX

Also available from Pitman Publishing

Operations Management

This major new textbook has been written to give students a clear, well-structured and interesting treatment of operations management. It successfully provides both a logical path through the activities of operations management and an understanding of the strategic context in which operations managers work.

The book is structured around the popular design, planning and control model, but does not separate planning from control activities. The improvement activities of operations have been covered in a separate part of the book to reflect the responsibility of operations managers to continually improve the performance of their operations. Throughout the book, service operations are treated with the same level of seriousness as manufacturing operations.

In general, the book is:
- **strategic** in its perspective of the manager's contribution to the organisation's long term success;
- **conceptual** in the way it explains the reasons why operations managers need to take decisions in each area;
- **comprehensive** in its coverage of the significant ideas which are relevant to most types of operation;
- **practical** in the way it looks at the issues and difficulties involved in making operations management decisions;
- **international** in its use of materials and examples;
- **balanced** in its treatment of the various types of organisation which create products and services.

The book is enhanced by a range of distinctive features including:
- a wealth of illustrations and real-life examples;
- personal profiles at the end of each chapter, based on interviews with practising operations managers;
- short case exercises and questions at the end of every chapter;
- discussion questions;
- the use of two colours throughout the text and diagrams.

'An excellent balance of services and manufacturing ... A top class European textbook ... A refreshing approach to operations management.'
Paul Walley, Lecturer in Operations Management at Loughborough University Business School

'... an important contribution to the European literature.'
Professor Roland van Dierdonck, De Vlerick School of Management, University of Ghent, Belgium

Nigel Slack is the A.E. Higgs Professor of Manufacturing Policy and Strategy, **Stuart Chambers** is a Lecturer in Operations Management and **Robert Johnston** is a Reader in Operations Management. All are based at Warwick University Business School.
Alan Harrison is a Research Fellow at Cranfield University Business School.
Christine Harland lectures at the University of Bath.

0 273 60316 7

Project Management and Project Network Techniques

Building on the foundations of the successful *Critical Path Analysis*, this new text has been substantlally revised in order to include the management concepts of project management. The book focuses on the introduction of project management in established industrial concerns, on risk assessment and on quality in projects.

This text looks at what defines a project and at the new techniques available to project managers. It is divided into two parts: the first part deals with the managerial aspects of project management such as organisation and planning; the second, with project management methods such as Activity-on-Arrow and Activity-on-Node networks. Written in a user-friendly style, the book contains numorical and essay-style questions and a glossary of terms.

Professor Keith Lockyer is Emeritus Professor of Operations Management, University of Bradford and **Dr James Gordon** is a Project Management Consultant, Chairman of the BSI Committee on Project Management, Convener ISO Working Group on Guidelines to Quality in Project Management.

0 273 61454 1

Principles of Operations Management

This text is an ideal introduction to operations management for all non-specialists, both new students and those with some management experience.

Principles of Operations Management tackles all the main areas of operations management in a clear, no-nonsense way. The text begins by explaining what an operations manager does and goes on to set this in an international context.

Principles of Operations Management:

- covers everything that any student on a modular operations management course will need to know;
- is written in a succinct, no-nonsense style;
- is clearly laid out for ease of use.

Dr Mike Harrison is Head of the Division of Operations and Information Management, The Business School, Staffordshire University.

0 273 61450 9